COBBETT'S

TOUR IN SCOTLAND

MR WILLIAM COBBETT.

COBBETT'S

TOUR IN SCOTLAND

BY WILLIAM COBBETT
(1763–1835)

———————

EDITED, ANNOTATED AND WITH
INTRODUCTION AND APPENDICES
BY

DANIEL GREEN

———————

FOREWORD BY

LORD GRIMOND

———————

ABERDEEN UNIVERSITY PRESS

This edition first published 1984
Aberdeen University Press
A member of the Pergamon Group
© Daniel Green 1984

The publisher acknowledges subsidy from the
Scottish Arts Council towards the publication
of this volume

British Library Cataloguing in Publication Data
Cobbett, William
    Cobbett's tour in Scotland
    1. Scotland—Description and travel—1801–1900
    I. Title   II. Green, Daniel
    914.11'0473   DA865
    ISBN 0 08 030376 5
    ISBN 0 08 030384 6 Pbk

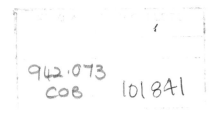
PRINTED IN GREAT BRITAIN
THE UNIVERSITY PRESS
ABERDEEN

FOREWORD

BY LORD GRIMOND

The tradition in which Cobbett stood has a long history. It is exemplified by Dr Johnson, Cobbett, Belloc, Chesterton and some more modern adherents to whom I shall come.

The tradition has no name that I am aware of. It might be called Tory-Populist or Radical Reactionary. It has some affinity (though not strong) with the Christian Democrat and Agrarian parties on the continent. As the tradition, though influential, has never exercised anything like dominance, being indeed essentially anti-government, its adherents have often sought outlets and activities in different directions. Cobbett began as a Tory and ended as a radical. Belloc was a Liberal MP. This diversity, added to the lack of a distinctive name, can be somewhat bewildering. Let us for the purpose at least of this introduction call it The Cobbett Tradition. That at least will please the shade of that conceited man. We must think of it not as a faction of its own, still less as a political party but as an outlook which has affected politicians of different parties and writers outside any party.

What then are the characteristics of the Cobbett tradition? A concern for individual welfare. That sets it apart from abstract authoritarian doctrines such as Communism. But that concern alone does not put a distinctive stamp upon it. A concern for the welfare of individuals usually leads to some genuflection towards equality. But for the Cobbett tradition, equality has no virtue in itself. Certainly the tradition accepts Parliamentary democracy in which votes count equally. But the tradition also sees the welfare of individuals as being much dependant on organisation and has no objection to hierarchies or aristocracies. In this it differs from some liberals and all

anarchists. The Cobbett tradition accepts Burke's view of the
state—an organic growth not a product of theory. It sees the
state as having a limited role. The state is not to be used either
for the aggrandisement of a class or as the weapon of a creed.
In this it differs from state socialism. It believes in a society
based on rights, obligations and private property. It is suspicious of the déclassé and the déraciné. It is anti-Imperialist.
Men should be rooted in their country and their community.
Firmly planted on their own property, small men can resist
both tyranny and the snares of the slippery, rootless
manipulators. For the tradition is wary of financiers, inter-
national business, large corporations, paper money and financial jugglery. It tends to be anti-semitic because the Jews seem
too often to be rootless financiers. It values land and admires
the farmer. Indeed it tends to have a romantic attachment to
an ideal mediaeval and feudal never-never land. It has a nos-
talgic dream of a Britain of cottages and castles, jousts, beer,
banquets and Merrie England, but it rejects the deference and
complacency of the Tory.

It is indeed within Britain very much an English tradition.
No one speaks much of Merrie Scotland, Ireland or Wales. But
the Cobbett tradition has adherents outside England, for
instance, A G MacDonnell and some of the Irish priesthood.
As it is English it is insular. It tends towards Catholicism and
the higher reaches of the Episcopalian churches. For its essence
is that it admires authority—but a perfect authority, dealing
justly, guaranteeing freedom; an authority received and
accepted as of the natural and national order. That sort of
authority is more likely to be found in heaven than on earth.
Enjoying the pleasures of the body, particularly food and
drink, it does not share the anaemic aesthetics of the pre-
Raphaelites. But it appreciates art, beauty and particularly
conversation and writing.

Of course few in the Cobbett tradition embraced all these
views and fewer still were prepared for the life they recommended. But this last failing is common to all philosophers,
economists and politicians. Dr Johnson and Chesterton would
not have made good farmers or even country gentlemen. Their
physique imposed literary rather than pedestrian rambles.

The Cobbett tradition has another side to it. While reverent towards God, it is irreverent towards man. It enjoys lampoons and schoolboy humour. It likes taking the mickey out of the great — Johnson's letter to Lord Chesterfield. It pursues personal vendettas by way of bad-form jokes — Cobbett passim. It is often silly. The silliness ranges from Dr Johnson kicking a stone to refute Berkeley, through some of Chesterton's tropes to Cobbett's attacks on the 'Feelosofers' and Malthus. Malthus, cleverer and as compassionate, was nicer (in the end more influential — through Keynes) than Cobbett. Cobbett did not understand him (though his views were simple). Making fun of what you do not understand but of which you are vaguely jealous and frightened is the reaction of not very nice small boys — the sort of boys who stone to death unfamiliar animals.

Where does this examination of the Cobbett tradition land us today? In *Private Eye*. *Private Eye* is the embodiment of the tradition. It is *The Register* come to life. We have the same scurrility, the same schoolboy humour, the nicknames, the repetitions of abuse (Cobbett's 'Bloody Old Times', Ingram's 'Getsmuchworse'), the diatribes against sometimes not very important figures.

The Cobbett tradition is always valuable — never more so than when the Establishment arrogates to itself special powers and privileges, when corruption, perks and nepotism take the place of obligations and the state through incompetence or bureaucratic selfseeking becomes the enemy rather than the protector of the body politic. That was a danger in Cobbett's time, and is a danger again today. The Cobbett tradition represents a welcome anti-state strand in politics. Without it we would be left with a choice of parties all of which are more or less statist. It is essential always to have critics who, like Cobbett and *Private Eye*, do not want to rule. We should be most grateful therefore to Daniel Green for following up his excellent life of Cobbett with a new edition of *Cobbett's Tour in Scotland*.

The tour began in 1832 with the approach to Scotland through northern England. Yorkshire, Lancashire, Durham and Newcastle upon Tyne were rising on the swell of the industrial revolution. But they were little known in the South and Cobbett was a South of England man. The first point to be made is that *The Tour* is a striking sight of the North through

fresh eyes. Cobbett was a practised journalist. One would expect therefore a lively account for contemporary readers — perhaps less exciting a hundred and fifty years on. But I find his
story still very readable. Among other skills he has that trick of
the effective pamphleteer — making repetition bearable. What,
however, I find most intriguing are some side winds, so to
speak, from his main narrative. His main narrative being concerned with a journey undertaken to preach the radical cause.
We are not, rather curiously I think, given any of the substance
of his innumerable lectures. Instead we are regaled by a full
recital of adulatory addresses. Except as an insight into
Cobbett's character and evidence of how the reforming case
was pursued, these are not of much interest.

But I am intrigued by some of Cobbett's measuring rods. He
appears to have judged the clemency of a region by the
number of oaks and its prosperity by the number of parish
churches and villages. Good and relevant tests they seem now
that he has mentioned them but I never thought of them before. I wonder what the equivalent tests would be today?
Numbers of motor cars? Restaurants? Extensions on houses?
Gardens? (In Orkney increased prosperity in my time is most
obvious in the quantity of flowers now grown) Or absence of
tower blocks?

His observations, always accurate, are sometimes surprising.
He does not seem to have disapproved of industrial growth. He
found the Durham miners well housed and well fed. He must
have passed through the East Lothian coalfield which we have
been brought up to believe was an example of capitalism at its
worst — trucks pulled by semi-naked women, poor wages, and
not so long before Cobbett, conditions of slavery. Surely the
great radical agitator, the highly inquisitive investigator,
would have noticed and commented upon such conditions? He
does not seem to have done so. It was the condition of the agricultural workers in the Lothians which appalled him.

The system by which farm servants were accommodated in
bothies or chaumers continued up to at least the Second World
War. Cobbett found these to be long dormitories, cold, dirty
and dark — stables for men. He was horrified by the poor food
and low wages provided for the inmates, contrasting their dank
prisons with the cheerful cottages in which he alleges their

southern counterparts browsed upon good bread and meat and vegetables (other than the hated potato). It was probably a bad system and at its worst perhaps in Cobbett's day. But when I knew it, it was only single men who lived in the bothy. Many farmers' wives, who cooked for them, were good and lavish cooks and even in Cobbett's time some of the rations, for instance of milk, seem to have been generous. Cobbett having known hunger in the Army was obsessed by food — and rightly so. On returning through England he praised the way in which farm servants were looked after by the farmers; the bothy system at its best was somewhat similar.

We get a picture of large scale 'progressive' farming as it existed in southern Scotland in the first half of the last century. We can discern fore-runners of today's woes. Do the grain growers in eastern England now grub up the hedges from greed? Turnip fields of fifty acres were noted by Cobbett: vast stack-yards produced by factory methods and threshed by steam. Again he is on the whole complimentary about Scottish sheep and cattle. Yet the days were not so long past when this stock driven down from the Highlands was raised in conditions where few beasts survived the winter. Cobbett contrasts the agricultural opulence of southern Scotland with the barren wastes of Surrey.

Taking Cobbett on southern Scotland with Osgood Mackenzie's *A Hundred Years in the Highlands* (just later) and Professor Youngson's *After the 'Forty-five* (somewhat earlier) we should by now have revised the popular notions about the rural Scotland of our forebears.

Again the growing factories of central Scotland and Glasgow seem to have aroused no revolutionary indignation. Indeed they are hardly mentioned though the Carron Ironworks is approved. New Lanark is neither understood nor approved. Owen is treated to some silly jibes. That Cobbett had no interest in machinery is not remarkable but that he had no concern about the results of the industrial system, surely is. It says something about Cobbett's character. He was a selfish, opinionated man taken up with proving his opinions right. He was interested largely in agriculture, fruit growing, and to some extent in finance — as well of course as in politics. But it also says something about the agitation which led to the first

Reform Bill. It was not a revolt of the poor but of the middle classes. The reformers were not much concerned with living conditions and the hardships of labour herded into the big cities. If sympathetic and sometimes indignant about the sentences imposed on the industrial agitators Cobbett and his middle-class admirers had no wish to overturn the system.

Cobbett's conversion from loathing to admiration of the Scots was typical. He often leapt to conclusions based on prejudice. It is also a little comic. I suspect all these adulatory addresses had something to do with it.

This *Tour* is still to be recommended as history, as comment upon life which is still worthy of attention and as further evidence of the Cobbett tradition—a tradition to be studied and fostered.

CONTENTS

MR WILLIAM COBBETT *FRONTISPIECE*

FOREWORD BY LORD GRIMOND v

INTRODUCTION BY DANIEL GREEN xiii

TOUR IN SCOTLAND

APPENDICES

A SPEECHES AT THE GLASGOW DINNER 130

B COBBETT'S SCOTOPHOBIA 134

C THE NEWSPAPERS AND COBBETT 144

NOTES 157

BIOGRAPHICAL INDEX 183

INTRODUCTION

It would be fair to claim that William Cobbett (1763–1835) was the most prolific, influential, and widely-read publicist of his day. None the less there is remarkably little of the great body of work he produced that is still available to the general public. The twelve volumes of *Porcupine's Works* and the eighty-nine of his *Political Register* can be found in their entirety only in the statute libraries. Of all the books he wrote, only *Cottage Economy*, *Advice to Young Men*, and *The English Gardener* are currently in print. To these one must add, of course, *Rural Rides*, the work with which he is most commonly associated, and the one that has never, in the last century and a half, been long out of print. The same cannot be said of *Cobbett's Tour in Scotland*, which was, effectively, the last of the *Rides* to be published in book form.

As with all the earlier *Rides*, the *Tour* first appeared as a series of weekly articles published in the *Register*; in this case in copies dating from 29 September to 24 November 1832. Just as most of the earlier *Rides*, covering the period from 1821 to 1830, had been collected together and published in book form in that latter year, so the *Tour* articles were also published, in a small, duodecimo volume, in January 1833. The first 82 of that work's 264 pages covered Cobbett's progress towards the Tweed through 'the four Northern Counties of England'. When his son, James Paul Cobbett, published his enlarged and annotated edition of the *Rides* in 1853, he included passages from this part of the later book in his work, but nothing that his father had written after he left Alnwick. These apart, *Cobbett's Tour in Scotland* has only been re-published once since its original publication in 1833.

In 1930, a century after the publication of the first *Rural*

Rides, Peter Davies produced a limited, three-volume edition of all the *Rides* which included the whole of the *Scottish Tour*. That fine edition was superbly edited and annotated by the late G D H Cole, the *doyen* of Cobbett biographers and scholars. All who now study Cobbett owe much to that particular edition, and I would wish here to acknowledge how much Cole's Notes and Biographical Index have guided me in the preparation of this volume.

Unfortunately, that particular edition of *Rural Rides* is now as much of a bibliophile's rarity as the original 1833 edition of the *Scottish Tour*. As a consequence, anyone who wants to know what Cobbett wrote about Scotland on his first and last visit to that country, will probably have to go to a library in order to satisfy his curiosity. The principal, though not the only reason for this edition, therefore, is that it offers the general public access to the least-known section of Cobbett's best-known work.

Nevertheless the *Tour* is not, for a number of reasons, offered to the reader in its entirety. The length and the cost of a complete, and completely annotated edition were one consideration. Another was the fact that passages from the English part of the *Tour* were contained in the 1853 edition of *Rural Rides*, which is still available to the general public in Messrs Dent's *Everyman's Library*. Finally, it was thought that, by restricting the work to Cobbett's travels in Scotland, one could isolate the only one of his *Rides* — Ireland apart — that took him abroad, since for Cobbett, as for so many other Englishmen of his time, Scotland was still a foreign, and largely unknown land. It is for those reasons that this edition starts with the first entry written on Scottish soil, that is, from page 82 of the original text, and omits almost all that he wrote about his return journey once he had again crossed the Tweed — i.e. pages 228 to 245 of the original.

Everyman's Library, which has done so much to keep the 1853 edition of *Rural Rides* in print, publishes that work under the classification of 'Travel'. Cobbett would have been gratified by the survival of his book, but puzzled by its classification. The *Rides*, which started in 1821 and were continued, intermittently, until within a year of his death, were never undertaken in order to collect material for either a travel book or a 'country' one. He was, first and foremost, a political writer travelling for political purposes. This may explain why *Rural Rides*, minor classic though it is, is now less frequently read than it used to be. Remarkably little journalism survives even the generation it was written for. Such of it as does, survives in spite of the ephemerality of most forms of journalism, political journalism included.

If *Rural Rides* is still read, it is surely because of Cobbett's personality, style, and digressive habits of thought. He was, above everything else, one of those most cherished of all British institutions, a 'character'. His picaresque career, and the impact he made on his age and his contemporaries, would have confirmed him as one even if he had written no more and no better than any other polemicist. In fact he was, as Hazlitt said of him, 'not only unquestionably the most powerful political writer of the present day, but one of the best writers in the language'. He was arguably the first English journalist to make the difficult transition from writing political leaders to leading a political party. In addition, he was certainly one of the most professional, versatile, opinionated and self-regarding men ever to put pen to paper. He had, in short, almost all the qualities required of a 'character'.

It was because he was so self-regarding that he always thought of himself as his own best hero, and an example, under every circumstance, to the heathen. He was always very willing, therefore, to stray from his ostensible subject in order to write about himself. That is why there is more to be learnt *about* Cobbett *from* Cobbett than there is from any of the numerous biographies he has inspired — my own included. This is especially so in the case of *Rural Rides*. That work took so long to complete that it acquired, largely because of its digressions, many of the characteristics of a diary and some of the qualities of an autobiography. And yet, as has already been said, it was intended to be a political work.

It is perhaps idle to enquire what Cobbett's political philosophy was. Apart from a rooted hatred of poverty, novelty, and anything he conceived to be unjust, he had none worth the mentioning. He devoted forty years of his life to politics without ever being consistent or even entirely logical in any of his several different political attitudes, and he was seldom capable of agreeing for any length of time, with anyone. Inconsistency, he claimed, was a political virtue. It allowed a man to learn from experience. That was why he despised all dogmatics, theorists, system-mongers and 'feelosofers' who claimed to have a complete political solution for everything. So, although he moved, politically, in what many would consider to be a widdershins direction, having been a High Tory when young and a Radical in his old age, he paid not the slightest attention to those he had deserted.

Lord Cockburn, the eminent Edinburgh Whig, once said of Cobbett that he was a politician of the belly rather than the intellect. If an enduring hatred of injustice and an honest belief in the absolute validity of one's opinions of the moment reside in the belly, then Lord Cockburn was right. What he ignored, however, was the fact that Cobbett was such an outstandingly talented polemicist that he could make it seem the most natural thing in the world for a man to keep his opinions in his belly rather than in his brain. Anyone who differed from Cobbett in any particular naturally thought otherwise, and declared that he was too passionate, pugnacious, prejudiced and pig-headed for rational political argument. Yet none of those qualities prevented the *Political Register* from developing into the most influential political weekly in the history of British journalism: one that soon became required reading in political circles in Europe and the United States as well as in Britain.

Whatever Cobbett may or may not have achieved as a politician, he was certainly the most skilful controversialist of his day. He was a master of all forms of chop-logic argument, and a pioneer of what some would describe as 'investigative journalism', and others as 'muck-raking'. He was constitutionally scurrilous, but his savage sense of humour often transformed the personal and vulgar abuse he heaped on his opponents into an entertainment even his victims could enjoy. He was moralistic, didactic, narrow-minded, sentimental, prejudiced, and, one suspects, a great deal of a humbug in spite of his absolute belief in his own integrity. But he made people laugh at themselves, and that is probably the most valuable gift a political polemicist can possess. A man with so many human weaknesses and so much talent cannot avoid being more interesting than any number of entirely rational, run-of-the-mill politicians and political journalists.

He was, moreover, an innovative writer and a master of the English language. In an age when most other writers loaded their sentences with Ciceronian orotundities or Gothic fancies, he wrote a plain, vigorous prose which skilfully followed the patterns and rhythms of the spoken word. That perhaps is why, now that we all write in the demotic, his writings seem strangely modern in their style, if not in their subject matter.

Cobbett may have been a somewhat blinkered traveller who allowed himself to see little more than what he wanted to see to prove a point. But what he did see he could describe to perfection, for he had a retentive memory, was sharply observant, and was quick to perceive what others might ignore. He loved and understood nature and, although he always looked at a landscape with a farmer's eye, and at the figures peopling it with a politician's, the scene he eventually described would, at its best, have some of the colour to be found in a Turner painting, and some of the precision and sharpness to be found in a Stubbs.

If *Rural Rides* remains in print, then, it is largely because it provides such a valuable record of its author's idiosyncracies, and of a countryside and a country way of life that were disappearing even as he described them. That is, it is now read because of its digressions and in spite of its politics. Such is far less the case with his *Tour*, a circumstance which may help to explain why it is out of print and the earlier *Rides* are not. If the *Tour* is to be introduced to the modern reader, it has to be introduced for what it is, a sustained exercise in political electioneering. Even G D H Cole, who was as much of a political animal as Cobbett, and more truly a Radical, tended to believe that the *Tour* was over political. It was, he wrote, 'brimful of politics and political abuse, so much so that Cobbett sometimes seems to forget that he is touring at all'.

What Cole may have ignored when comparing the *Tour* with those earlier *Rides* were the political necessities of that particular year. It was a momentous period in British political history. The Reform Bill had, at last, been passed, but no General Election had, as yet, been called. Everyone knew that Parliament was about to be reformed, but people differed over what Reform would mean. Cobbett, at least, knew what he wanted Reform to mean, and it was in an attempt to turn his wishes into reality that he embarked on his tour. He was as close to being single-minded as he could ever be, and this prevented him, to a large extent, from indulging himself in his writing. He had, in short, less time to indulge in the digressions and the descriptive writing which were the principal attractions of the earlier *Rides*. He confidently believed that his time had now come. The hated borough-mongers had been defeated. Some, though not enough, of the common people would be given a voice in electing the new House of Commons. If he could rouse them to it, they would support him in his purpose which was, to put it briefly, to create a third force in British Parliamentary politics. He was, or so he thought, 'about to break the mould of British politics'.

That, above all, was what the tour was for, and that, in the main, is what the *Tour* is about. The student of politics should find it interesting for that reason alone, for I know of no better account of politics and electioneering in Scotland during those few stirring months when many hoped or feared that a political revolution was about to occur. This edition has not, however, been prepared solely for students of political history. Those who find such political echoes tedious, should still persevere with the *Tour*, even though they read it skippingly. They will find it contains a sometimes unflattering self-portrait of Cobbett in his old age, and Cobbett was always sufficiently a 'character' to be amusing. They will also come across several colourful descriptions of a Scotland that has very largely vanished and be given an opportunity to flavour the polemics of a more robust age than our own. Such things, they may think, deserve their perseverence, and it has been in order to encourage them to persevere that this edition has been provided with aids in the form of Notes, Appendices, and a Biographical Index. Ancient political arguments, vendettas and scandals seldom come alive unless they are put in their context. If that has been done, they are seldom less interesting than anything we can find in our Sunday newspapers, or in *Private Eye*, that latter-day, cut-down version of *Cobbett's Political Register*. The reader who is already at home in the period, and with Cobbett, is entitled to ignore such intrusive addenda. He should concentrate, instead, on the text. This has been taken, verbatim, from the 1833 edition and checked against the original *Register* articles for such discrepancies as arose from Cobbett's hurried editing. It should be added that, although he was an eminent grammarian, his punctuation, spelling, and typographical devices are not always those we are accustomed to.

What remains to be done in this Introduction is to outline the political situation at that time, *as Cobbett saw it* and to give a brief explanation of how the tour was conducted and in what particulars it differed from earlier *Rides*.

The Reform Bill, in its ultimate form, received the Royal Assent on 7 June 1832, something that was only briefly noticed in the *Register*. Cobbett reserved his rejoicing for the 8 July, when he organised a great 'Chopstick Festival' at Sutton Scotney. That was a day he described in a long *Register* article as one of the happiest of his life. It was spent in the company of his fellow-farmers and of those farm labourers who were his cherished 'chopsticks'. He was, moreover, on his home territory, as close to his birthplace at Farnham as he was to Botley where he had farmed so pleasurably for so many years. 'Every thing,' he wrote, 'was right; every thing was pleasant.' He, who was already, though perhaps unjustly, being referred to as the 'the father of Reform' had, indeed, a signal victory to celebrate. But it was no more than one victory in a long-fought campaign he would be engaged in until the day of his death.

It was in pursuance of this *lutta continua*, therefore, that the *Register* of 25 August 1832 published a notice headed *Intended Tour.* In it Cobbett announced that he was about to embark on a journey that would take him from Coventry to some of the principal industrial towns in the North of England. Thereafter, he would cross the Tweed at Berwick and proceed, by way of Edinburgh, Dunfermline, Kincardine and Falkirk, to Glasgow, Paisley and Greenock. Then, if a General Election had not been called in the meantime, he proposed to cross to Ireland, another country he had not, as yet, visited. He was, in short, to visit, lecture and electioneer in those newly-enfranchised constituencies in England and Scotland in which candidates of his own way of thinking stood most chance of being elected. 'SCOTLAND', he wrote, 'I have always wished to see; especially the people of PAISLEY and GLASGOW. . . . The conduct of the Scotch with regard to this question of reform, has been, from first to last, exemplary beyond description; and they are now setting an example to the whole kingdom of good sense and public spirit beyond all praise.' By which he meant that, ever since the 1790s, the Scottish Radicals of Clydeside and the Central Belt had been particularly active in meeting, marching, petitioning, and occasionally rioting in the cause of Reform.

In Ireland he sought potential Parliamentary allies rather than potential Parliamentary followers. He had given strong support to the Catholic Emancipation Act of 1829, which had put Daniel O'Connell in Parliament at the head of a small but vociferous party of Irish Nationalists. There were many subjects on which Cobbett and O'Connell disagreed, but Cobbett was already looking forward towards that Parliamentary alliance of British Radicals and Irish Nationalists that would so often prove to be a powerful factor in British politics. So it was that Cobbett wrote: 'As I shall, I dare say, very soon be a *lawgiver*, I hold it necessary that I should *see* all the people to govern whom I am to assist in making laws. I am particularly desirous to see IRELAND; because of all matters that can engage our attention, none are of so much importance as those which affect Ireland.'

It will be noticed that Cobbett was now confident after twenty-five years of failing to get elected in one constituency after another, that nothing, this time, could prevent his success. The Manchester Radicals had invited him to stand as one of their candidates in that newly-enfranchised, two-member constituency. In the nearby and similar constituency of Oldham, John Fielden, the enlightened and immensely popular industrialist had refused to be nominated as one of the Radical candidates unless his friend, William Cobbett, was invited to stand as the other. Cobbett, initially, preferred Manchester, but consented to fight Oldham as well.

It was, in fact, a more winnable seat for, as the General Election approached, the Reform movement in Manchester was disrupted by factionalism. The Potters (q.v.), who were wealthy industrialists lately turned bankers, exerted great influence in Manchester Reform circles. They had, originally, supported Cobbett's candidature, although the invitation to stand had come from the Radical, rather than the 'moderate' Reformers, most of whom came from the working classes. The Potters, however, were men of property and 'moderates', and the rioting that had preceded the passing of the Reform Act had convinced them that the Radicals were dangerously Jacobinical. They switched their support, therefore to the Whig candidate who, although a Reformer, was a sufficiently moderate one.[1] Tom Potter went so far as to declare that he would 'sell the coat from his back rather than that Cobbett should be member for Manchester'. There was no such opposition in Oldham, where it was thought that the combination of Fielden and Cobbett, local Radical hero and national one, would prove unbeatable. And so, eventually, it was.

The Potters's backsliding enraged Cobbett, and a great deal of mutual blackguarding ensued. The Potters sent pamphlets to Glasgow warning the Reformers there to have nothing to do with Cobbett, and reminding them of all the scandals attached to his past. Cobbett, for his part, filled his *Register* articles, and so, ultimately, his book, with a series of abusive attacks on the Potters and their circle. This was doubly a pity. There was so much abuse of the Potters, and so much of it made tedious reading, that the balance of the book was disturbed. Cobbett, who had blackguarded and been blackguarded by far greater men, was shooting at sitting ducks.

The Manchester schism mirrored the sectarianism that had developed throughout the Reform movement. The country had, as a whole, been forced to accept that Cobbet had been right when he offered the politicians the choice between Reform and revolution. The riots and violence of 1831 and 1832 had made this almost self-evident, and Wellington's failure to form an anti-Reform administration had completed the process. All but the most die-hard Tories were Reformers now, and the Reform movement had developed into such a broad church that sectarianism had become inevitable.

The Tories, having swallowed Reform, looked to the Whigs to keep it 'moderate'. This they were very willing to do. In spite of their new, middle-class followers, and in spite of the 'liberal' doctrines of the Whig 'feelosofers', theirs was still the party of the oligarchs. Even the most 'liberal' and 'feelosofical' of these were members of a generation for whom the French Revolution had served as a fearful warning of what could result from any excess of 'democratical' zeal. Moreover 1830 and the troubles in France, Belgium and Poland, had convinced them that the spirit of '89 still lived. They were determined, therefore, that the Reform Act should be a once-and-for-all measure, since it was clear to them that any movement towards universal suffrage must be a move towards universal anarchy.

Cobbett thought otherwise. The 'great changes' he demanded had been listed by him in the fourteen propositions he had advanced in his *Manchester Lectures* the previous year, and the Act had conceded none of these. Nevertheless, he was prepared, for the moment, to accept the Act as it stood, since he felt confident that it provided an opportunity to transform the Radicals from an extra-Parliamentary and incipiently illegal party into a Parliamentary one, acting within the constitution, and destroying 'moderation' from within. It was to ensure this that he undertook the tour and split from the 'ultra-Radicals' who were all for having nothing to do with the Act since it failed to provide for universal male suffrage, secret ballots, and annual Parliaments.

Cobbett had always disliked the Whigs, whom he had once supported, even more than he disliked the Tories, whom he had also once supported. He believed Lord Grey to be a genuine rather than a reluctant Reformer, but he hated and mistrusted Brougham, who seemed likely to replace him, and almost all the rest of the Whig Ministers. He had personal reasons, moreover, for his hatred. A year earlier, that same adminstration had attempted to ruin him and, perhaps, silence him for ever by putting him on trial for sedition, If that attempt had failed, it was partly because it was so clearly a manufactured case, and partly because he had subpoenaed Grey and the best part of his Cabinet. Although he had not been allowed to put them in the witness box, he had so bullied and lectured them in the course of his defence as to convince judge, jury, and a large part of the public that this was no more than a shabby conspiracy to silence the one man in England who could claim to speak for, and with the voice of, the commons of England.

He had concluded his defence on that occasion in this

manner. 'If I am compelled to meet death in some stinking dungeon into which you have the means of cramming me, my last breath shall be employed in praying God to bless my country, and to curse the Whigs for everlasting; and revenge I bequeath to my children and to the labourers of England.'

As it turned out, he had more reasons for blessing the Whigs than for cursing them. He left the King's Bench a free man and something of a national hero, and from then on carried a martyr's halo in his pocket to be exhibited whenever it suited him to produce it. It is difficult to see what more political advantage he could have gained from that encounter.

Nevertheless he continued to hate the Whigs, not least because it was politically expedient to do so. If he was to achieve his ambition of creating a third force in British politics, he had to do something more than getting as many Radicals as he could elected to Parliament. He also had to discredit the two traditional parties and the two-party system. Consequently, when he got to Edinburgh, he would shock his audience in that eminently respectable and Whiggish city by declaring that, in point of villainy, there was nothing to choose as between the moderately reformist Whigs and the anti-reformist Tories. The latter were 'impudently, basely and intrepidly tyrannical'. The former were 'equally tyrannical, but with the words liberty and freedom continually on their lips. The one party was more brazen, the other more false.' He followed this up from Glasgow with a *Register* article in which he wrote: 'It is no longer Whig-faction against Tory-faction; but both these factions combined against the *phalanx of the people*. They think I am likely to be one of the leaders of that phalanx; and, therefore, rat never sighed for the destruction of cat so sincerely as they sigh for mine.'

His other purpose, which was to ensure the election of a substantial number of Radicals, he had disclosed just as soon as the Reform Bill had become law. The *Register* of 9 June 1832 had contained an article headed *Lectures*. 'NOW', he had announced, 'is the time for EXERTION! . . . For ME now to neglect anything within my power, would not only be an abandonment of my duty towards my country, but a stupid foregoing of my own unquestionable right. . . . What we want now is, a common understanding . . . with regard to the

choosing of proper men for Parliament. . . . To this subject I
shall call the attention of my readers *next week*, when I shall
NAME MEN, whom I think ought to be chosen. . . . But,
besides work with the PEN, I am resolved to work with the
TONGUE.'

The work with the pen did indeed start the following week.
Over the next six months the *Register* was full of puffs for those
Radical candidates Cobbett considered to be 'proper men for
Parliament' accompanied by violent and scurrilous criticisms
of their opponents. As for the tongue, after exercising it in a
series of lectures in London, Hampshire and the Isle of Wight,
Cobbett decided, as has been seen, that he could exercise it
more profitably in those newly enfranchised constituencies in
the north of England and the south-west of Scotland where
Radicals were more likely to win seats. There was a certain
irony in the fact that his native South Country was, under
current conditions, unfavourable electioneering territory. The
smallholders and farm labourers who provided such enthusiastic audiences for him, had not been enfranchised as the £10
householder had been in the towns. So he, who had so mistrusted and resisted industrialisation, had to look to the new
factory towns for seats and support.

This, then, was the over-riding reason for the *Tour*. Once
the reader accepts that this was an account of a barn-storming,
electioneering visit undertaken in the run-up to a uniquely
important General Election the special character of this last of
the *Rides* will become apparent. It is true that all of the previous ones had their political purposes, but they had been of a
general and evangelising nature. Then he had been riding as
missionary at large to the nation. Now he had specific seats to
win and a Radical Parliamentary Party to create.

The earlier *Rides* had taken him, at his own pace, and on
horseback, through familiar farming country, although the
later ones had occasionally led him to the industrial Midlands.
For the most part, however, he had travelled as a fellow-farmer
and a neighbour. He had had time to talk to those he met on
the way, to look over hedges and comment on the crops, to take
tracks and bridle paths, to spend a day or two with friends and
to indulge, perhaps, in a hare course or a day's shooting. Now
he travelled solely by stage coach and post chaise through a

foreign land and amongst strangers. The distances he had to cover forbade delays and diversions, for audiences waited for him at the end of each day's journey. He saw little more of the countryside than could be observed from a coach window, or that might be shown to him by some new Scottish acquaintance in what few leisure hours were left to him. He was constantly invited to inspect factories and machines although such things had never interested him, and he was never as much at home in the Scottish landscape and farmscape as he would have been in the south of England.

All of these things affected the quality of his descriptive writing, for write he had to, whether he was travelling or not. There was always copy for that week's *Register* and a dead-line to meet, and it had been his invariable custom to rise with the sun and devote the hours before breakfast to that task. Now, however, there was also that evening's lecture to prepare and, perhaps, a political speech or two and a reply to an Address. These bit into the time he could devote to his articles, even though he was now dictating everything to his secretary, who was probably, at that time, James Gutsell.

Lecturing had, by this time, become more of a financial necessity than a political requirement. If, at that moment, his political fame had never been higher, his fortunes had never been lower. He had to lecture, and to be paid for lecturing, if he was to travel at all. He was famous enough and orator enough to attract large audiences and, although he dropped the entrance charge, or even lectured for nothing to working-class audiences, he expected to earn considerable sums from middle-class ones.

He himself described his Scottish tour as a 'speechifying' one, and when it was over he calculated what it had entailed. He had, he wrote, travelled more than fourteen hundred miles in eighty-seven days, given twenty-five speeches out-of-doors, delivered fifty lectures, and spoken three times at public dinners. In addition to all this, he had written thirteen *Registers*, frequently contributing more than forty thousand words to a single number. He had indeed to work hard for his politics and his lecture money.

Such things help to explain why the *Tour* was less felicitously written than the earlier *Rides*. But there were also, by now, other considerations. He was in his seventieth year and, although he still showed much of his former vigour, he already entertained some intimations of mortality. For the very first time, such phrases as 'If God spares me' and 'God willing' crept into his writing. He had always been an extraordinarily strong and active man but by now he was also an extraordinarily stout one. He had, for some years past, suffered from a hernia, for which he wore a truss, and like most heavy men he suffered from bronchial trouble.

He had, in fact, no more than another three years to live, and his health would have broken down before then. Yet one cannot believe, on the evidence of all that he accomplished between September 1832 and June 1833, that he was any less powerful, physically, than he had always been. The strains of the tour have been mentioned. It had to be cut short to allow him to rush back to London to prepare for the General Election. Ten weeks later he had taken his seat as the member for Oldham after a hard-fought campaign. He was present for every sitting of the first session and spoke on some hundred and fifty occasions and generally to a hostile House which he defied to shout him down.

There was no sign, at this time, that his physical powers were weakening. He was still, in point of vigour, twice the man most men half his age could ever hope to be. There was some evidence, however, that his mind was weakening. He had always subscribed to the conspiratorial theory of history and he had, in his political career, made more enemies and suffered more reverses than most. It was not altogether surprising, therefore, that he began, in his later years, to suffer from a persecution complex, although it is surprising that it had, by this time, extended to his family. Two years earlier he had written, in *Advice to Young Men*, what was, in effect, a eulogy of, and a guide to, domestic happiness, and had used his own marriage and his own family as illustrations of how this could be achieved. Yet his domestic life, which had indeed been a happy one for more than thirty years, was at that moment collapsing in ruins. He accused the wife he had held up as a model of affection and faithfulness, and the children whose virtues and fondness were the product of the care and love bestowed upon them, of having joined in a conspiracy against him. The following year he cut himself off from them completely, and refused to admit them to his presence until he lay on his death-bed.

If one adds to this a degree of self-approbation that had, by now, some traces of megalomania about it, one can understand why Macaulay wrote that Cobbett, in his final years, was evidently mad. 'His faculties were impaired by age, and the late hours of the House probably assisted to enfeeble his body & consequently his mind. His egotism and his suspicion that everybody was in a plot against him increased and at last attained such a height that he was really as mad as Rousseau.'

Macaulay was a Whig and a 'feelosofer' and had suffered from Cobbett's pen as a consequence, so one need not take him too literally. Cobbett's political speeches certainly showed few signs of any weakening of the political passions that had possessed him ever since he had first started pamphleteering in Philadelphia, forty years earlier. But when one compares the *Tour* with the earlier *Rides*, it is not difficult to believe that his mind, if not yet weakened, had become clouded. Even if one allows for all the strains of the tour and the fact that copy was dictated, often in haste, and sent off unrevised, there is still too much in it that suggests a falling-off in his once very considerable powers as a writer. There is too much often pointless abuse, too many repetitions, too much that is disjointed and rambling for it to be worthy of the author of *Rural Rides*, although a lesser writer might have claimed it as a masterpiece. Cobbett had never been what editors and publishers call a disciplined writer, possibly because he had always been his own editor and publisher. In the *Tour*, however, he often gives the impression of having completely lost control of his material as he wanders backwards and forwards in space and time, or interrupts what he was saying in order to avenge some former or imagined insult.

Yet felicities there are. He had always favoured an epistolary style for his more important articles, and these were generally addressed to important men. But none of them read as well as the two *Letters to the Chopsticks* he wrote from Edinburgh. His descriptions of the 'bothy' system are fine and sympathetic pieces of writing. If he did not do as well by Scottish farming as he had always done in England it was probably because he displayed an almost naive surprise at discovering that the Scots farmed at all. He had come north expecting little more than barren mountains and boggy wastes. Nevertheless, some of his descriptions of Scottish livestock could still be used as examples of what to look for in a beast.

Cobbett was at his best when it came to describing a landscape that had delighted him. A farmscape he would always judge by the state of the crops, but a landscape had to have trees and running water before it could please him. He had little time for landscapes and descriptive writing whilst he was in Scotland, and he apologised to his readers for it. 'I shall', he wrote, 'probably not have room for my notices relative to the country, the scenery, the orchards, and other things on the banks of the CLYDE, until my next . . . I must do full justice to the *political part* of these my CALEDONIAN adventures this, after all, being the matter of the greatest importance.' He wrote that when he was at a spot he described as 'the most interesting spot of earth that I ever set my foot upon in the course of my long and rambling life'. He was, in short, seeing the Falls of the Clyde for the first time, and it is heartening to know that in his 'next' he gave as fine a description of that landscape as any he had ever written in England or America.

He was still the master of the sudden and unexpected phrase which, on second reading, seems difficult to better. Who but Cobbett would have described a particularly large apple tree as one 'in whose shade fifty oxen could lie?' Who else would have described Brougham as 'a gourmandiser of praise?' Or who, anticipating Lord Grey's reaction when reading the next number of the *Register* would have written, 'He will curl his lip, just as they did when Noah was stepping into the Ark?'

The abuse heaped on the 'feelosofers', the 'renegadoes' and such as the Potter gang is, on the whole, tedious, largely because it was seriously meant and the product of obsessions. But there are still traces of the scurrilous wit with which, as 'Peter Porcupine', the young Cobbett had delighted and shocked post-colonial America. What modern gossip writer could be as delicately ribald as Cobbett was when reviving the sad story of 'Duke' Gawler and the octogenarian Duke of Roxburghe, who robbed Gawler of his inheritance by siring an heir on his new, and twenty-year-old Duchess? What modern

political journalist could or would do as much to a former
Chancellor of the Exchequer as Cobbett did to Vansittart?

But finally, we have to return to the fact that it was an electioneering tour. That is always an occasion, as all politicians
know, for repeating a few well-tried slogans at each stopping
place, for abusing one's opponents, and for praising oneself
and anyone who seems likely to be a supporter. So some, at
least, of the tedious abuse in the book should be attributed to
politics rather than to persecution mania. Nor were all the
boasting and puffing and fulsome responses to fulsome addresses symptoms of megalomania. Cobbett had to boast to persuade his audiences that he and his followers were the only
fellows who could, if elected, chastise the Whigs, scourge the
Tories, and rid Westminster and the country of corruption.

It was equally essential that those audiences should be flattered, and, in this instance, Cobbett needed to lay his flattery
on with a shovel, for he had a personal and particular difficulty
to explain away. He had, and deserved to have, a reputation as
a Scotophobe. How he had earned that reputation is discussed
in Appendix B. The London newspapers, always hostile to
him, had joyfully predicted that he would get no farther into
Scotland than the north bank of the Tweed. The Scots he had
so frequently insulted and traduced would throw him back into
the river. The *Scotsman* was confident that its patriotic readers
would see that he was thrown into the nearest ditch.

The newspapers were indulging in wish-fulfilment. Enthusiasm for Reform proved stronger than injured national pride.
Cobbett was given a lion's welcome. The question of his Scotophobia was only once referred to, and that in a most delicate
manner when he was welcomed by the Glasgow factory delegates. For the rest, nothing was made of his regrettable
prejudice, and a great deal was made of his wisdom, courage,
honesty, talents and compassion. Cobbett, in return, assured
the Scots that they were the best, the most industrious, and the
most estimable people on earth—with, of course, the exception
of the 'feelosofers' and 'renegadoes'.

Such a climate of mutual admiration led Cobbett to write, 'I
knew very well that I had the *Scotchies* on my side', which was
not, after all, the most tactful way of describing it. But, since
the 'Scotchies' did not object, Cobbett felt free to crow over the

'bloody old *Times*' and all the other newspapers, and to invite Lord Grey and the Whigs to reflect on the fact that he had even the Scots behind him.

Cobbett seldom, if ever, apologised for anything he had done or said. But when he got back to London, some compunction for past attitudes must have intruded. He wrote a Preface to his book in which he came dangerously close to apologising to the Scots for his alleged Scotophobia. It was an involved apology in which he explained that he had never, in fact, been a Scotophobe, or, if he had, it was because, as an Englishman, it was part of his racial inheritance, and if it was, his had never been a general prejudice but a particularised one. In short, he had always loved, and admired the Scots except for those of them, presumably, who were Whigs, Tories, or 'feelosofers'. He underlined this fact by mentioning that some of his best friends had been Scots.

The back pages of the *Register* regularly contained advertisements for Cobbett's past and present publications. A new one appeared on 5 January 1833. It ran, 'COBBETT'S TOUR IN SCOTLAND, including the four Northern Counties of England, will be published on Thursday, the 10. of January, in a neat volume, price 2s.6d., bound in boards.'

The instant book is not, as we tend to believe, a product of modern journalism and modern technology. The *Tour* was published a mere thirteen weeks after Cobbett had written the first line in Newcastle-upon-Tyne. He had also, in that period, done a great deal of travelling, lecturing, and electioneering, besides fighting a General Election. It is, by any standards, a remarkable feat of book production, and a tribute to the talents, passion, industry and vigour of one of the most remarkable men of his day.

Oldhamstocks Mains

COBBETT'S

TOUR IN SCOTLAND

IN THE AUTUMN OF THE YEAR
1832

BY WILLIAM COBBETT

M.P. FOR OLDHAM

LONDON

PUBLISHED AT 11, BOLT COURT, FLEET STREET:

AND MAY BE HAD OF ALL BOOKSELLERS

1833

DEDICATION

TO THE PEOPLE OF THE BOROUGH OF OLDHAM, IN
LANCASHIRE

MY FRIENDS,

I beg you to receive this little book, the first that I have published
since you did me the honour to choose me to be one of your representatives in the House of Commons; I beg you to accept it as a mark of
the sincerity of my gratitude towards you, as a mark of my admiration of your sense and of your public virtue; and, moreover, I beg you
to accept of it as containing a record of the patriotic sentiments of
the people of Scotland, and of the approbation, which they, beforehand, gave to that choice which you have made.[1] The old and sound
maxim, with all oppressors, is, "*Divide and oppress;*" and, the
oppressions, which this kingdom (formerly three kingdoms) has so
long had to endure, have, in a great measure, arisen from the means
which have been found for acting upon that crafty and malignant
maxim. These means have been afforded by the *prejudices*, which
arose from the innumerable falsehoods (many of which have become
proverbs), which have been sedulously propagated and perpetuated
by those who found their own interest in the oppressing of us. To be
powerful and free; to be able to beat down all oppressors beneath our
feet, *cordial union* amongst us all is the only thing wanted; but, to
secure that happy union, we must first *know one another well*; and,
that you may well know our brethren of Scotland; that you may well
know what they and their country are; that the latter is by no means
that which we have hitherto thought it to be; and that they
themselves are worthy of our highest esteem and of our warmest
affection, the following pages are sent forth to the world, and are
addressed in a more particular manner to you, by

Your faithful friend
And most obedient Servant,

WM. COBBETT.

London, 28. Dec. 1832.

3

PREFACE

The publication of this TOUR has been put off longer than I could
have wished. I intended to put it to the press immediately on my
return from Scotland to London, which return took place on the
23rd of November; but, upon my arrival in London, I found that the
Parliament would be dissolved in a week or ten days from that time;
that I must be compelled to go very soon back to Lancashire; and I
found so much business upon my hands, during the short space between my return to London and the day of the dissolution of Parliament, that it was impossible for me to find time for the writing of this
short preface, and for attending to the sheets of the work as would
have gone through the press.

With regard to THE MATTER contained in this little book, it consists, as the reader is already apprised, of a record of my observations, made during the TOUR described in the title-page; and also of
a record of transactions, rather of a political nature, in which I
myself was a principal actor. I have inserted the divers parts,
according to the date of the place and time, at which, and when,
they were first written. In giving an account of the reception which I
met with on my *Tour*, I have thought, that justice to myself as well as
to my friends required, that I should preserve the several addresses
presented to me, without leaving out even the names which were
signed to them. There can be no doubt that every one who signed any
one of these addresses will be pleased to see his name thus recorded,
more especially as he thus put down his name before the event which
has lately taken place at OLDHAM.

In some few instances I have made small alterations, of a verbal
nature, and here and there I have enlarged my observations and state-
ments of facts; but, generally speaking, I have not found it necessary
to make alterations or additions in the part which was already
written. I have made what I deem a very interesting *addition* relative

to the resources of the *Highlands* of Scotland, and their comparative value with some parts of England; and this addition seemed to me to be necessary, in order to give my readers something like correct notions with regard to that part of their kingdom, which has always been so greatly undervalued, not only by Englishmen, but by all the rest of the world.

The MOTIVES to the making of this publication, are, to communicate to everybody, as far as I am able, correct notions relative to Scotland; its soil; its products; its state, as to the well-being or ill-being of the people; but, above all things, it is my desire to assist in doing justice to the character, political as well as moral, public as well as private, national as well as social, of our brethren in that very much misrepresented part of the kingdom. This is a duty particularly incumbent upon me; for, though I never have carried my notions of the sterility and worthlessness of Scotland, and of the niggardly character of its inhabitants, to the extent which many others have; though I have, in reprobating the conduct of the *"booing" pro-consular feelosofers*, always made them an exception in favour of the *people* of Scotland; though I have always done this, still, I could not prevent myself from imbibing, in some degree, the prejudices, which a long train of causes, beginning to operate nearly a thousand years ago, have implanted in the minds of Englishmen; though I had intimately known, for many years, such great numbers of Scotchmen, for whom I had the greatest regard, still the prejudices, the false notions, lay lurking in my mind; and in spite of my desire always to do justice towards everybody,[1] the injustice would slip out, even without my perceiving it. In any other man it would have been of some importance that these erroneous notions should be corrected; but, in me, whose writings I might fairly presume, extended to every part of the civilized world, it became of very great importance; and it became my bounded duty to do that justice, which I have endeavoured to do in the following pages; and to make, by a true statement of facts, derived from ocular proof, that atonement for past errors, which I have in these pages endeavoured to make.

From how many pairs of English lips have I heard the exclamation: "Good God! who would have thought that Scotland was such a country! What monstrous lies we have been told about that country and people!" And, which has pleased me exceedingly, not one man have I met with to whom the discovery does not seem to have given delight. If I had before wanted a motive to give further extension to my account of Scotland, these exclamations would have been motives sufficient; for, they would have proved, that bare justice demanded that, which, by this publication, I am now endeavouring to do.

Were it *possible*, that either this statement of motives, or that any part of the work itself, could be, by even the most perverse of human beings, ascribed to any desire on my part to curry favour with the SCOTCH, or to any selfish desire whatsoever; were this only possible, I am afraid, that I should not have had the courage to make this statement; but, as this is completely impossible, I make it as being the just due of the people of Scotland, for whose well-being, whose honour, whose prosperity, whose lasting peace and happiness, I have as great a regard, as I have for the well-being, prosperity and happiness of those who inhabit the spot where I myself was born.

WM. COBBETT

London, 28. Dec. 1832

COBBETT'S TOUR

Edinburgh, 14 Oct., 1832.

My proceedings at this city must be reserved for description after I have brought my readers forward from ALNWICK, in Northumberland, at which place I wrote my last *Register*, to this famous capital of Scotland; to *unknow* that which I have known in consequence of my coming to which, is what I would not experience for "all the gold in the Bank of England," which most of my readers will perhaps say, is no great deal!

From ALNWICK to BELFORD, which is about fourteen miles, we first leave behind us, with every feeling of contempt which haughtiness and emptiness can excite in the human mind, the endless *turrets* and *lions* of the descendant of SMITHSON, commonly called PERCY, whose father, CANNING and ELLIS and FRERE[1] so unmercifully ridiculed under the name of "DUKE SMITHSON," in a poem entitled "The Duke and the taxing-man;" the Duke having committed the sin of endeavouring to evade PITT'S assessed taxes. There was a flag flying on the battlements to indicate to the vassals around that the descendant of HOTSPUR was present in the castle.[2] Leaving all this behind us, we came along through better land than that between MORPETH and ALNWICK. There was some wheat out, and some oats also; and one field of very fine oats, not cut. No trees worthy of the name, except a few ASH, and those very bad. As we advanced, the farms grew larger and the land better: the turnips everywhere fine. I saw a flock of small birds; and I do not recollect having seen any small bird this side of Yorkshire, except in the warm plantations of Mr. DONKIN, of NEWCASTLE. At about seven miles from ALNWICK, I saw the sea to the right, and, for a rarity, a village-church. Thereabouts, they tell me, is the seat of Lord GREY, and of his brother, *General* GREY, who, as I was told, being at ALNWICK on the day when I was expected there to lecture, and being told of it, expressed his surprise to find that the people were going to hear me, observing, that my lecturing was all a *humbug*; in which the *General* would have found himself very much deceived, if he had heard me put it to a very numerous and sensible audience, whether they really thought that they ought to be taxed to pay *three generals* for every regiment of foot and horse in our elegant service;[3] and whether they did not think that the elector would deserve to be trampled to death under a cavalry horse's feet, who would give his vote to a candidate that would not pledge himself to put an end to this monstrous waste of our money. If the *General* had heard the sort of answer which the audience gave to these questions, he would not have thought the lecturing "*a humbug*."

Here we get amongst the mischief. Here the farms are enormous; the stack-yards containing from fifty to a hundred stacks each, and each stack containing from five to ten large southern wagon-loads of sheaves. Here the thrashing-machines are turned by STEAM-ENGINES; here the labourers live in a sort of *barracks*: that is to say, long sheds with stone walls, and covered with what are called pantiles. They have neither gardens nor privies nor back-doors, and seem altogether to be kept in the same way as if they were under military discipline. There are no villages; no scattered cottages; no up-stairs; one little window, and one door-way to each dwelling in the shed or barrack. A large farm-house, and large buildings for the cattle and implements; one farmer drawing to one spot the produce of the whole country all around; a sort of manufactory of corn and meat, the proceeds of which go, with very little deduction, into the pocket of the big landlord, there being no such thing as a small proprietor to be seen, though the land is exceedingly fine and produces the most abundant crops: the good part of the produce all sent away; and those who make it all, compelled to feed upon those things (as I shall hereafter more particularly show) which we in the South give to horses and to hogs. This, readers of the *Register*; this is the scene, chopsticks[4] of Kent, Sussex, Hampshire, Wiltshire, and Berkshire; this is the scene, and these the "*country people*" in which, and amongst whom, were born and bred those Ministers who sent VAUGHAN and ALDERSON and DENMAN and WILDE to execute the SPECIAL COMMISSIONS[5] in the South!

All the remainder of the way, through BELFORD and to BERWICK, the land continues to get, if possible, better and better; the turnips incomparably finer; the stack-yards increasing in number and big-ness of stacks; the steam-chimneys taller and taller; and the horrible

barracks longer and longer, and more and more hateful to the sight.
Gracious God! have these fellows the impudence; have they the insolent assurance, to hope to be able to bring the people of Kent, Sussex
and Surrey, into this state? This is "*rural life*" with the devil to it! But
it is useless to waste one's indignation upon the subject: their
emigration schemes and their poor-law schemes will all be blasted;
and they themselves will be the subject of ridicule and contempt for
ages to come.

I descend to the TWEED; and now for the "antalluct!" As I went
over the bridge, my mind, filled with reflecting on those who had
crossed it before me; saying to myself, "This has been the pass of all
those pestiferous *feelosofers*[6] whom I have been combating for so
long, and who have done so much mischief to their own country as
well as mine:" saying this to myself, and thinking, at the same time,
of the dreadful menace of the "SCOTSMAN," and of that "*national
debt of revenge*" that he said Scotland owed me; and with my mind
thus filled, I could not help crossing myself as I passed this celebrated
bridge.

BERWICK, which is a good solid town, and has a river into which
small vessels come to take away the corn from the *corn-factories*, and
which was formerly a strongly fortified place, is regarded, by law, as
being neither England or Scotland, but a separate dominion; and,
thinking that this was a safe place, I intended to stay here the night
of Monday, the 8th, in order to prepare myself a little before I
actually got into Scotland; but, seeing placards up enjoining the
observance of the *fast* on account of the cholera morbus, and being
rather hungry at the time, I, travelling by post-chaise, resolved to
push on another stage, in order to avoid giving offence by indulging
my appetite in such a state of things; therefore, on I came, exclaim-
ing as the chaise got upon Scotch Ground: "Angels and ministers of
grace defend me!" happening to remember so much of some prayer
or play, or something which I have now forgotten. It was plagiarism,
to be sure; but I committed it involuntarily, and I wish Lord
BROUGHAM could say as much with regard to the diverse acts of
plunder that he has committed upon me.[7]

Coming out of BERWICK, we have the sea to our right for some
time, with no trees, stone walls, very fine land, and very fine turnips.
After this, there come a rocky shore and hilly poor ground for a
short space. At about four miles from BERWICK, the sea gets farther
off, the land beautiful, the turnips fifty acres in a piece, fresh and

fine, and the land clean as a flower-garden; and thus, with great stack-yards and long barracks here and there on each side of us, we come down to the village of AYTON, and to the beautiful park and gardens of Mr. FORDYCE! "Fired at the sound, my Genius spreads her wings," and urges me to ask Mr. CREEVEY, my formidable rival at OLDHAM,[8] whether this is that same FORDYCE, who was once *surveyor of crown lands*, and also *collector-general of the taxes in Scotland*; and who was, somehow or other, related to the Duchess of GORDON; and who had AN ACCOUNT, about which account Mr. CREEVEY had given notice of a motion, and which motion he was, somehow or other, prevented from making when PITT was last in office; and, further, whether Mr. CREEVEY, if he have a seat in the reformed Parliament, will revive the motion now; or whether he will give me the information that I may revive it, if I should happen to be in that Parliament; for, though this may be the successor of that Mr. FORDYCE, Mr. CREEVEY, who is a lawyer, knows better than I do, that the crown acknowledges no laches[9] and that the act of *Elizabeth* will hunt public money as a pack of hounds hunt a fox, from cover to cover.

AYTON consists of a parcel of very homely stone houses; but the people seem to look very well, and particularly the boys, who all wear a sort of stiff caps, and who look rosy and hearty. When we get farther on, the land gets poor and hilly; the road twists about among the hills, and follows (towards its source) a little run of water, on the sides of which are some narrow meadows. The hills are here covered with scrubby woods, very much like those in the poorest parts of Hampshire and Dorsetshire. At the end of fourteen miles from BERWICK, I came to HOUNDSWOOD Inn, a place for changing horses; and I liked the look of the place so well, the house seemed so convenient and clean, and the landlord so civil and intelligent a man, that I resolved to stop here all night, which I did; in order to steady my head a little, and to accustom it to that large and fresh supply of "*antalluct*" which it had been imbibing ever since I crossed the TWEED. All these new ideas about thrashing-machines *worked by steam*[10]; corn-weavers, kept in barracks, without back-doors, or privies; all these new ideas, of such vast importance in rural philosophy, especially when I found myself in Dr. BLACK's *native country*, and recollected with what urgency he had pressed upon us of the South, the *prudence* of his countrymen in *checking population* by resorting to *illegitimate* indulgences[11] instead of *loading* themselves with wives; all these new ideas wanted a little digesting in my mind, before I could, with common prudence, proceed to present myself before critics so severe as those which I must naturally expect to meet with at the fountain-head of *feelosofy* itself, where there were (as I had been told at NEWCASTLE) *six or seven newspapers*, all assailing me with the greatest virulence.

On Tuesday morning, my heart thumping against my ribs, off I dashed at as round a pace as I could prevail on the post-boy to drive. For about five miles the land continued the same as before; a little sort of *moor*, in which they dig peat, the valley narrow, the hills on the side rocky, cultivated here and there a little, the rest of the ground growing scrubby firs or wyns; but a great number of Cheviot-hill sheep feeding on them; and very pretty sheep these are. They have no horns, are white all over, legs not long, body very truss, rather larger and a great deal prettier than the South-down sheep. The Highland sheep, of which you do not see a great many here, have black faces, black legs, and very long, very white, and coarse wool. They are very beautiful little sheep; and I will certainly endeavour to get a breed of them to put upon the heaths in Surrey,[12] where, I think, they would soon supplant the little miserable things we call *heath-croppers*. My Lord HOLLAND has always some of these *Highland sheep* at Kensington, in his beautiful park and farm, which he disfigured and half-spoiled, during the building madness of his colleague, ROBINSON's *"matchless prosperity"*[13] of 1824 and 1825. When in the former of those years, I saw "ADDISON-ROAD" come and cut his beautiful farm across, and when I saw "*Cato Cottage*" and "*Homer Villa*" start up on the side of that road, I said, my Lord (and I am very sorry for it) will pay pretty dearly for his taste for the "*classics.*" These "*classics*" are, sometimes, not very safe guides even in matters of a merely literary nature. So long, however, as you confine your enthusiasm to paper and print, you merely expose yourself to ridicule; but when your taste pushes you on to the levelling of banks, the tearing up of trees, the felling of oaks fifty years old, and, above all the rest, to dabbling in brick and mortar, the *classics* become most perilous and pernicious companions! The *Cheviot-hill* sheep have rather short wool, and are very pretty sheep in all respects, but I dare say that the mutton of the *Highlanders* is better; because my Lord HOLLAND must know all about the matter; and I know that he has had a supply of these sheep at KENSINGTON for a great many years.

Along here we see black and red cows, very small compared with those in Durham and Northumberland. The oxen, some without horns and some with horns, and chiefly black, all come from the Highlands, and are all excellent for fatting. There are immense fairs, which are here called *Trysts*, at which these cattle are sold, and from which they go all over the south of Scotland and all over England, except Sussex and Kent, where the Welsh cattle are the favourites. These oxen, fed upon the turnips of this country, and without any hay, will get quite fat during the autumnal and winter months; and the beef in Northumberland and in Scotland is as good as any in the world.

There are some oats out here yet, and some wheat out also. But now, at about seven or eight miles from HOUNDSWOOD, we get through the hills and out of this little narrow valley; we see the sea to our right, and the fine level country opens before us. Here we entered into what is called EAST-LOTHIAN; and just at a little village called "*Cockburn's Path*," where there is the second church that I have seen since I quitted BERWICK, we get into the county of HADDINGTON, where we see the sea all along upon our right till we get to DUNBAR (a distance of sixteen miles from HOUNDSWOOD), and such corn-fields, such fields of turnips, such turnips in those fields, such stack-yards, and such a total absence of dwelling-houses, as never, surely, were before seen in any country upon earth. You very frequently see more than a hundred stacks in one yard, each containing, on an average, from fifteen to twenty English quarters of wheat or of oats; all built in the neatest manner; thatched extremely well, the thatch bound down by exterior bands, spars not being in use owing to the scarcity of wood. In some of these yards the thrashing-machine is worked by horses, but in the greater part by steam; and where the coals are at a distance, by wind or water; so that in this country of the finest land that ever was seen, all the elements seem to have been pressed into the amiable service of sweeping the people from the face of the earth, in order that the whole amount of the produce may go into the hands of a small number of persons, that they may squander it at London, at Paris, or at Rome. Before we got into DUNBAR we found the road (which is very fine and broad) actually covered with carts,[14] generally drawn by one horse, all loaded with sacks of corn. For several miles it appeared to be a regular cavalcade of carts, each carrying about twelve English sacks of corn, and all going to DUNBAR, which is a little sea-port (though a large town) apparently made for the express purpose of robbing Scotland of all its produce, and of conveying it away to be squandered in scenes of dissipation, of gambling, and of every other vice tending to vitiate man and enfeeble a nation.

Between HOUNDSWOOD and DUNBAR, we came to ROXBURGH-PARK,[15] which has near it a sort of village consisting of very bad-.looking houses, with the people looking very hearty and by no means badly dressed, especially the little boys and girls, whose good looks I have admired ever since I entered Scotland; and about whom the parents seem to care much more than they do about their houses or themselves. They do not put boys to work hard when they are young, as they do in England; and, therefore, they are straighter and nimbler on foot; but here is a total carelessness about the *dwelling-place*. You see no such thing as a little garden before the door; and none of those numerous ornaments and those conveniences about the labourers' dwellings, which are the pride of England, and by which it is distinguished from all the other countries in the world. The dwelling-place of a *mere working countryman* in the United States of America is, generally, a miserable shed, all the *round-about* of which appears to have no owner at all.

They told us that the Duchess of ROXBURGH lived at this ROXBURGH-PARK, which is a very fine place, and very well wooded, and at which I could not look without thinking of BURDETT's *second*[16] poor "*Duke Gawler*", whose learned heir apparent is, or recently was, a candidate for the city of NORWICH, as mentioned in my *Register* of some time back,[17] where I gave the history of old Sir JAMES INNIS's getting the dukedom, marrying a young wife at four-score, having a son by her, which son is now a minor, and which wife is now the duchess living in this park. Faith! if GAWLER had got this dukedom, his heir would not need a sinecure place in the Chancery, and his brother would not need a commissionership along with SENIOR, and the "*reporther*" COULSON, whom BROUGHAM has set to work, under the name of a *poor-law commission*,[18] to digest a plan for an entire new distribution of the revenues of all the Englishmen's estates, from the lord down to the forty-shilling freeholder; for to this dukedom of ROXBURGH appertains an immense estate in the county of that name, which is bounded to the south and the west by the CHEVIOT HILLS, and through which, from one end of the county to the other, runs one branch of the TWEED; the south-eastern part being bounded by the TWEED itself, having on the banks land, if possible, still finer than this land of the LOTHIANS, Lord! how "DUKE

GAWLER" would have revelled in the possession of this estate! His heir apparent would have had DICK GURNEY for a huntsman, instead of creeping under the gabardine of this brewer-banker, in order to be shuffled into a seat for the city of NORWICH, in consequence of the recommendation of the famous patriot BURDETT, who used to teach us the absolute necessity of "*tearing the leaves out of the accursed Red Book,*"[19] and who has now the idiot-like folly and impudence to be trying to thrust one of the tax-eating HOBHOUSES into a seat for the city of BATH.

At DUNBAR, in the town, and going across the upper end of the main street, which is so wide as to be worthy of being called an oblong square instead of a street; across the end of this street stands the very plain, but very solid and very noble-looking house of my Lord LAUDERDALE, on whom I should certainly have called to pay my respects, if I had had time, his Lordship having been, upon several occasions, personally civil to me.

At about three miles from DUNBAR, we see, away to our right, standing upon a high hill, with beautiful woods about it, and looking over the sea, the house of the Earl of HADDINGTON, whose fine estate sweeps, we are told, all around this county; and which is very far from being destitute of trees. At about five or six miles from DUNBAR we came, at a place called BELTONFORD, to the bunch of farms rendered so famous by the monstrous farming and cattle concerns of that Mr. RENNIE, the account of whose failure occupied, some time ago, so much space in the London newspapers; and whose affairs really seem to have been upon a scale such as states or sovereigns might engage in.

> "Ill habits gathered by unseen degrees;
> As brooks make rivers, rivers swell to seas."

This couplet, which has been a proverb ever since it was first published, is applicable to this agricultural madness. Mr. RENNIE never thought beforehand, never dreamed before he began to stretch out, of the lengths to which he would be finally led. Here, again, and at every other step, we behold the fatal effects of the accursed paper-money.[20] What was there to check a sanguine and enterprising mind in pursuit of wealth, when money was to be had, in any quantity, by merely dipping a pen into an ink-stand, and writing a few words upon a little bit of paper? Such a man had no need of reflection, if the system then existing could have continued; if the system of *"cheap-currency,"* so eulogised by that profound statesman Lord HOWICK, could have continued, Mr. RENNIE must have gone on increasing in wealth; but it could not continue; foreign nations would not suffer us to have bank-notes to so great an amount passing along with gold; and then the system blew up, and Mr. RENNIE was destroyed; and destroyed, too, without having ever suspected the possibility of it, and without, even to this hour, clearly understanding the cause. In such a case a man is not to be accused of dishonesty; the wrongs which he does are not the wrongs of intention; he is impelled by unseen causes; and he is no more answerable for the consequences than is the man who, being knocked down by another, falls upon a child and presses it to death. But here is the dilemma; either the innumerable persons who have, in the manner of Mr. RENNIE, scattered ruin and misery around them; either these persons have all been criminal, or this is the foolishest or the wickedest Government that ever was tolerated upon the face of this earth; an alternative, which, if put to the vote, would be decided in favour of the latter proposition, by nine hundred out of every thousand men in the kingdom.

The country continues much about the same all the way to HADDINGTON; only it has more woods, and these very beautiful, consisting, however, chiefly of *beech, ash, sycamore,* and *birch,* though with here and there an *oak tree* of small size. Before we reach HADDINGTON, we see innumerable carts carrying the corn towards that town. Here are fields with trees round them like the finest and largest fields in Sussex and Kent. About two miles before we get to HADDINGTON, Sir JOHN SINCLAIR'S house and estate lie a little way on our left, and Lord DALKEITH'S farther on in the same direction, in a fine, well-wooded, beautiful valley; land as fine as it is possible to be; a hundred acres of turnips in one piece; and, as I am very well informed, with forty tons of bulbs upon an English acre. Everything is abundant here but people, who have been studiously swept from the land; and for which, by the laws of God as well as man, this Government is answerable; and it is not by way of joke that I express my hope, that it will be made to confess its errors, or that it will be punished for intention of mischief.

HADDINGTON is a large, a good, and solid town; and, being situated in the midst of so fine a country, must in the mere business of supplying the farms, besides being an immense mart for corn, possess a great deal of wealth. After we quit HADDINGTON, we come to a place called TRANENT, which is a sort of a colliery town; here are collieries and rail-roads; and the county, as well as the town of HADDINGTON, are supplied with coals from this source. Coming on from this place to MUSSELBURGH, we see the mouth of the FIRTH of FORTH, away to our right; and down there, close by the sea, lies that PRESTONPANS, rendered famous by the bloody battle fought at that place. Here we look across the FIRTH into the fine county of FIFE, and see the Highlands begin to rise up beyond KINROSS and the FIRTH of TAY. The prospect here is very beautiful, and thus we go on to MUSSELBURGH, which is a sort of place of resort for EDINBURGH people in the summer. It is called a village, but it is in reality a very fine town for the greater part of it. From this place, close along by the water-side we come to another village called PORTOBELLO, and then to EDINBURGH itself, at which I arrived about half-past two o'clock, and took up my quarters in the house of a friend, of whom I must not more particularly speak until I am placed beyond the possibility of being in his house after he shall have seen this account. Here, then, I was, in that city, of which I had heard and read so much; of which I had spoken in terms, not one of which was to be retracted as long as I was in it; and my reception in which, six news-papers here, to say nothing of the hundreds in England (the bloody old *Times*[21] by no means excepted), had, for more than a month, been labouring to render not only mortifying and disgraceful but even personally perilous! And here it was, in this renowned capital of Scotland, that I was destined, without even uttering a single word in my defence, to crown my triumph over all these atrocious calumnia-tors, and over the base and detestable men in power, who had employed the mercenary wretches to vomit forth their calumnies.

But, before I proceed to endeavour to describe to my English readers this beautiful city, and its still more beautiful environs, I must endeavour to perform a task far more interesting to us all, and especially to the people of Scotland, gratitude on my part to whom, would render the performance of this task a bounden duty, even if England had no interest in it; but the fact is that it is interesting to all of us alike; and, if I discharge it as I ought, in a manner commensur-ate with the importance of the subject, I shall receive the lasting thanks of every good man in the kingdom.

Let me look back, then, over this fine country, from the TWEED to the FIRTH of FORTH. When at NEWCASTLE, I learned that *Scotch vagrants* were regularly sent from that place back into Scotland by *pass-carts*; that the conveyance of them was *contracted for*; and that the contractor recieved two pounds two shillings for each journey; that this contractor put them down at a place called KYLOWE or KELSO, a place five miles distant from BELFORD, on the road to BERWICK; that the vagrants were delivered into the custody of a police-officer, who saw them deposited in the parish in Scotland named in the pass; and that the contractor had sometimes taken the same individuals as often as ten or twelve times! These facts, of the correctness of which there can be no doubt, may be useful to Lord BROUGHAM's most wise *commission*, the great object of which is to get rid of the English poor-laws; that is to say, those just laws, which, before they were violated by STURGES BOURNE's bills, ensured to the working people of England something like a due share in the produce of the earth, in compensation for the loss of that patrimony which the aristocracy had taken away from them at that season of enormous robbery and plunder most falsely called the Reformation. These facts, so astounding, so unanswerable, may serve also (and I hope they will) to make Mr. O'CONNELL less positive, and less pertinacious, in opposition to the ONLY measure that can ever make Ireland a country fit for either a poor or a rich man to live in.[22] These facts may (and I trust they will) serve the further purpose of inducing my dignitary, Dr. BLACK (who is spoken of with great respect here), to hesitate before he another time holds out the labourers of Scotland as an example to be followed by the *chopsticks* of the South. He does not, indeed, persevere, like Mr. O'CONNELL, to revile the institution of poor-laws; but still, he talks of the *ignorance* of my countrymen, the chopsticks; he imputes the fires to their *ignorance* and not to a *sense of their wrongs*; he contrasts their turbulent behaviour with the *quiet submission* of the labourers of Scotland, whom he represents as being WELL OFF in consequence of *their fewness in number*; he ascribes the suffering of the labourers of England to the *excess of their numbers*, and not to the weight of the taxes and the low wages which those taxes compel the farmer to wish to pay. These are most pernicious errors; errors that have produced the greatest evils; and errors which it shall be my duty to dissipate, if I find myself equal to the task.

With regard to the poor-laws; before any one is impudent enough to propose to abolish them, or to change them (except back again to their original state), let him hunt throughout Scotland and Ireland, and there find an *English vagrant*; there find a *pass-cart* to convey

beggars back again to England. This is the first thing to do before a
pack of Scotch and Irish renegadoes get together to hatch the means
of robbing the working people of England of the compensation of
their patrimony, as the people of Scotland and Ireland have been
robbed. Before any quack be impudent enought to propose to
abolish English poor-laws, let him stop the *pass-carts*, which are
constantly in movement to carry out of England, and to toss back
upon their own soil, the destitute people of Scotland and Ireland.

Here is a thing calling itself *"a Government"* and a *"paternal
Government"* too, having three countries under its management, out
of two of which distressed persons are continually prowling into the
third; and that third is as constantly engaged in carrying these
distressed person back again by force, and tossing them back upon
the soil from which they have made their incursions; and this work of
carrying back (causing great expense) is constantly going on through
numerous channels every year of our lives, from the first of January
to the thirty-first of December: and with all this before their eyes, this
"paternal Government" is incessantly at work, hatching schemes for
reducing the third country to the situation of the other two! It is
useless to rage; and, there being *a liberal Whig Ministry* in power, I
stifle my feelings, and refrain from doing justice in characterising
this Government.

But now, Dr. BLACK, about the famous *"antalluct"* of the
labourers of Scotland, and the *ignorance* of the chopsticks of the
South; those causes of turbulence in the latter, and of the quiet submission in the former. You are a Scotchman, Doctor; but you know
nothing about Scotland. You live in England; but you know nothing
about England. *Books* have been your teachers; and that which you
know about the characters, the capacities, and especially the *motives*
of living authors, ought to warn you against trusting the stuff put
forth by the scribbling coxcombs, fools, and knaves that are dead. I,
taking permission to use the words of the apostle, "bear witness of
that which I have seen." It is not yet a week since I set my foot in
Scotland; yet I have seen enough to make me clearly understand the
ground-work of all your errors relative to this most important of all
human matters.

I find that there is a sort of poor-laws *in some parts of Scotland*;
that the counties bordering on the sea, through which I have come,
that the county of FIFE, and others, some of the rich parts of
Scotland; that this city, that PAISLEY, GLASGOW, GREENOCK, have

compulsory assessments for the relief of the poor; but that, in all the interior, and over the far greater part of Scotland, there is no such provision, and that the destitute depend entirely upon collections at the church-doors, and upon other alms voluntarily given. The people of England compelled the Government to give them a legal claim upon the land generally in lieu of their *patrimony*, which consisted of efficient and substantial relief out of the tithes. The people of Scotland, embroiled and torn to pieces by conflicting tyrants; and the people of Ireland, kept down by the iron arm of the greedy aristocracy in England; had not the power to compel their rulers to do them justice, and give them compensation for the loss of their patrimony. Therefore these two countries were robbed without compensation ever obtained; and therefore it is that destitute persons prowl from them into England, and that the English destitute persons stay at home.

Even Scotch charity does a great deal, and the distribution of the alms being committed to their exemplary parochial ministers, a great deal is done to alleviate the sufferings of the destitute. In the rich counties and the great towns where the assessment is compulsory, it is nevertheless extremely defective. It is a *fixed sum for the year*. In this city it is six per cent. on the rental; but then (which is a subject to be treated of another time) the judges, and every one belonging to the courts, claim an exemption; very unjustly, to be sure, but they claim it, and they have it; and thus about a thousand of the richest men in the city pay nothing towards the relief of the poor. The sum thus raised is found to be very inadequate: here, in this fine and beautiful city, with as much real piety as is to be found in any place in the world; with ministers as diligent, and with a whole people as charitable, the assessments fall so much short of the necessities of the case, that the suffering and the beggary, though so much checked by the proud stomachs of the people, surpass, in a ten-fold degree, that which is to be found in any place in England; and if I were to say in a fifty-fold degree, I do not think that I should go beyond the fact. From everything that I can learn, nothing can exceed the diligence, the pains, the disinterestedness, with which the funds raised for the poor at EDINBURGH are managed; and yet such is the distress and such the beggary! Well, then, what does this prove? It proves the wisdom as well as the justice of the act of Elizabeth; it proves that, to make the relief what it ought to be, there must at all times be, as in England *and the United States of America*, a power to collect, not a certain sum during the year, but as much as shall be wanted during the year, and the adoption of measures to secure the due application as well as an efficient collection.

Having now shown that even in Scotland necessity has dictated something in the way of compulsory assessment, leaving Mr. O'CONNELL to reflect on these and on the foregoing facts, and respectfully suggesting to him to consider whether it might not be as well to sweep beggary out of Ireland first, and then for us to discuss, when the people shall have their backs covered and their bellies filled, the question about a repeal of the Union; leaving Mr. O'CONNELL and these matters here, let me now, Dr. BLACK, turn to you again, and talk to you about that famous "*antalluct*" beforementioned, that keeps the labourers of the North so quiet, while those of the South are so turbulent; and about that "*moral restraint*" of the nasty-pensioned-parson[23] MALTHUS, and that "*prudence in abstaining from marriage*" which makes the labourers of Scotland so WELL OFF; because, Doctor, it is the last-mentioned matter which is the great thing of all.

Now, then, let me tell you how those persons are off, whom you wish the labourers of England to imitate, and with whom you wish them to change situations. But I will not address myself to you here. I will address myself to the chopsticks of the South; and this part of this *Register* I hereby direct my printers to take out of the *Register*, after they have printed off the edition, and to put it in a half sheet or quarter sheet of demy paper, with a title to it, just such as I shall here give. I hereby direct them to print ten thousand copies of this address; to put at the bottom of it, price ONE PENNY; and I hereby direct the person keeping my shop at *Bolt-court*, to sell these addresses at *five shillings a hundred*; or at *three shillings for fifty*. Now, then, Doctor, BROUGHAM and MALTHUS and LORD HOWICK and STURGES BOURNE and BROUGHAM's other poor-law commissioners, SENIOR and COULSON the *reporther*, and HARRY GAWLER (the Duke's brother) and *Malthusian* BURDETT, and all the whole crew, shall find that I have not come to Scotland for nothing.

COBBETT'S ADVICE
TO THE CHOPSTICKS
OF

Kent, Sussex, Surrey, Hampshire, Wiltshire, Dorsetshire, Berkshire, Norfolk, Suffolk, Essex; and of all the other Counties in the South of England.

Edinburgh, 14. *Oct.* 1832.

My Friends, — This is the finest city that I ever saw in my life, though it is about five hundred miles to the north of the southern part of Dorsetshire; but neither the beauty of this city, nor its distance from your and my home, has made me forget you, and particularly poor COOK and Farmer BOYES and the men that were transported in 1830. I have some *advice* to offer you, the object of which is to induce you resolutely to maintain the rights which, agreeably to the laws of our country, we all inherit from our forefathers. Amongst these rights are, the right to live in the country of our birth; the right to have a living out of the land of our birth in exchange for our labour duly and honestly performed; the right, in case we fall into distress, to have our wants sufficiently relieved out of the produce of the land, whether that distress arise from sickness, from decrepitude, from old age, or from inability to find employment; because there are laws, and those laws are just, to punish us if we be idle or dissolute.

There is a reform of the Parliament; and, it is touching your conduct as connected with this reform, that I am about to offer you my advice; but before I do that, I must speak to you about what I have seen in Scotland, of which this fine city is the capital. You know that many gentlemen in England have *Scotch bailiffs*; and that these Scotch bailiffs, particularly CALLENDAR, the bailiff of Sir THOMAS BARING, in Hampshire, and another one or two whose names I have now forgotten, were principal witnesses against the men who were brought to trial for breaking thrashing-machines, and other acts of that sort in 1830. You know that these bailiffs are always telling you how good and obedient the labourers are in Scotland, and how WELL OFF they are; and yet they tell you that there are no poor-laws in Scotland.

All this appears very wonderful to you. The Government and the parsons tell you the same thing; and they tell you, that if you were as well-behaved as the Scotch, and as quiet, you would be as well off as they are. They say, that it is your *ignorance* that makes you not like to live upon potatoes while those who live upon the tithes and the taxes have the meat and the bread. They tell you that you would be better off if you were but as sensible and would be as quiet as the Scotch labourers. Now, then, I will tell you how well off the Scotch labourers are; and then you will judge whether you have been wise or foolish, in what you have been lawfully doing for two years past, with a view to making your living a little better than it was.

This city is fifty-six miles from the river TWEED, which separates England from Scotland. I have come through the country in a post-chaise, stopped one night upon the road, and have made every inquiry, in order that I might be able to ascertain the exact state of the labourers on the land. With the exception of about seven miles, the land is the finest that I ever saw in my life, though I have seen every fine vale in every county in England; and in the United States of America I never saw any land a tenth part so good. You will know what the land is when I tell you, that it is by no means uncommon for it to produce seven English quarters of wheat upon one English acre, and forty tons of turnips upon one English acre;[24] and that there are, almost in every half mile, from fifty to a hundred acres of turnips in one piece, sometimes *white* turnips and sometimes *Swedes*; all in rows as straight as a line, and without a weed ever to be seen in any of these beautiful fields.

Oh! how you will wish to be here! "Lord," you will say to your-selves, "what pretty villages there must be there; what nice churches and church-yards; oh! and what preciously nice ale-houses! Come, Jack, let us set off to Scotland! What nice gardens we shall have to our cottages there! What beautiful flowers our wives will have climbing up about the windows, and on both sides of the path leading from the wicket up to the door'. And what prancing and barking pigs we shall have, running out upon the common, and what a flock of geese, grazing upon the green!"

Stop! stop! I have not come to listen to you, but to make you listen to me; let me tell you, then, that there is neither village, nor church, nor ale-house, nor garden, nor cottage, nor flowers, nor pig, nor goose, nor common, nor green; but the thing is thus: 1. The farms of a whole country are, generally speaking, the property of one lord; 2. They are so large, that the corn-stacks frequently amount to more than a hundred upon one farm, each stack having in it, on an aver-age, from fifteen to twenty English quarters of corn; 3. The farmer's house is a house big enough and fine enough for a gentleman to live in; the farm-yard is a square, with buildings on the sides of it for horses, cattle, and implements; the stack-yard is on one side of this, the stacks all in rows, and the place as big as a little town. 4. On the side of the farm-yard next to the stack-yard there is a place to thrash corn in; and there is, close by this, always a thrashing machine, sometimes worked by horses, sometimes by water, sometimes by wind, and sometimes by steam, there being no such thing as a barn or a flail in the whole country.

"Well," say you, "but, out of such a quantity of corn and of beef and of mutton, there must some come to the share of the chopsticks to be sure?" Don't be *too sure* yet; but hold your tongue, and hear my story. The single labourers are kept in this manner: about four of them are put into a shed, quite away from the farm-house and out of the farm-yard; which shed, Dr. JAMIESON, in his Dictionary, calls a "boothie," a place, says he, where labouring servants are lodged. A boothie means a little booth; and here these men live and sleep, having certain allowance of oat, barley, and pea meal, upon which they live, mixing it with water, or with milk when they are allowed the use of a cow, which they have to milk themselves. They are allowed some little matter of money besides to buy clothes with; but they never dream of being allowed to set their foot within the walls of the farm-house. They hire for the year, under very severe punishment in case of misbehaviour or quitting service; they cannot have fresh service, without *a character* from the *last master*, and also a character from the *minister of the parish!*

Pretty well, that, for a knife-and-fork chopstick of Sussex, who has been used to sit round the fire with the master and the mistress, and to pull about and tickle the laughing maids! Pretty well, *that!* But it is the life of the married labourer that will delight you. Upon a steam-engine farm there are, perhaps, eight or ten of these. There is, at a considerable distance from the farm-yard, a sort of *barrack* erected for these to live in. It is a long shed, stone walls and pantile roof, and divided into a certain number of *boothies*, each having a door and one little window, all the doors being on one side of the shed, and there being no *back-doors*; and as to a *privy*, no such thing, for them, appears ever to be thought of. The ground, in front of the shed, is wide or narrow according to circumstances, but quite smooth; merely a place to walk upon. Each distinct *boothie* is about seventeen feet one way and fifteen feet the other way, as nearly as my eye could determine. There is no ceiling, and no floor but the earth. In this place a man and his wife and family have to live. When they go into it there is nothing but the four bare walls, and the tiles over their heads, and a small fire-place. To make the most of the room, they, at their own cost, erect *births*[25], like those in a barrack-room, which they get up into when they go to bed; and here they are, the man, his wife, and a parcel of children, squeezed up in this miserable hole, with their meal and their washing tackle, and all their other things; and yet it is quite surprising to behold how decent the women endeavour to keep the place. These women (for I found all the men out at work) appeared to be most industrious creatures, to be extremely obliging, and of good disposition; and the shame is that they are permitted to enjoy so small a portion of the fruit of their labours, of all their cares.

But if their dwelling-place is bad, their food is worse, being fed upon exactly that which we feed hogs and horses upon. The married man receives in money about four pounds for the whole year; and he has besides sixty bushels of oats, thirty bushels of barley, twelve bushels of peas, and three bushels of potatoes, with ground allowed him to plant potatoes. The master gives him the keep of a cow for the year round; but he must find the cow himself: he pays for his own fuel; he must find a woman to reap for twenty whole days in the harvest, as payment for the rent of his *boothie*; he has no wheat; the meal altogether amounts to about six pounds for every day in the year; the oatmeal is eaten in porridge; the barley-meal and the pea-meal are mixed together, and baked into a sort of cakes upon an iron plate put over the fire; they sometimes get a pig and feed it upon the potatoes.

Thus they never have one bit of wheaten bread or of wheaten flour, nor of beef nor mutton, though the land is covered with wheat and cattle. The hiring is for a year, beginning on the 26th of May, and not at Michaelmas:[26] the farmer takes the man, just at the season to get the sweat out of him; and if he die, he dies when the main work is done. The labourer is wholly at the mercy of the master, who, if he will not keep him beyond the year, can totally ruin him, by refusing him a character. The cow is a thing more in name than reality; she may be about to calve when the 26th of May comes; the wife may be in a situation to make removal perilous to her life. This family has NO HOME; and no home can any man be said to have who can thus be dislodged every year of his life at the will of a master.[27] It very frequently happens that the poor creatures are compelled to sell their cow for next to nothing; and, indeed, the *necessity of character from the last employer* makes the man a real slave, worse off than the negro by many degrees; for here there is neither law to ensure him relief, nor motive in the master to attend to his health or to preserve his life.

There, chopsticks of Sussex, you can now see what English scoundrels, calling themselves "gentlemen," get Scotch bailiffs for. These bailiffs are generally the sons of some of these farmers, recommended to the grinding ruffians of England by the grinding ruffians in Scotland. Six days, from daylight to dark, these good and laborious and patient and kind people labour. On an average they have six English miles to go to any church. Here are twelve miles to walk on the Sunday; and the consequence is, that they very seldom go. But, say you, what do they do with all the wheat and all the beef and all the mutton, and what becomes of the money that they are sold for? Why, the cattle and sheep walk into England upon their legs; the wheat is put into ships to be sent to London, or elsewhere; and as to the money that these are sold for, the farmer is allowed to have a little of it; but almost the whole of it is sent away to the landlord, to be gambled or otherwise squandered away at LONDON, at PARIS, or at ROME. The rent of the land is enormous: four, five, six, or seven pounds for an English acre: the farmer is not allowed to get much; almost the whole of the produce of these fine lands goes into the pockets of the lords; the labourers are their slaves, and the farmers their slave-drivers. The farm-yards are, in fact, *factories* for making corn and meat, carried on principally by the means of horses and machinery. There are no people; and these men seem to think that people are unnecessary to a state. I came over a tract of country a great deal bigger than the county of Suffolk, with only three towns in it, and a couple of villages, while the county of Suffolk has twenty-nine market towns and 491 villages. Yet our precious Government seems to wish to reduce England to the state of Scotland; and you are reproached and abused and called ignorant, because you will not reside in a "*boothie*," and live upon the food which we give to horses and to hogs! Take one more fact, at which you will not wonder; that, though Northumberland is but a poor county compared with this that I have been describing, the poor Scotch labourers get away into England whenever they can. There is a great and fine town called NEWCASTLE-UPON-TYNE, from which, and its neighbourhood, the coals go into our country. The poor Scotchmen flee from their fine and rich lands to beg their bread there; and there they are put into caravans and brought back to Scotland by force, as the Irish are sent from LONDON, from MANCHESTER, from BIRMINGHAM, and other great towns in the South.[28] Is not this the greatest shame that ever was witnessed under the sun! And shall not we be resolved to prevent our country from being reduced to a similar state; shall not we venture, if necessary, our limbs and our lives, rather than not endeavour to cause, by all legal means, a change in the condition of the labourers of these two ill-treated countries? What! shall any lord tell me, or tell any one of you, that you have not a right to be in England as well as he has? Will he tell you that he has a right to lay all his lands *waste*, or lay them into sheep-walks, and drive the people from them? A stupid land-owner might say so, and might attempt to do it; but detestable must be the Government that would suffer him even to begin in the work of giving effect to his wish. God did not make the land for the few, but for the many. Civil society invented property, but gave it not that absolute character which would enable a few owners to extirpate the people, as they appear to be endeavouring to do in Scotland. Our English law effectually guards against the effects of so villainous a disposition; it gives to all men a right to maintenance out of the produce of the earth: it justly gives to the necessitous poor a claim prior to that of the owner of the land. The law has been greatly impaired by the acts of STURGES BOURNE, which created the select vestries[29] and introduced hired overseers into the parishes. It is my intention to use all the means in my power to get these acts repealed; and it is upon this subject that I am now about to give you my advice. You see the situation of the Scotch and the Irish, in consequence of a want of the poor-laws; and the design manifestly has been, and yet is, to go on by degrees stripping England of the poor-laws. STURGES BOURNE's acts were a great stretch in this direction; let us, therefore, use all our strength legally to annihilate these acts.

Your case is this. For a thousand years, your forefathers were, in case of necessity, relieved out of the produce of the TITHES, and were never suffered to know the pinchings of want. When the tithes were taken away by the aristocracy, and by them kept to themselves, or given wholly to the parsons, your forefathers insisted upon a provision being made for them out of the land, as a compensation for that which had been taken away by the aristocracy and the parsons. That compensation was given them in the rates as settled by the poor-law. To take away those rates would, therefore, be to violate the agreement, which gave you as much right to receive, in the case of need, relief out of the land, as it left the land-owner a right to his rent. STURGES BOURNE's acts have not, indeed, openly violated the agreement; but they have done it in a covert and indirect manner, by taking away the power of the native overseer to administer relief, and by taking away the equal rights of rate-payers to vote in the vestry.

To get these acts repealed is our first duty, and ought to be our earliest care; and I do most strongly urge you to attend at all elections, *whether you have votes or not*,[30] and to demand of the candidates that they will vote for the repeal of these acts. I exhort you to be ready with petitions[31] in support of those members of Parliament who shall demand this repeal. Though, according to the Reform Bill, you are not *to vote*, yet you have *the right of petitioning*; and if you make use of that right, and in a proper manner, we shall never again see those days of degradation of which we have now seen so many.

As God has now blessed us with a harvest such as the oldest man living scarcely ever saw, I hope that you are all enjoying the fruits of it, in proportion to the labours that you have performed, and to the sobriety and care that you have practised and exercised. I shall be glad, when I see you again, to find you better off than when I saw you last; I confide in your resolution to maintain your present rights unimpaired, and in your efforts to recover those that have been lost; and, in that hope,

I remain, your faithful friend,

Wm. COBBETT.

There, Dr. BLACK, now talk about your *"antalluct"* as long as you please. What a Sussex chopstick would say if he were asked to live with his family in one of these *"boothies,"* I do not exactly know; but this I know, that I should not like to be the man to make the proposition to him, especially *if he had a bill-hook in his hand!* Slow as is the motion of his tongue and legs, his hands would move quickly enough in such a case. In short, Doctor, you have never seen, and you can know nothing of, the labourers of either country. If you had seen a great deal of the docile and cheerfully submitting labourers of Scotland, you could know still less than you know now about the glum and stubborn chaps in the South, whom neither interest, nor threats, nor certainty of punishment, will move to do that which they think they ought not to be commanded to do. They will not, even if they greatly gain by it, do anything out of the track of their habits and prejudices. Yet, in their stubborn adherence to their words, and in their perfect sincerity, a sensible man finds a compensation for their untowardness; but the rules which may very well apply to one of these sets of men, may be wholly inapplicable to the other. And, as to the *"antalluct,"* be you assured, Doctor, that the Scotch labourers would not be a bit less intellectual, if they were to sit down to dinner every day, to wheaten bread and meat, with knives and forks and plates, and a nice clean cloth every Sunday, as they do yet in a considerable part of the farm-houses in the southern counties of England.

I now come back to this delightful and beautiful city. I thought that BRISTOL, taking in its heights and CLIFTON and its rocks and its river, was the finest city in the world; but EDINBURGH with its castle, its hills, its pretty little sea-port, conveniently detached from it, its vale of rich land lying all around, its lofty hills in the back ground, its views across the FIRTH: I think little of its streets, and its rows of fine houses, though all built of stone, and though everything in LONDON and BATH is beggary to these; I think nothing of *Holyrood House*; but I think a great deal of the fine and well-ordered streets of shops; of the regularity which you perceive everywhere in the management of business; and I think still more of the absence of all that foppishness, and that affectation of carelessness, and that impudent assumption of superiority, that you see in almost all the young men that you meet with in the fashionable parts of the great towns in England. I was not disappointed; for I expected to find EDINBURGH the finest city in the kingdom. Conversations at NEWCASTLE, and with many Scotch gentlemen for years past, had prepared me for this; but still the reality has greatly surpassed every idea that I had formed about it. The *people*, however, still exceed the place: here all is civility; you do not meet with rudeness, or even with a want of a disposition to oblige, even in persons in the lowest state of life. A friend took me round the environs of the city; he had a turnpike ticket, received at the first gate which cleared five or six gates. It was sufficient for him to *tell* the future gate-keepers that he had it. When I saw that, I said to myself, "Nota bene: Gate-keepers take people's word in Scotland; a thing that I have not seen before since I left *Long Island*."[32]

In this tour round the city we went by a very beautiful little country-house, at which Mr. JEFFREY, the Lord Advocate,[33] lives. He

did not do me the honour to attend my lectures on account of ill-
health, which cause I am very sorry for; for it will require health and
spirits, too, for him to buffet the storm that is about to spring up,
unless his party be prepared to do a great many things of which they
appear not as yet to have dreamed. In the course of this little tour I
went to, and to the top of, the ancient CRAIGMILLAR Castle, which
stands on a rock at about three miles from EDINBURGH and from
which you see the castle and all the city of EDINBURGH; and you look
across the Firth of FORTH, and, beyond it, and over the county of
FIFE, and the Firth of TAY, see the Highlands rise up. It appears that
part of this castle was demolished by the English, when that merciless
monster Henry the Eighth invaded Scotland in order to *compel the
young Queen of Scots to marry his son*, Prince Edward! So this
ruffian, who was marrying and beheading wives himself all his life-
time, actually undertook a war for a purpose like this! This young
queen lost her life at last, by the hands of the myrmidons of his
savage daughter; but, at any rate, she enjoyed some years of happiness in France; and one minute of it she never would have had, being
in the hands of a TUDOR.[34]

This castle has round it, with some exceptions as to form, a circle,
the diameter of which is about ten miles, of land, which lets on an
average for seven pounds the English acre. It lets the higher certainly, for being in the neighbourhood of a city like EDINBURGH; but not
much higher. Here is an area of seventy-five square miles; and here
ought to be, according to the scale of the county of Suffolk, about
thirty-two churches and thirty-two villages around them; and with
the exception of MUSSELBURGH, there is but one, or at least I could
see but one; and is it possible that among so many *really* learned and
really clever men as these are at EDINBURGH, not one should be
found to perceive the vast difference in this respect between this city
and all the cities in England, and to perceive, too, how much greater
and more famous EDINBURGH would be, if it were surrounded, as it
ought to be, with market-towns and numerous villages? You cannot
open your eyes, look in what direction you will, without perceiving
that Scotland is robbed of its wealth and of its character by a stupid
and unnational nobility. And, if the reformed Parliament do its
duty, it will do by Scotland as HENRY *the Seventh* did by England;
and we shall very soon see villages rise up in Scotland, and see a stop
put to the caravan bringing back to the North vagrants from NEW-
CASTLE.

With regard to my *lecturing concerns*, which are of far less importance than any other of the subjects of this volume, I have to observe, in justice to my hearers, that better manners never were exhibited in this world than by my audiences here; and that, though I have seldom failed to experience great cordiality and great indulgence, never have these been exceeded at any of the numerous places at which I have thought it my duty to offer my opinions. The four lectures were advertised in the following words:

"1. On the necessity of a great change in the management of the affairs of the nation; on the numerous grievances inflicted on the country by the boroughmonger parliaments; and on the duty of the electors to pledge candidates to measures which shall remove those grievances.[35]

2. On the nature of the pledges which electors ought to insist upon, before they give their votes; and on the justice and necessity of the measures to which they would be bound by those pledges, including amongst those measures a total abolition of tithes, lay as well as clerical, in all parts of the kingdom.

3. On the injustice of taxing the people to pay interest to those who are called fundholders; and on the resources possessed by the nation, for making, from motives of indulgence and compassion, such provision for a part of the fundholders as may be found necessary to preserve them from utter ruin.

4. On the mischiefs and iniquity of paper-money generally, and on the necessity of putting a stop, as speedily as possible, to all paper-money of every description."

These subjects I went through at the *Adelphi Theatre*, before an audience consisting of rather better than a thousand persons. That which was wanting in me (and a plenty was wanting) was amply made up for by the good-nature, the indulgence, and the kindness of the audience. I had not read the vile newspapers (for I never do)[36] but my friends had; and they who do not know so well as I do the effect of such publications, were greatly alarmed lest I should meet with a hostile reception. I uniformly told them not to be afraid: they were surprised at my confidence; but they found it amply justified by the event. The truth is that, in the first place, the Scotch are a sensible people. When you have fools to deal with, you do not know what may happen. Then, that which I had to utter was so true; and yet, uttered in this bold manner so *new*; besides, there were my hundred volumes of books written by my own hand;[37] there was my battle with this powerful and malignant Government for more than a quarter of a century, ending with its last foul attack, and my triumphant defence, in the *Court of the King's Bench*; and here was I, an utter stranger, five hundred miles from my home, to make an appeal to reason and to justice: under such circumstances, to have doubted of a patient hearing, would have been to show very little knowledge of mankind in general, and no knowledge at all of the people of Scotland; but my reception very far exceeded my hopes. Every man that I have met with at EDINBURGH has been as kind to me as if he were my brother. Young men are always more zealous than those of an advanced age; and the conduct of the young men of EDINBURGH towards me has been such as it is impossible for me adequately to describe.

It was desirable that I should give one lecture at a place, and upon terms that would enable the working people to attend, without hindrance to their occupations and without a tax upon their purse. For this purpose, a very large room was engaged last night, where I attended, and where I harangued for the better part of two hours; and I wish the Lord Advocate had been well enough to have been present; for then he might have had a foretaste of that which is to come. Upon this occasion an ADDRESS was presented to me, to which, after the manner of *"other great men,"* I had prepared a written answer, contrary to my usual practice; but which I though proper to do on this occasion, in order to show that I deemed this a matter of very great importance, as I really did mean it. With the insertion of this address, preceded by the very neat speech of Mr. DUN, followed by the names which were attached to it at a very short notice, and those names followed by my answer, I shall now conclude this long, and I am afraid the reader will think it wearisome account of my entrance into Scotland.[38]

Mr. B. F. Dun, teacher, in presenting the Address, said,

"Sir, — I am deputed by a respectable body of my fellow-citizens to present you with a congratulatory address on your visit to this city. We have long observed your strenuous, indefatigable, and disinterested exertions in the cause of Reform; and glad are we that those exertions have not been made in vain. A march in human affairs has commenced, and although you have been hitherto

seven years in advance, we trust that now you and all genuine Reformers will march hand-in-hand till there be obtained a radical
reform, and an utter extinction of all monopolies, corruptions,
and abuses. We are proud to avow, Sir, that we owe whatever political information we do possess, to your writings, and we are satisfied that in addressing you we are only expressing the sentiments
of thousands of the inhabitants of this city. It is gratifying to be
able to state that no sooner had the humble individual who has
now the honour to wait upon you drawn up this address, and
scarcely was the ink dry, than the names of many of our respectable fellow-citizens were attached to it. With your permission I
shall now read it."

To WILLIAM COBBETT, Esq.

Edinburgh, 13. October 1832.

Sir, — We, the undersigned, respectfully take leave to express the
gratification afforded us by your arrival in the metropolis of
Scotland.

Unknown to you even by name, with no other excuse for the liberty
which we have taken than the admiration and respect which the
worth of your character and the splendour of your talents generally
excite, we have come forward thus publically to bear testimony to
your unremitting, and we rejoice to say, *successful efforts in the
cause of Reform.*

In you we do not so much behold WILLIAM COBBETT, the ablest of
writers, the most consummate politician, as the fearless, the uncom-
promising advocate of the rights of the people. Fully convinced that
your writings have been the means of exposing that system of misrule
by which the many have been so long plundered for the gains of the
few, and by which *the usurpation of a grasping aristocracy has been
perpetuated*, we earnestly hope that you may be preserved to us for
many years, and that your health may remain unimpaired, so that
you shall have the happiness of witnessing, as well as procuring those
objects dearest to all disinterested and patriotic men, — the blessings
of *cheap government, cheap law, cheap religion, cheap bread,* and a
good day's payment for a good day's work.

You, Sir, to whom the political world owes so much, need scarcely
be informed that there are many of the *inhabitants of this city* who

will always rejoice in your success. Should you, as we confidently anticipate, be *be one of the members* in the people's reformed House of Parliament, we have no doubt that your voice will ever be raised in the *cause of the working classes* — that you will be the unflinching supporter of civil and religious liberty — and that no exertions shall be wanting on your part to root out every species of corruption and abuse from whatever source it may emanate, and whoever may be its supporters. That patriotism which has led you to advocate out of Parliament those healing measures which we fondly expect to be the mighty realities of what is termed the Reform Bill, will, we are confident, incite you in Parliament, with your usual ability, and by arguments completely irrefragable, to render reform NOT A DEAD LETTER, but a measure of practical utility to the country at large.

In this city where the *newspaper press* has enlisted itself under the banners of *one or other of the two parties* who have alternatively assumed the reins of Government, it is most gratifying to us to be able to state that you, who it is well known will allow no compromise, no party considerations, to influence your opinions, have *numerous and daily increasing friends.*

That their esteem and regard may long continue, is the sincere wish of

Sir,

Your most obedient servants,

[There follow approximately 520 signatures and addresses]

MR. COBBETT'S ANSWER

Gentlemen, — I thank you very sincerely for this mark of your esteem, which, though some persons may be surprised at my receiving it, is by no means matter of surprise with me. The nation in general would naturally suppose that the virulence and falsehoods of the base newspapers would produce some effect upon your minds prejudicial to me: your conduct upon this occasion will convince the whole country, that my judgement was correct, when I despised the efforts of those vehicles of slander, and relied upon your penetration and your justice.

To make the grasping part of the aristocracy recoil from its usurpations, and loosen its grasp, has long been a principal object of my labours; and never will I desist from the pursuit until the working man, in whatever calling of life, shall have his full share of the fruits of the earth and of his own labour.

Gentlemen, it was the labourers of the South[39] who compelled the Ministers to bring in the Reform Bill; it was principally the great towns that compelled them to carry it to the last stage; and it was again those great towns that produced the final result. The work has been the people's from the beginning to the end; and for the Reform Bill not to be "*a dead letter,*" the people must still carry on the work; first, by choosing proper members where they can; and above all things, by coming to the support of those members who shall be found able and ready to support their cause in the house.

I do not say, Gentlemen, that I receive an address at Edinburgh with a greater degree of pleasure than I should receive one at any other place; but I receive this address with a very singular pleasure, because it gives a contradiction in terms the most striking, to the assertion of that infamous press which has pursued me with its viperous tongue, from the banks of the Thames to the banks of the Firth of Forth. Therefore, Gentlemen, you are entitled to my partic-ular thanks; in rendering you which, I shall be joined by every true friend of our country, from the Isle of Wight to the north of the Highlands of Scotland.

Glasgow, 19. October, 1832

On Monday morning, the 15th of October, I went in a carriage, furn-ished by my kind friends at EDINBURGH, who accompanied me in it, to a place called QUEEN'S-FERRY, where you cross the FIRTH of FORTH, to go over to a little place called NORTH FERRY, whence I went in a post-chaise to the ancient town of DUNFERMLINE. But before I proceed to give a further account of my progress, I must observe on something that I left behind me at EDINBURGH, namely the *Caledonian Mercury* news-paper, promulgating in one of its columns of the 15. October, Mr. DUN'S address to me at the *Waterloo Room*, the address itself and my answer to that address; and in addition to this, the editor's statement, "that the large *Waterloo Room* was *crowded to excess* long before the hour appointed; that, on his entrance, Mr. Cobbett was *greeted with repeated rounds of applause*; and that, at the conclusion of the lecture, *thanks* were given him in the shape of *three general cheers*; and that he was *again cheered* when he drove off from the door of the hotel."

In another column of the same paper is the following, which the *Caledonian* gentleman had the justice, the good taste, and the sound judgement to extract and insert from that rumble-tumble of filth and beastly ignorance, called the *Globe*[1] newspaper: —

"COBBETT. — Cobbett, who has by this time, we suppose, commenced his lectures at Edinburgh, *has been (doubtless) receiving an overflow of that sort of tribute to which his frequent scurrilous abuse of Scotland and Scotsmen has so naturally advanced a claim.* The *Caledonian Mercury*, received today, contains an *elaborate article,* in which the almost inconceivable contradictions and inconsistencies of the oracle of the *Register* are duly set forth. In a general way, this, of course, conveys nothing but that which all the world knew before;[2] but as a *refresher* for the modern Athenians, preparatory to the opening of a lecture, it is a *formidable affair.*"

Thus we have a specimen of the expectations of this beastly crew of hirelings. Here was this stupid oaf, who is scribbling in a dirty news-paper in London, while the army-list represents him as a brevet colonel on full pay doing duty at CHATHAM barracks, and while we are taxed to the tune of five hundred a year, to pay him for his CHATHAM services; here was he, cherishing in his beastly mind the thought that I should be hissed and hooted out of EDINBURGH; or, as another newspaper of that city had advised, flung into the deepest and dirtiest ditch that could be found: and this thought we see coming into his brutal head, in consequence of "*an elaborate article,*" which has been put forth by this very identical *Caledonian Mercury*! But, though this might not much surprise one, coming from a blundering skull, the produce of potatoes, and filled with blubber instead of brains, it really is a matter of surprise that the editor of the *Caledonian Mercury*, a name at once descriptive of a sensible people, and of uncommon science and literary acumen; it is really a matter of astonishment to see these two things put forth in a paper under such a title, and in one and the same number.

Enough of these envious, malignant, mercenary, mean and cowardly wretches; but not enough, and never enough, of the people of EDINBURGH, of all classes, with regard to their conduct towards me; and, self-gratification aside, this is a matter of very great importance, in a *public* point of view; because, somehow or another, no matter how it has happened, but, somehow or another, my name has become identified with certain great measures, involving a *total change* in the manner of conducting the affairs of this kingdom. No matter how it has happened; but *it is so*. Therefore Lord GREY, if he be not blinded by the set who surround him, must, in this one fact, see quite enough to induce him to believe that it is utterly impossible that the Government should proceed at all, if it attempt to get along without making something like *that sort of change* for which I have so long been contending. I beseech him to think of this matter seriously; and not to imagine that this unequivocal popularity of mine is a thing confined to the breasts of the *working people*. It was not of these that the audiences at the theatre of EDINBURGH were composed. It was not with these that I was invited to dine in that city of science of all sorts. The popularity did not, and could not, arise from any cause other than that which I have stated. I knew not one single soul in that city; my notification in the *Register* that I intended to go to EDINBURGH, brought me a letter from Messrs. CHADWICK and IRELAND, merchants, whom I had neither ever seen or heard of before in my life.[3] The price of entrance at the theatre was, on account of the high charge made for the use of it, a great deal higher than I could have wished, and necessarily excluded working men; and yet that theatre was crammed full from beginning to end. There was nothing in my writings; nothing in my character, except that it had been vilified more than that of any other man that ever lived; nothing in my station in life; no possibility of my ever being able to make a return for any favours received. Therefore, my reception and my treatment are to be ascribed solely to the favour with which my political principles and my well-known endeavours and intentions are viewed. Perhaps Lord GREY does not think it worth his while to read my *Register*; if so, that is his fault and not mine; if he do, let him ponder well upon what I have now said, before he listen to the advice of those who would make him believe that he can get on with a reformed parliament *without making any great change*.

In returning, now, to my most delightful tour: upon leaving EDINBURGH, along the very finest turnpike-road that I ever saw, the cause-ways on the sides of which are edged with white stone, and the gutters paved as nicely as those of a street; in leaving EDINBURGH we came closely by the castle, which I had not seen at so short a distance before, and up into which I would not go, seeing that there were *soldiers* there; for merely speaking to any one of whom (he choosing to swear that I had endeavoured to seduce him to desert, or quit his post) *I might have been hanged by the neck till I was dead*, according to a law originally drawn up by SCOTT ELDON, passed for the life of the "good old king," revived again (on the motion of SCOTT ELDON) when his worthy eldest son came to the throne, and *now kept in full force* by the liberty-loving Whigs!

This castle, like the Christian church, is built upon a rock, which rock is very lofty, and almost perpendicular; so that it is a most interesting and magnificent spectacle, especially if your are on any eminence at a little distance from the city; infinitely grander and more interesting than St. Paul's from BATTERSEA Rise. I remember nothing of the sort equal to it, except the view of LINCOLN cathedral. As you come out of the city, you see the very pretty and convenient port of LEITH, about a mile and a half away to the right; the Firth of FORTH is before you; the beautiful county of FIFE on the other side of that; and the Highlands rising up in the distant view. Just at coming into the country, losing sight of the water, you get into the estate of Lord ROSEBERRY, which is one of the finest estates in Scotland. It has everything; fine fields, fine pastures, fine woods, immense tracks of beautiful turnips, stack-yards with a hundred stacks in each; all, however, rendered mournful to me by the sight of the thrashing-machine and of the beggarly barrack, in which are doomed to live on oats, barley, peas and potatoes, those without whose labour all this land would be worthless, having neither woods, nor stacks, nor turnips, nor herds of cattle, nor flocks of sheep.

After just seeing the top of Lord ROSEBERRY's house, which lies down pretty nearly to the Firth, in a fine glade between two lofty woods, we came to the QUEEN'S-FERRY, took leave of our friends, and sailed across the FIRTH, in a large boat, which took us over in about ten minutes, seeing the mouth of the Firth away to our right, and seeing four large *men-of-war* lying in ordinary about a mile up to our left.[4] In that direction, too, we saw the grand mansion of Lord HOPETOUN, in a very beautiful situation, in a well-wooded park, forming part of his immense estate, which is, they say, another of the finest in Scotland. These descriptions do not accord with my former ideas of Scotland, though I knew that there were some very fine lands and places in this country; but it is my business truly to describe that which I have seen, paying no regard to what I formerly thought upon the subject.

From the NORTH FERRY to DUNFERMLINE, the country, which

belongs, I am told, chiefly to Lord MORAY, and then farther on to Lord ELGIN, and is in the county of FIFE, is nearly level; the land not so good as that in EAST and MID-LOTHIAN, but still very good; the farms large as before; the turnip-fields prodigious; and uniformly good beyond description; this being the country for turnips, because the FLY never destroys them as it does in England; which, when they hear it, will make English farmers cease to wonder that the crops are so uniformly good.

DUNFERMLINE, which is now a place for the manufactory of table-cloths and table-covers, contains about twelve or fourteen thousand inhabitants, and is, like all other manufacturing places, more abundant in small and mean houses than in houses of a different description. It is, nevertheless, a good solid town, and is to return one member to Parliament, who is, they say, quite worthy of its sensible and spirited inhabitants, a good part of whom, in spite of a dreadful alarm about the cholera morbus, attended in a chapel, from the pulpit of which I harangued them on the necessity of driving out at the door, or tossing out of the window, any candidate, who offering himself as their *representative*, should have the audacity to tell them, that it was beneath him to pledge himself to do that which they wanted him to do for them. After the harangue, I spent a most pleasant evening (which I made too long) amongst these intelligent and zealous men of DUNFERMLINE, and promised to send them a small collection of my books for the use of their *Political Union*;[5] which I shall do as soon as I get home.

This town is celebrated for the abbey that formerly was here, and has been the burial-place of several of the Scottish kings, particularly of the renowned ROBERT BRUCE, whose tomb is just opposite the pulpit in the church, and whose names are written, or rather the letters of them are fixed up, round the spire of this church.

From DUNFERMLINE, I had engaged to go to FALKIRK, which, together with other places, is now to send one member to Parliament. We left DUNFERMLINE about noon on Tuesday, the 16. of October, had to go fourteen miles to KINCARDINE, a little town on that side of the FIRTH of FORTH, and then to cross the ferry to go to FALKIRK, at a distance of six miles from the ferry. The land upon leaving DUNFERMLINE, appears to be as fine as any can be in the world; the pastures are very fine, and also the trees; the people are within the reach of fish; and there is nothing wanting, apparently, that God himself could have given to man except fuel; and that is here given in coals, which may be dug out of every field, and which are so cheap as to be hardly worthy of being accounted a part of the expense of a family. Yet, in the midst of all this, how fares the man who labours on the land? What share of its produce does he enjoy? These questions must receive their answer in another address to the *chopsticks* of the South.

COBBETT'S ADVICE
(2nd ADDRESS)
TO THE CHOPSTICKS
OF

Kent, Sussex, Surrey, Hampshire, Wiltshire, Dorsetshire, Berkshire, Oxfordshire, Buckinghamshire, Norfolk, Suffolk, Essex; and all the other Counties in the South of England.

Glasgow, 19. October, 1832.

MY FRIENDS,

In my former address I described to you how the *married* labourers of Scotland were treated, in what places they lived, and what they lived upon: I am now going to describe to you how the *single* men live; I mean the farming men, who are what the law calls servants in husbandry. I mentioned to you before, that these men are lodged, a parcel of them together, in a sort of shed, and that they are never suffered to eat or drink, or even set their foot in the farm-house any more than the oxen or pigs are; but I had not then examined the matter with my own eyes and ears, which I have now done; and I shall, therefore, now give you an account of the whole thing, and shall give you my advice how to act so as to prevent yourselves or your children from ever being brought into the same state.

On Tuesday last, the 16th of this month, I went to the farm of a Farmer REID, near the town of DUNFERMLINE. The land is as fine as man ever set his eyes on, having on it some of the finest turnips that you ever saw; and there being in the stack-yard about three-score stacks, perhaps each containing from fifteen to twenty quarters of corn; fine oxen and hogs in the yard, and fine cows and sheep in the pastures. I told you before, that the single men lived in a sort of shed, which is here called a *"boothie;"* and the farmer upon this farm, living near a town, and being said to use his people rather better than the common run, I wished to see with my own eyes the *"boothie"* upon this farm and the men in it.

The custom here is for the men to plough with a pair of horses; to go out at daylight; come in at twelve o'clock, and stay in till two; then go out again and plough till night; and I have seen many of them plough till sunset. COKE of Norfolk brought this practice from Scotland to Norfolk; and it has spread over a good part of England. It is a very bad practice, though I adopted it for some time, and, I found no advantage to me, while it was a great slavery both to the horses and the men.

I went to the *"boothie"* between twelve and one o'clock, in order that I might find the men at home, and see what they had for their dinner. I found the *"boothie"* to be a shed, with a fire-place in it to burn coals, in, with one doorway, and one little window. The floor was the ground. There were three wooden bedsteads, nailed together like the births in a barrack-room, with boards for the bottom of them. The bedding seemed to be very coarse sheeting with coarse woollen things at the top; and all seemed to be such as similar things must be where there is nobody but men to look after them. There were six men, all at home; one sitting upon a stool, four upon the sides of the births, and one standing talking to me. Though it was Monday, their beards, especially of two of them, appeared to be some days old.[6] There were ten or twelve bushels of coals lying in a heap in one corner of the place, which was as nearly as I could guess, about sixteen or eighteen feet square. There was no back-door to the place, and no privy. There were some loose potatoes lying under one of the births.

Now, for the wages of these men. In the first place the average wages of these single farming men are about ten pounds a year, or not quite four shillings a week. Then they are found provisions in the following manner: each has allowed him two pecks of coarse oatmeal a week, and three *"choppins"* of milk a day, and a *"choppin"* is, I believe, equal to an English quart. They have to use this meal, which weighs about seventeen pounds, either by mixing it with cold water or with hot; they put some of it into a bowl, pour some boiling water upon it, then stir it about and eat it; and they call this BROSE; and you will be sure to remember that name. When they use milk with the meal they use it in the same way that they do the water. I saw some of the brose mixed up ready to eat; and this is by no means bad stuff, only there ought to be half-a-pound of good meat to eat along with it. The Americans make "brose" of the corn-meal; but then they make their brose with milk instead of water, and they send it down their throats in company with buttered beef-steaks. And if here was some bacon along with the brose, I should think the brose very proper; because, in this country, oats are more easily grown in some parts than wheat is. These men were not troubled with cooking utensils. They had a large iron saucepan and five or six brose-bowls; and they are never troubled with those clattering things, knives, forks, plates, vinegar-cruets, salt-cellars, pepper-boxes, mustard-pots, table-cloths, or tables.

Now, I shall not attempt any general description of this treatment of those who make all the crops to come; but I advise you to *look well at it*; and I recommend to you to do everything within your power that is lawful for you to do, in order to show your hatred of, and to *cause to suffer*, any one that shall attempt to reduce you to this state. The meal and the milk are not worth more than eighteen-pence a week; the shed is worth nothing; and here are these men, who work for so many hours in a day, who are so laborious, so obedient, so civil, so honest, and amongst the best people in the world, receiving for a whole week less than an American labourer receives for one day's work not half so hard as the work of these men. This shed is stuck up generally away from the farm-yard, which is surrounded with good buildings, in which the cattle are lodged quite as well as these men, and in which young pigs are fed a great deal better. There were three sacks of meal standing in this shed, just as you see them standing in our farm-houses filled with barley-meal for the feeding of pigs. The *farm-house*, standing on one side of the yard, is always a sort of gentleman's house, in which there are several maids to wait upon the gentleman and lady, and a boy to wait upon them too. There is generally a BAILIFF upon these farms, who is very often a relation of the farmer; and, if he be a single man, he has either a small "*boothie*" to himself, or a place boarded off in a larger "*boothie*;" and he is a sort of sergeant or corporal over the common men, who are continually under his eye day and night; and who being firmly bound for the year, cannot quit their service till the year be out.

It is from this source that the *"agricultural gentlemen,"* as they call themselves, in England, have been supplied with SCOTCH BAILIFFS, who are so justly detested by you. The Scotch land-owners, who suck up and carry away almost the whole produce of the earth, have told the English land-owners how they manage the matter here. The English fellows find that they can get nobody in England to treat men in such a way, and, therefore, they bring them up from Scotland, and they pick out the hardest and most cruel fellows that they can find in Scotland; so that we have not, by any means, a fair specimen, even of Scotch bailiffs; because nineteen twentieths of them would not do the savage things which the English tyrants want them to do. Well enough may you complain of Scotch bailiffs; and, wherever you find one, you always find the employer to be a grinding, hard-hearted man, and I advise you to have your eye upon every man who has a Scotch bailiff; for, you may be very sure, that his intention is to bring you down to the shed and to the brose; to prevent you from ever seeing knife or fork, or bread again, and to have you considered as being nothing better than the cattle.

I shall address another paper to you before I leave Scotland; and in the meanwhile it is right to tell you that every good man in this country (and the far greater portion of them are very good men) detest these agricultural tyrants as much as you and I do. The tyrants take the produce of the land and carry it all away, and treat worse than horses and dogs those who make the produce to come. When a labouring man offends one of these tyrants, he is doomed to starve, or to get away out of the country; and the poor creatures go away from some of the richest lands in the world, and get into England to beg; and then they are sent back again as vagrants. And this, my friends, is the state to which it has been attempted to reduce the labourers of England. Have your eyes open; be resolved to maintain all your rights; *be resolute* in it; and then you will not only preserve yourselves from this horrible degradation; but you will rescue from it your oppressed fellow-subjects and brethren, the labourers of Scotland.

I am your faithful friend,

Wm. COBBETT.

Directing (as I hereby do) my printers to print off, in the same manner as directed last week, *ten thousand copies* of this address to

the chopsticks with *price a penny* at the bottom of each, and with
intimating to my readers that, by application at BOLT-COURT,[7] they
may have them at five shillings for a hundred, or fifty for three
shillings; with these matters thus settled, I now proceed on my
journey from DUNFERMLINE to FALKIRK; the land on both sides of
the road extremely fine. We do not, for several miles, see the FIRTH
of FORTH; but it is not far to our left. The farms are very fine;
turnips surprisingly fine; large woods; rows of trees by the sides of the
road; the trees vigorous and fresh and lofty; as beautiful a country,
taken altogether (abating only the want of vine-covered cottages and
little gardens), as I ever went through in all my life. At four or five
miles from DUNFERMLINE we come to a long village called TORY-
BURN, the houses in general having no up-stairs; all the buildings
extremely ugly and mean; and yet the village is manifestly in a state
of rapid decay, many of the houses being empty, and many of them
tumbling down. This village, we perceive as soon as we quit it, has
been principally created by the fishing; for here we find ourselves
with the FIRTH of FORTH close down by our left, and we see little
houses here and there all along the shore. A little farther on we see
the woods of CULROSS, down to our left near the water; and upon the
road where we are, we come to a mansion, and pretty place called
TORY. Here we are getting amongst old friends; for here resides Sir
JOHN ERSKINE, brother and successor of Sir JAMES ERSKINE (and not
Sir WILLIAM as I thought) who is now dead, and succeeded by his
brother JOHN, and which Sir JAMES was husband No. 1. of our Lady
LOUISA PAGET[8], who, as the newspapers told us, and as the courts
decided, had No. 2. in Sir GEORGE MURRAY, who is now canvassing
for a seat in PERTHSHIRE, just over the hills to our right! The newspapers, and the courts too, may have belied her ladyship and in that
case I shall be singularly happy, if she will afford me the means to
send over the world a contradiction with regard to this affair; for I
have long felt a particular interest in the affairs of her ladyship, who
is, to make use of the words of a friend at DUNFERMLINE, "amongst
the most fascinating of all the fascinating creatures in this world;"
besides which, she is, in some respects, a person belonging to the
people; and I do not think the worse of myself for being a sort of
shareholder in a case like this. My Lord COCHRANE used to say,
"That a man might eat mutton till he become a sheep." And a lady
might eat taxes till she become taxes, however fascinating she may be
on the outside. This fascinating creature, though the daughter of the

Earl of UXBRIDGE, and the sister of the Marquis of ANGLESEA, had one pension given her while she was a maiden, and another at her marriage to Sir JAMES ERSKINE. And BURDETT, when he was a noisy patriot, and when he was teaching us the necessity of "tearing the leaves out of the accursed *Red Book*," with just as much zeal as he is now praising the King and the Queen, and urging the people of BATH to elect a placeman who was nursed on sinecure pap,[9] used never to omit to mention the particular case of our fascinating Lady LOUISA, though he might as well have mentioned Lady JULIANA HAY, whom little SANCHO, his colleague, at once brewer and right honourable privy-counsellor, led to the altar a little while ago from the pension-list, where she had been sticking for *twenty-one years at the least*, though the daughter of one marquis, and the sister of another. Faith! she may be sticking on the pension-list yet, for anything that I know to the contrary! But we will know all about this by-and-by: we will have bright Lord ALTHORP'S *reasons* for heaping money upon these ladies, while those who till the land live upon "brose," and while those who make the clothing have not half enough to eat. Aye, and we will put Daddy BURDETT to the test, too. We will see whether he will help to tear the leaves out of the "accursed *Red Book*;" whether he will help to endeavour to produce so much of an equitable adjustment as may induce the brewer privy-counsellor to give us back the amount of the receivings of Lady JULIANA.

Quitting TORY, which is a very pretty place, we come, a little farther on, to the very beautiful house and park of Sir ROBERT PRESTON, who is now the owner of CULROSS, which lies away to our left on the side of a very beautiful bend in the Firth of Forth, in a little detached part of the great county of PERTH, and divided from it by the small county of CLACKMANNAN, from the chief town of which Lord ERSKINE took his title. CULROSS is a very beautiful spot. Rising up and bending round by the side of the water. As beautiful a place as any to be found about the *Isle of Wight* or the SOUTH-AMPTON Water. It was impossible for me to see it without thinking of the NEW-FOREST, NETLEY-ABBEY woods, and particularly of that HOLLY-HILL[10] at which once resided that Lord COCHRANE, who was born at this CULROSS, it then being the estate of his father; and to reflect on whose treatment always fills me with indignation inexpressible, knowing as I did, and as I do, that, even if the thing imputed to him had been a crime, he was innocent of that crime; and remembering, as I do, all the base means that were used to render him despicable in the eyes of the people, whom he had served in Parliament with more zeal and fidelity than any man that I have ever known, my Lord RADNOR only expected; and who was more capable and more disinterestedly disposed to serve his country in arms than any man that I have ever known in my life.

Before we get to KINCARDINE, where we are to cross at the ferry, we go over about a mile or so of poor heathy ground, thousands upon thousands of acres the like of which any one may see in my native country of Surrey. Here, a few miles to our right, we see the OCHILL hills, running along from east to west, and dividing the country of FIFE from the county of PERTH. These hills are not called *Highlands*, though they are very lofty. As we approach KINCARDINE, the view is by far the finest that I ever beheld. We are in the midst of beautiful land on each side of us; the hills before-mentioned continue rising to our right; on our left we have the Firth of FORTH, and then the fine level lands between that and FALKIRK, and at the back of those rising up the very hills which divide the county of EDINBURGH from those of PEEBLES and LANARK; while a little to our right and in our front, the Firth of FORTH takes another beautiful bend, with flat lands on the side of it; then come hills rising one above another, and behind those, we see, at a distance, perhaps from twenty to fifty miles, the tops of the Highlands called the BEN-CHOCAN, the BEN-LIDDI, CRAIG-BENYON (all of them conical mountains of a prodigious height); and, lastly, the tip of the "lofty BEN-LOMOND" itself, which really seems to touch the sky; which has been the subject of so many sonnets and so many songs, and the syllables composing the name of which are as sweet and as sonorous as the mountain itself is majestic. Very near to the little town of KINCARDINE, where the ferry is, is a very fine house, built by Lord KEITH, looking down into the Firth of FORTH. We crossed the ferry in five minutes; and, getting into a post-chaise which met us by appointment, we proceeded to FALKIRK over a level country called the CARSE of FALKIRK, just like the Fens of Cambridgeshire and Lincolnshire; and, apparently, producing, like them, everlasting crops of wheat and of beans. Here they dig coals everywhere; and close by FALKIRK there is the famous CARRON iron-foundery. Before we get there, there is a country-house, on our right, called KINNAIRD HOUSE, which was the place of residence of the famous traveller, Mr. BRUCE; and, to the honour of the people here, they seem to reverence the place on that account. The CARRON works, prodigious as they are, naturally brings a numerous working

population about them; and here is such a population, differing in
no material respect from those of the manufacturing towns of Lancashire, Staffordshire, and Yorkshire.

Before we got into FALKIRK, we crossed the famous canal which
connects the waters of the ATLANTIC with those of the GERMAN
OCEAN, coming out of the Firth of FORTH, and ending, as we shall
by-and-by see, in the CLYDE between GREENOCK and GLASGOW. The
manner in which such a thing so apparently wonderful has been
effected, neither my taste nor my time will induce me to endeavour
to describe; it is sufficient for me to know that the thing is, and sufficient for the far greater part of my readers to know, that, by the
means of this canal, goods, of any weight, are much more easily sent
from GREENOCK and GLASGOW to EDINBURGH, than from LONDON
to BARNET or to UXBRIDGE.

At FALKIRK, my friends (BROUGHAM and TOM POTTER will say
that "they are fools," but it is the FACT that we have to do with) rang
the church bells in honour of my arrival, and received me with a
hearty shout at the door of the hotel. Now, stop a bit. Is it not worth
while for Lord GREY to think a little about this, and to turn again to
that which I more particularly address to him in the early part of this
article? As to the gabbling, hair-brained, feelosofizing BROUGHAM
and his crew; as to poor spiteful things like the tallowman[11] and the
brewer privy-counsellors; as to these creatures, who know that they
must be nothing if my doctrines and my propositions prevail; as to
these creatures, all the addresses presented to me; all the honours
with which I have been received by thousands upon thousands, of
whom I knew not a single soul; all the heaps of money (more than
sixty pounds a night) paid for going to applaud me at the theatre,
even at Edinburgh. All these, and all the rest which I have still to
relate up to this day, will, with the "*feelosofers*," the tallow-man and
brewer privy-counsellors, only operate in this way. Perceiving that if
my doctrines prevail, they must either go to rake the kennel or black
shoes, they will think of nothing but of means which they think calculated to counteract me; they will be racking their stupid skulls for
tricks and contrivances to be carried on in conjunction with, and by
the instrumentally of, such creatures as the POTTERS and BAXTER
and SHUTTLEWORTH and their companion the Irish mountebank,[12]
through the means of which very identical reptiles, they have now
been sending pamphlets (*bearing the name of their mountebank
companion*) to their correspondents in EDINBURGH, FALKIRK,

GLASGOW, PAISLEY, and GREENOCK; these pamphlets pointing out particularly my writings (*when I was in* PHILADELPHIA)[13] against MUIR and the other Scotch reformers who were transported by PITT and DUNDAS; the stupid POTTERS and BAXTER and SHUTTLEWORTH, not seeming to think it possible that those writings are seven-and-thirty years old; that I was then only thirty years old myself, or thereabouts; that I was then living in a country where an all-predominant *French* party praised MUIR and his companions; and that that was enough, and ought to have been enough for me, who was an *Englishman*, and who knew nothing at all about the merits or demerits of MUIR and his affair; the vulgar and rich sots of Manchester not seeming to think it possible that the Scotch had discernment enough to perceive these things: all these vermin, the BURDETTS, THOMSONS, the HOBHOUSES, the POTTERS, and the like, not forgetting SERGEANT WILDE, and his brother judge DENMAN, whose exploits in the case of Farmer BOYES and poor COOK, and in the case of the poor *Taffy*,[14] too, may possibly yet be remembered: that all these vermin should see no prospect of escape from something or other unpleasant, unless I can be put down, and that they should entertain the hope of accomplishing the thing; seeing that their stupidity is equal to their spite, is of no more consequence to the public, than it is whether I crush a parcel of cockroaches with my foot, or sweep them into a fire with a broom; but, what the views and EXPECTATIONS of my Lord GREY are, with regard to this matter, is of *tremendous consequence to the whole nation, and particularly to my Lord Grey himself.*

I shall return to this matter by-and-by, when I have proceeded further with the account of my tour. At FALKIRK I lectured from the pulpit of a chapel, as I had done at the town of DUNFERMLINE; spent a very pleasant evening in a company of the most respectable tradesmen of the town, with whom I sat up so much beyond my usual hour, that I had not time to breakfast before I came off at eight o'clock in the morning, when I departed amidst the cordial farewells of very numerous friends. At first, the flat land continues for a mile or two, on our way from FALKIRK to GLASGOW; but soon after we get upon *high land*. The English reader will take care not to confound *high lands* with *Highlands*. The former are like HAMPSTEAD and HIGHGATE, and EPSOM downs, compared with the land approaching the Thames; but the Highlands are chains or groups of mountains in variety of forms and of heights, such as the imagination can never form to itself; they are *rocks*, the base of some of which is many miles across, and the points and edges of which, when not actually lost in the clouds, seem to touch the sky. This distinction my readers will be so good as to bear in mind. We are now, then, upon some of this high land; and, with the exception of the little bit which I mentioned in Berwickshire, and the still smaller bit in FIFESHIRE, I now, for the first time, saw poor land in Scotland. Here it is generally a sour clay. The ground is too high and too cold for oaks; and, as no other trees like clay, everything of the tree kind is scrubby. In some places there is peat. In one part of the journey, we passed by BONNY-MUIR,[15] which means pretty-moor; on an accusation for designing to assemble a rebel army on which, the Scotch reformers suffered so cruelly in 1820, when as was then said, the infamous spies were so numerous, that every man looked upon every other man as a spy unless he personally knew him. These *"paternal"* exploits of the THING, in the exposing of which, and in defending the Scotch reformers, *I only* was heard, was forgotten by the shuffling fellows at the Three Golden Balls[16] at Manchester, but it was not forgotten by the good people in Scotland; and particularly by the reformers in GLASGOW, who sent me a written vote of thanks in 1820, and who now, joined by nine-tenths of the whole community, have been showing their gratitude to me in person. And, do these muckworm creatures, the POTTERS, the grubbing TADCASTER fellows, imagine that, merely with their promises to pay printed upon bits of paper, and with their three golden balls; and do the cackling SHUTTLE-WORTH and pompous BAXTER and full-blooded Yankee DYER; do they imagine that they, with the aid of a mere real mountebank player, coming piping-hot from the cauldron of Sergeant WILDE, being the fellow-labourer of *"our Charley"* in London: do they imagine, are they such complete brute beasts as to imagine, that they could persuade, not the Scotch *people*, (for the thought would be worthy of death!) but even one single half-dozen of Scotch plough-men, or Scotch weavers! If I, where in the Court of King's Bench, and having the group of Whig Ministers before me, stood in need of all my contempt to relieve me from the danger of suffocation at the thought of *running away* from the "GREYS and the BROUGHAMS and the LAMBS and the RUSSELS;" what, oh God! what am I to stand in need of to prevent me from expiring at the thought of being checked for one moment in my course by such nasty creeping things as the POTTERS and the SHUTTLEWORTHS and the BAXTERS!

We came by the stage-coach; and in the coach there were three very sensible and polite gentlemen, one of whom, a very nice young man, was a hop-merchant and wine-merchant; and as, somehow or another, he began to say something about hops, I took an opportunity of showing off my at-once-extensive and minute knowledge of the subject, from the planting of the plant to the bagging and selling of the hops, naming particular places eminent for the growth of the article. By-and-by, the gentleman began to talk politics; from participating in which I carefully abstained, sitting as silent and looking as demure, as the country people say, as girls who have made a slip in their time do at a christening, there being a *baby* in the case in both instances. But, by-and-by, the conversation began to turn upon myself, and I thought it necessary to take the earliest opportunity to apprise the gentleman of my identity; and the hop-merchant having said, "I should like to hear him speak," I said, you do hear him now, Sir: an explanation took place, of course; and whatever might be the sentiments of any one of the three, all was very pleasant. The hop-merchant then came back to our old subject, expressing his astonishment that I, who had so constantly been engaged in pursuits of quite a different nature, should understand *so minutely* every little circumstance belonging to the raising and harvesting and curing and vending of hops; an astonishment which was, doubtless, removed when I told him, that the first work that I ever did in my life, was to tie the hop-shoots round the bottom of the poles with rushes; and that even as soon as I could stand upon my feet, those feet used to help to trample the rushes, spread upon the floor for the purpose, in order to make them pliant to tie with. Seeing that I had thus begun at the very bottom of the business, his wonder must have ceased that I understood so much about hops. After showing him, that, if the infernal duty were taken off, *which costs more in the collection* than its gross amount; after showing him the monstrous effect of this hinderance of the gift of God coming to our hands; after making it clear to him that the brewers of EDINBURGH ale would have for nine-pence, instead of three shillings, the hops which they now use, if this monstrous piece of foolery on the part of the Government were put an end to; after this I bragged a little about having been born in the parish of FARNHAM, which produces the best hops in the universe, feeling bold, seeing that no Kentish, or Sussex, or Worcestershire man was present. For, there is a tenderness upon this subject, which scarcely falls short of that when a young lady fortune is the object of rivalship. My amanuensis, who is a *Sussex* man, was, to my perfect convenience, on the outside of the coach; or, it is very likely that I should have been less forward to indulge in this little instance of human vanity. I promised this young gentleman, that when he came to London, I would take him down and show him the plantations and the people in my country, which, I told him, was very beautiful, and where he would see hop-works in their highest perfection. If he should see this, I hereby repeat my invitation, just observing that it will be as *well*, if, while he is there, he does not say anything to excite a suspicion in the minds of the people that he thinks it is possible that there may be hops in some other part of the world equal to the "FARNHAM." Guarding against *this*, I will warrant him a most cordial reception.

When we got to GLASGOW, we alighted at a hotel; and though I was engaged to take up my quarters at the house of Mr. DAVID BELL, CLYDE BUILDINGS, as I had not breakfasted, I therefore set to that work at the inn, without loss of time, upon everything that is good, but particularly upon some *tender* beef-steaks; a thing which I have not met with before in more than one out of ten beef-steak jobs in my life; and, I may as well stop here to observe, that which I have omitted before, that all the beef that I have tasted in Scotland has been excellent. It appears to come from the little oxen which the Highlands send down in such droves; and a score of which, please God to give me life, I will have next year in Surrey. I should suppose that these little oxen, when well fatted, weigh about twenty score, which is about the weight of a Hampshire hog eighteen months or two years old.[17] The joints are, of course, small compared with the general run of beef in London. A sirloin appears to be no very great deal larger than a loin of large veal, rump and all. The meat is exceedingly fine in the grain; and these little creatures will fat where a Devonshire or Lincolnshire ox would half starve. My project is to get a score of them, let them run upon the common till the corn-tops and blades are fit to cut, then feed them with them; after that with mangel-wurzel or Swedish turnips, and have them fat as butter in the months of March, April, and May. I have never seen a piece of pork in Scotland, and there are very few pigs to be seen, though I saw in Berwickshire a litter of the half *wild* breed; that breed having been brought from the Mediterranean by my Lord LAUDERDALE's son or brother. The mutton at GLASGOW is chiefly from the black-faced Highland sheep; and, if it have age (four or five years old), it is exceedingly fine, though the same pains are not bestowed in making mutton fat here as are bestowed in England; and the same may be said of the beef; and the reader will recollect that the Scotch youth, who came to me at KENSINGTON, would not eat his breakfast that my daughter had prepared for him because the beef was "*vary fot*;" and, really, my rage upon that occasion would have been less violent, if I had known that the general taste of his countrymen was against very fat meat. These little black-faced sheep, which may easily be made as fat as you please, shall some of them march into Surrey, or be carried in a steam-boat; and my Lord HOLLAND, who, to my certain knowledge, has been eating this mutton these twenty years, ought to have told us the secret long ago. I think a flock of these little sheep and a drove of these little oxen, are amongst the most pleasing sights that I ever beheld.

So much for the meat of Scotland; and now I am talking about victuals, let me observe, first, that the wheaten bread, of which there is an abundance in all the towns, is just about as good as it is in London; that, besides this, there are oat-cakes made very thin, which are very nice things of the bread kind, it being understood that I am speaking of such as are made in the houses of gentlemen, merchants, and persons who do not very rigidly adhere to the saving of expense; for there are some of these cakes which rank with the "*brose*" mentioned in the former part of this article. Then the oatmeal, when ground and dressed in a nice manner, is made into porridge, just in the same manner as the Americans make the cornmeal into *mush*, and it is eaten with milk just in the same manner. Every morning but one, while I was at Edinburgh, it formed the principal part of my breakfast; and I greatly preferred it, and should always prefer it, to toasted bread and butter, to muffins, to crumpets, to bread and butter, or to hot rolls. This is the living in Scotland, along with plenty of eggs, very fine butter, and either Ayrshire or English cheese; and everywhere you see a sufficiency of good victuals (including poultry and game); you see it without ostentation; you see it without being compelled to sit whole hours over it; you see everything good, and everything sensibly done with regard to the victuals; and as to the drink, just as in England, you always see ten times too much of it; and I verily believe that I shall be the first human being that ever came into Scotland and went out of it again, without tasting wine, spirits, beer, or cider. Everyone drinks too much; and it is not just to reproach the working people with drunkenness, if you, whose bodily exertions do not tend to provoke thirst, set them the mischievous example, by indulging in drink, until habit renders it a sort of necessary of life. While all the world seem astonished at the wonderful labours that I am performing now, I feel that I am leading a very lazy life. The reason is, that I am always sober; always well (whatever the POTTERS may think of it); and, therefore, always fit to be doing *something*, and always wanting to be doing something.

I shall lose sight of my *"tour"* presently, if I do not come back to it. I had scarcely begun my breakfast, when the room was crowded with friends, who, in consequence of a mistake which I had committed, had gone to another inn to receive me. To name individuals in such a case would be improper, when all were equally entitled to my thanks. As soon as I was ready Mr. Bell brought a carriage, and took me home to his elegant and pleasantly situated house, in which I now write; from which I go to-morrow by the steam boat to GREENOCK, and to which I shall return, after having been at GREENOCK, PAISLEY, and HAMILTON; and then, in a day or two, set off to England by the way of CARLISLE, stopping a day at OLDHAM, and another at MANCHESTER, hunting out the POTTERS from their hole by way of episode. And now what *am* I to say of this GLASGOW, which is at once a city of the greatest beauty, a commercial town, and a place of manufactures also very great. It is MANCHESTER and LIVERPOOL in one (on a smaller scale) with regard to commerce and manufactures; but, besides this, here is the *City* of GLASGOW, built in a style, and beautiful in all ways, very little short of the New Town of EDINBURGH. The new Exchange is a most magnificent place; and, indeed, the whole of the city, compared to which the plastered-up Regent Street is beggarly, is as fine as anything that I ever saw, the New Town of EDINBURGH excepted.[18] The whole is built of beautiful white stone; and doors, windows, and everything, bespeak solid worth, without any taste for ostentation or show. The manufacturing part, with the tall chimneys and the smoke, is at the east end of the city, and somewhat separated from it; so that there is very little smoke in GLASGOW. The river CLYDE runs down through the city; and ships come up and lie by the wharfs for the better part of a mile. Goods are here taken out or shipped with the greatest convenience. Higher up than the point to which the ships come, there are three bridges, which cross the CLYDE, for the convenience of going quickly from one side of the city to the other. By the side of the river, above the bridges, there is a place modestly called GLASGOW-GREEN, containing about a hundred English acres of land, which is in very fine green sward, and is at all times open for the citizens to go for their recreation.

Having three lectures to deliver here, and having engaged to go to GREENOCK the day after the delivery of the third, I had no time to walk about; but Mr. BELL has been so good as to take me round in a carriage, that I might not go away in a state of ignorance with regard to the extent and character of so important a place. I will give an account of this pleasant ride, by inserting a paragraph from the *Glasgow Chronicle* of this day; to Mr. PRENTICE the editor of which, I take this opportunity of expressing my best thanks for a series of civilities, far too great for me to repay in an adequate manner:—

"On Thursday, Mr. Cobbett, accompanied by Mr. Bell, in a carriage and pair, visited various parts of the city. Setting out from Clyde-buildings, they proceeded by Carlton-place, along the Old Bridge, and then westward by the north side of the river to York-street, up that street to Argyle-street, thence to Buchan-street, up St. Vincent-street, Hope-street, and West George's-street, round Blythwood-square by Montague-place, down Bath-street, from which Mr. Cobbett saw the shipping in the canal at Port-Dundas. Proceeding down Buchanan-street by St. Vincent-place, round George's-square by South Hanover-street, and Ingram-street to the Royal Exchange, where Mr. Cobbett alighted, and walked round the Great Room. Mr. Cobbett expressed much admiration at the splendour of the building, and the elegance and extent of the Great Room. The party then proceeded down Queen-street, Argyle-street, Glassford-street, Ingram-street, Montrose-street, George's-street, to the University, where Professor Mylne received Mr. Cobbett, and showed him the Museum, the College, the Faculty-hall, &c., all of which Mr. Cobbett seemed much pleased with, and laughed heartily at the prospect of his being elected Lord Rector. From the College Mr. Cobbett proceeded up High-street to the Royal Infirmary and Cathedral; from thence down High-street, Saltmarket-street, and drove round the Green, which he admired exceedingly, and calculated by the eye that it contained above a hundred acres. Mr. Cobbett then visited Messrs. Henry Monteith and Co.'s Turkey red dyeing and print works at Rutherglen-bridge, and was received by Mr. George Rodger and Mr. Harvie, the managers. Mr. C. seemed much gratified by his visit to the works, and

acknowledged the attention paid to him by these gentlemen. Mr.
Douglas, being at Bridgeton on his canvass, accompanied Mr. C.
through the work. Mr. Cobbett then proceeded through Bridgeton,
by Canning-street, Green-street, Tureen-street, to Gallowgate-
street, and down that street, by the Barracks, to the Old Exchange,
where he alighted and visited the Tontine Coffee Room; Mr.
Cobbett very much admired the room, the buildings, and the
arcades of the Exchange. He then proceeded westward along the
Trongate and Argyle-street, up Queen-street to Upper St. Vincent-
street, and alighted to meet a party at dinner at Mr. John Boyle
Gray's. On passing the George Hotel, George-square, Mr. Cobbett,
observing two soldiers on duty, exclaimed, 'What are these soldiers
doing there?' which was explained to him. Altogether Mr. Cobbett
expressed himself much pleased at the extent and appearance of
Glasgow. We understand he will leave this city tomorrow for Greenock, but will return again here. Mr. Cobbett will, very probably,
visit some other establishments and places in Glasgow on his
return."

Greenock, 21. October, 1832.

After lecturing at GLASGOW, on Wednesday, Thursday, and Friday
nights, I set off by the steam-boat for this town yesterday morning at
eight o'clock, accompanied by my kind and generous entertainer,
Mr. BELL, by Mr. DOUGLAS, of BARLOCK, who is a candidate for
GLASGOW, and by Mr. GRAY. I had not time in writing at GLASGOW
to notice several things which I should not have omitted. There is the
finest, most convenient, and best-conducted *cattle market* that I ever
saw in my life. I do not like to see manufactories of any sort; but that
of Mr. MONTEITH, for the dyeing and printing of calicoes and shawls
and handkerchiefs, and upon a scale of prodigious magnitude, I did
go to see, and I saw it with wonder that I cannot describe. First, there
was a large room full of men, engaged in drawing, upon paper, the
flowers and other things which were to be imprinted on their cotton;
then there was another set to put these drawings upon blocks of
wood; then there was another to fasten on little pieces of copper upon
the wood; then there were others to engrave upon the copper, in
order to print, pretty nearly as printing work is carried on; then came
the men to mark the copper with the blocks according to the
drawings; and lastly came the printers, who carry on their work by

rollers, and effect their purposes in a manner so wonderful, that it almost makes one's head swim but to think of it. The buildings to this dyeing and printing concern are as large as no very inconsiderable country town.

I was not aware that GLASGOW was an ancient city; but I now find that it was the *see* of one of the archbishops of Scotland, which was divided into two archbishoprics, one in the east and one in the west; the *see* of the latter of which was GLASGOW, and that of the former ST. ANDREWS, in the county of FIFE. There is a college here of very ancient establishment, which, as the above paragraph relates, I went to see. Of the cathedral, only the nave and the chancel remain; the transepts appearing to have been demolished. It is very ancient, and was once very grand, though for a long time it appears to have been miserably neglected; but the two ends of it serve as churches to two parishes of the present inhabitants, which, however, seem not to be attended to with that care, and kept in that good state, that the other churches are.

With regard to the treatment that I received at GLASGOW, I cannot speak of it, until the next number of my *Register*; because I am to return to GLASGOW again, to be at a public dinner there on the 29th of this month: the *Register* will appear there before that day, and I wish not to be at GLASGOW when that *Register* shall be received there. My treatment, therefore, by the people generally, and especially by individuals, is a subject that must be reserved until my next *Register*; when I must also speak of this place, and of the treatment that I have received here. This present article I shall conclude with inserting an ADDRESS, which, on Friday last, I received at GLASGOW, from the reformers of NEWMILNS, AYRSHIRE, who came to me from that town (a distance of about twenty miles) for the express purpose of presenting me this address. If vulgar TOM POTTER and his mountebank companion; if the Whig-Judge, Sergeant WILDE, and DRAYTON, the auctioneer; if the tallow-man privy-counsellor, or the brewer privy-counsellor; if BROUGHAM and DENMAN and BROUGHAM's precious crew of poor-law commissioners; if these fellows could have seen and heard . . . Oh, no! what a fool I am! It would have produced no effect upon these conceited and stupid creatures; but if my Lord GREY could have seen the deputation that came twenty miles to bring me the following paper, and could have heard what they said, in addition to what they say in the paper itself, he would have said to himself: "If any considerable portion of such men as these think as these men think, and have formed the resolution that these men appear to have formed, I must adopt the propositions of COBBETT, or, after a vain struggle, sink in the attempt to resist them." The manner of presenting this ADDRESS, the hand-writing in which it was drawn up; the cleverness, the great talent displayed by the gentleman (a very young man) who presented it to me; the beautiful speech with which he prefaced the delivery of it into my hand; everything belonging to the matter would have dictated to a man of sense to exclaim, "The principles of this man must prevail, and his plans must be adopted." Here follows the address and the names subscribed to it; and let the base POTTERS, the stupid SHUTTLEWORTH, and BAXTER, read it, and then wait eagerly for the arrival of the bloody old *Times*, to see if it contain nothing to comfort them.

To WILLIAM COBBETT, Esq.

The reformers of Newmilns, Ayrshire, beg leave to congratulate you with feelings of the most unqualified gratification and delight upon your visit to the land of our nativity, which long did, and still does, contain hearts devoted to the cause of freedom. We have long and fondly cherished the hope of being enabled to address you in person, and thus we gladly avail ourselves of the present opportunity. Our long perusal of your unrivalled writings has kindled in us an attachment for you, which nothing but the hand of time can extinguish. Your manly and unwearied advocacy of the rights and usefulness of the working classes, has called, and will call forth, the thanks and acclamations of a grateful people. To the labours of your pen we are chiefly indebted for the exposure of the workings of the paper-money system; a system fraught alike with cruel oppression, and destruction to sound morality. The plan of an equitable adjustment brought forward by you in the Norfolk Petition,[1] and which you have ever since so ably advocated and defended, in conjunction with the other measures so clearly developed in the lectures delivered by you upon your fourteen propositions, we consider to be the only real cure for the miseries of a long-afflicted and injured people. And, sir, we will not, we cannot despair of justice being done to us so long as God in his goodness to you and our country, grants you health and strength to continue your exertions in our behalf. We rejoice in the triumph of the Reform Bill, although we know it to be short of our just and natural rights, as we trust it will be the means of your introduction into Parliament along with a sufficient number of other representatives pledged to and supported by the people, who will carry into effect your or similar measures, which will make our beloved country what she once was, and what nature has so admirably fitted her for by her geographical position, and by the strength, industry and ingenuity of her inhabitants, the queen of nations and the abode of liberty, peace and plenty.

That you may live to see your labours crowned with success: that you may descend to the grave amidst the tears of a grateful people, and that your memory may be cherished as the friend of your country, as long as its history shall continue, will be our unceasing prayer.

[There follow approximately 175 names.]

NEWMILNS is so situated, that I can go through it, in going from GLASGOW to get into the CARLISLE road; and, do this I will; unless something should happen to render the doing of it very inconvenient. I answered this address verbally, there being no time for doing it in any other manner. Precisely what I said I cannot now recollect; but I was so struck with the behaviour of the deputation, with their unfeigned attachment to me, whom they had never seen, and whom they are probably never to see again, that I was induced to trouble them at greater length, in my answer, than would, generally speaking, have been proper; but I took this opportunity of assuring these kind and clever young men, that, if I were chosen a member of Parliament, happen what would, I never would, for one single moment, be a party to a deceiving of the people; that I had taken a farm[2] as a place of retirement; and that, if I found the people of England so base as not to go hand in hand with the people of Scotland, and insist upon those things being done which ought to be done, I would retire to that farm, and never remain for one minute to give my countenance to a *sham*; that, however, I felt perfectly confident that the people in England would also do their duty; that they would insist that the work of the legislature should be done by *daylight*, and not carried on under the roof of a victualler, mixing legislative speeches with the rattling of knives, forks, plates, and dishes, the drawing of corks, and the jingling of glasses;[3] I trusted that the people would insist, that the work of law-giving should no longer be carried on in this manner; and that, in that case, they might rely upon my best efforts to the last moment of my health and strength

I have received very pressing invitations from the other side of the FIRTH of FORTH, and from STIRLING. Indeed from STIRLING, PERTH, DUNDEE, MONTROSE, ABERDEEN, ELGIN, in what is called the North of Scotland. If I were sure that Parliament would not be dissolved, I would go to these places now; but, as I have to do with a set of pretty gentlemen, some tallow-men and some brewers as well as privy-counsellors, whose business it seems to be to make human affairs uncertain, and human life a burden; I dare not move my body, at present, farther from the scene of action than I now am. If it please God to preserve my life, until the middle of next June, I will come to the North with one of my sons, and I will go into every county, and go even into the ORKNEYS, and see the good people there, to whom I taught the straw-plat manufacture.[4] I will go and see how the Highlanders live, and how they raise those pretty sheep and oxen that they send to be devoured by others. I will go and inquire upon the spot whether the natives of the county of SUTHERLAND were driven from the land of their birth by the countess of that name, and by her husband, the Marquis of STAFFORD; and if I be in Parliament, I will then endeavour to induce the nation, and through it the Parliament, to come to some settled determination relative to the right of land-owners to drive away the natives of the land, or to refuse them a share of its produce. It is high time that we come to some settled notions relative to this matter. I am very sorry that I cannot accept the invitations that have been given me now; but I will endeavour to show my gratitude by my visit next year.

Greenock, 22. Oct. 1832.[5]

It was high time that somebody should come to Scotland to be able to explain to Englishmen how this country has been treated. I, who had known so many Scotchmen ever since I was sixteen years old, who had had so many of them come to visit me, in the jail into which I was put for writing against the flogging of local-militia men;[6] I, even I, had strong feelings excited in my mind against Scotland generally (always expressly making great exceptions) by the scoundrelly "feelosofers," who preached up a doctrine tending to cause the people of England to be treated like cattle; even I could not make out how it was, that Scotland should spew forth so many of these monsters. I now see to the bottom of the whole thing. Those who have read the history of the Roman empire, know that it extended itself over all Europe; and that the farther any part of its subjects were from Rome, the worse they were treated by their governors (called pro-consuls) that were set over them. LA FONTAINE, in his beautiful tales, relates, that a man came before the senate from one of the distant provinces to complain of the monstrous injustice and cruelty exercised by the pro-consul in the province from which he came; that the senate heard his eloquent and indignant description with patience; and then laid their heads together to consider about the wrongs inflicted on this province, and about the answer they should give to this eloquent complainant; when, one of the senators said, "Make him himself pro-consul of his province, and you will hear no more complaints from him, I will warrant you." This was done, and the province was oppressed more than ever. Just thus has it been with Ireland and with Scotland, which have always been injured by the selfishness and treachery of those whose birth ought to have taught them to be their protectors; and, the renegado villanous "feelosofers," who have come to London from Scotland, have been, and are, the corrupt tools of the Scotch oligarchy for selling their own country, and of the English oligarchy for pillaging and enslaving the people of England. Here is this great commercial and fishing town of GREENOCK, with a population of thirty thousand souls, and with a custom-house like a palace, to have one member of Parliament, while the miserable town of THETFORD, in Norfolk, without any trade, in the middle of a barren bit of ground, and with a population of only 3,462 souls, to have two members of Parliament! A hundred instances, pretty nearly as shameful as this, might be pointed out; but, here is DUMBARTON, on the side of the CLYDE, at once commercial and manufacturing to a certain extent, having a population far surpassing that of CHIPPENHAM; but there must be two or three other towns added to DUMBARTON, making up about fifty thousand people, in order to entitle them to have *one* member, while the old rotten borough of CHIPPENHAM, which has only 5,270 people, is to have *two* members! How came the Scotch members in the house not to contend against this monstrous injustice? Ah, faith! nineteen-twentieths of them would have been glad if Scotland had had no members at all! But, as it is; bad as it is; monstrously unjust

as it is; it will put an end to the *pro-consulships*, and drive all the
"*land-clearing*" and poor-rate abolishing "feelosofers" to the devil,
who must be sighing for them as the bridegroom sighs for the bride.
It will be a happy meeting. As the coachman says, in TOM JONES, it is
very proper that there should be a hell for such monsters to go to.
However, as they may escape in the next world, I am for doing them
justice in this; and, If I have not been diligent enough heretofore, I
will *now*, at any rate, discharge my duty.

As a little specimen of the treatment which the Scotch pro-consuls
have suffered their country to receive, I will mention the conduct of
what is called the "TRINITY-HOUSE," with regard to pensioners.
This has been a great instrument in the hands of corruption. I must
explain a little the nature of it, before I proceed to the specimen
above-mentioned. This "TRINITY-HOUSE," as it is called, is a corporation, originally founded for the purpose of causing lighthouses,
buoys, and pilots to be provided for the purpose of securing safe
navigation into and out of our harbours. The members of it consist of
what are called "*elder brothers*;" and a great number of the aristocracy, who scarcely know a buoy from a tea-kettle, are "elder
brothers" of this concern, which has the fingering of immense sums
of money; a circumstance which you have already supposed, the
moment you heard that the *aristocracy* thought it an honour to
belong to it. These "elder brothers" get the money by taxes levied
upon ships, and all sorts of sea-vessels, and by the rents of estates,
which, at various times, good and public-spirited merchants and
other men have bequeathed to this corporation, from the most benevolent of motives, and for the purposes which they expected would
be answered by their bequests. A reformed Parliament, unless it will
want reforming again the first week, will ransack this monstrous
concern to the bottom, and teach the "elder brothers" that the
money is not to be expended upon grand dinners and the like. But at
present, I mean to speak only of the treatment which *Scotland
receives* from these "elder brothers;" and this, too, only in the particular case of its *pensioners*. A part of its funds is annually expended in
pensions given (or ought to be given) to meritorious seafaring
persons, having served principally in matters connected with
commercial navigation; and not with matters relating to the warlike
marine. These pensioners are naturally persons belonging to the
several commercial sea-ports; and, if the TRINITY-HOUSE were just
in bestowing these pensions, we should naturally find that the

number of pensioners at each commerical sea-port, would, in some degree, at any rate, correspond with the amount of trade and population of each sea-port respectively. In the year 1825, an account of the number of these pensioners was laid before the Parliament and published. In that account, the commercial towns were ranged in the following manner, with its numbers of pensioners against each; and, if the Scotch and Irish readers still want something to convince them of the tendency of the pro-consular government, let them look at this list.[7]

ENGLISH TOWNS

	Number of Pensioners		Number of Pensioners
Aberistwyth	17	Shieldses (the two) and	
Alonby	19	Newcastle	678
Berwick	52	Staith	280
Bideford	93	Stockton-upon-Tees	65
Bristol	72	Sunderland	150
Caernarvon	81	Workington	255
Dartmouth	177	Yarmouth	360
Exeter	179	Total for England	6,408
Fishguard	123		
Gainsborough	100	SCOTCH TOWNS.	
Ilfracombe	98		
Ipswich	67	Aberdeen	14
Liverpool	282	Montrose	91
London	3,741	Glasgow	2
Lymington	86	Greenock	5
Newbiggin	85	Total for Scotland	112
Newhaven	16		
Penzance	56	IRISH TOWN.	
Ramsgate	59		
Scarborough	158	Cork	60
Scilly	38	Total for Ireland	60

There, you scoundrelly "*feelosofers*," who sell your own country, and who come to point out to our oligarchy how they shall check the population and drive the people from the land; you renegado scoundrels; you base instruments of injustice, tyranny, and cruelty, who applauded the driving of the natives out of the county of

SUTHERLAND, and who are advising all insolent and stupid beasts of land-owners to desolate the villages, and drive out the people from Kent and from Sussex,[8] and to have a few slaves in *"boothies"* to raise corn and cattle for the French to come over and take at their pleasure; there, you renegado Scotch scoundrels, that is what you could never find out! But, it is what the Scotch reformers have seen long and long enough; and therefore it is that they gather round me on whom they can rely for my best efforts to put an end to these abominations.

What! your *"feelosofical"* blood, though put into you by the earth and the air of Scotland, can move, can it, tranquilly through your veins while you see the little miserable village of NEWBIGGIN, in Westmoreland, which contains only *a hundred and fifty-two souls,* have almost as many pensioners upon this list as the whole of Scotland put together, while GREENOCK has only *five,* GLASGOW only *two,* and many other towns of commerce not one! But NEWBIGGIN lies close by the rotten borough of APPLEBY! LONDON has no right to more than about a thousand of these pensioners; and yet it has more than one half of the whole. Do not these things want rectifying; and are you not the greatest villains that the world ever saw, or the most stupid of beasts, to be crying up the happiness of Scotland, and to be labouring to reduce England to a similar state? Only think of the monstrous partiality here exhibited. Here we see the little miserable port, which is hardly a port, of WORKINGTON, with *two hundred and fifty-five* pensioners, while GLASGOW has *two!* Aye, but WORKINGTON is close by the rotten borough of COCKERMOUTH; and the voters of COCKERMOUTH would naturally not be the worse for a pension, given under the name of seafaring men at WORKINGTON. Base and mercenary ruffians, your days of *"feelosofy"* and living in idleness are at an end; the reform, defective as it is, will destroy you as completely as if you had been shot or run through the body. No matter about *Whig* or *Tory*: the *people* will have these abominations put an end to; and you must take to the honest calling of sweeping the streets or blacking the shoes. I have a hundred times said, that, on general subjects, when speaking of your country, I made use of the word England, I wish to be understood as including every part of the kingdom. I know, that, for England herself to be happy and free, her laws (as they stood before the reign of George the Third) must be extended to, and firmly take root in, Scotland and in Ireland; I know that every lash given to either of these two countries inflicts a wound upon

England herself; I know that the accursed "*boothies*" of Scotland, and the accursed potato-diet of Ireland, tend to take the meat and the bread, and the knives, forks, and plates from the tables of the labourers of England. Therefore, a love of England herself would induce me to endeavour to cause justice to be done to Scotland and to Ireland; but, if that were not the case, I should hate myself if I were capable of keeping silence, being a witness of these monstrous oppressions.[9]

Paisley, 26 October, 1832.

In my last I had not time to say anything about my passage down the CLYDE from GLASGOW to GREENOCK; and for the reason there stated I spoke in a general manner, only, of my treatment at GLASGOW. I must now say upon that subject, that I was at the house of Mr. BELL, received as if I had been a father or a brother; that I dined there, and also at Mr. GRAY's (writer) with many of the first merchants of GLASGOW; that Mr. BELL's elegant and very pleasantly-situated house was at my service for the receiving of friends, deputations from the towns and villages around; and that, in short, If I had gone to that fine city and beautiful scene of commerce and manufactures at the same time; if I had gone thither with power to add to the riches of the place, and to dispense honours and favours around me in all directions, I could not have been received or treated with greater favour and kindness. Mr. PRENTICE, the very respectable and able editor of the *Glasgow Chronicle*, was the only person connected with the press with whom I came in immediate contact. I should want words to describe the extent of his good offices, had not experience furnished me with the means of adequately describing it by a contrast. I say then (and that will do justice even to him), that, in character and in conduct, he showed himself to be *precisely the contrary* of the infamous wretches, whom those two impudent women, ANNA BRODIE and FANNY WRIGHT, hire to write in the bloody old *Times*; precisely the contrary of what was that JACK WALTER, whom SCOTT ELDON made a justice of the peace, and who is now (monstrous impudence!) a Whig candidate for the county of Berks.; *precisely the contrary* of what this fellow was when he was manager of the bloody old *Times*.

As I mentioned before, Messrs. BELL, DOUGLAS of BARLOCH, and Mr. GRAY, accompanied us to GREENOCK, where we were received by the two Messrs. BAINE, who are great merchants there, and by my excellent and stanch old friends and adherents, Messrs. CAMERON, CAMPBELL, and others, respectable tradesmen in that town. Agreeably to appointment, we were lodged at Mr. BAINE's country house, about three quarters of a mile out of town, situated close on the bank of the Firth of CLYDE, with the little village of HELLENSBURGH on the other bank, and the Highlands rising up behind that.

The whole of the way down the CLYDE is interesting beyond description. It is a fine wide river at GLASGOW; gets wider and wider of course; but for several miles down it is walled on each side in the most complete manner. All the way down to our left we have Renfrewshire, very soon after we leave GLASGOW, which is in the county of Lanark. The land to our right is, first, a strip of levelish ground, with little country seats, with here and there a manufactory of some sort. To our left is an extended flat of very fine land. There are several considerable country seats, those of Lord BLANTYRE and of Mr. SPIERS of ELDERSLIE, in particular. At about half the way down, the town of DUMBARTON lies on our right; the castle of DUMBARTON, on a round and almost perpendicular rock standing out in the water, an object worth travelling from the Isle of Wight to this spot barely to see. The town of DUMBARTON lies down between two hills. The ground now becomes very hilly on our right, though it is generally cultivated for some distance back; and, behind these high grounds, the Highlands tower up; and this is the sort of coast which continues on to GREENOCK, and then continues all the way round to the corner of the main land opposite the ISLE of BUTE. About half way between DUMBARTON and GREENOCK is on our left the little sea-port called PORT-GLASGOW; and here the ground, from being flat as before, becomes rocky and lofty very near the shore, and thus continues all the way to GREENOCK

At about seven miles from GLASGOW we pass the mouth of the famous canal, which goes close by GLASGOW, close by FALKIRK, and which connects the Firth of CLYDE with the Firth of FORTH; and thus connects the waters of the ATLANTIC with those of the German Ocean. Near DUMBARTON we passed the spot where they say are the remains of the old Roman wall, which went from the Firth of CLYDE to the Firth of FORTH; and by the means of which those gentlemen thought proper to divide the Highlands from the Lowlands of Scotland. I may as well observe here, that the river CLYDE rises in the mountains which divide the county of EDINBURGH from the county of LANARK, and that other branches of it rise out of mountains that divide the counties of PEEBLES and DUMFRIES and AYR from the county of LANARK. The river FORTH rises at the foot of the famous mountain called BEN-LOMOND, and runs down through the country dividing PERTHSHIRE from STIRLINGSHIRE, and STIRLINGSHIRE from the county of CLACKMANNAN. All to the north of the canal which joins these two Firths is called the *North of Scotland*: the other is, of course, called the *South*.[1]

The harbour and bay of GREENOCK are very fine. The town, which consists of thirty thousand people, is built on a little flat, the high land beginning to rise up immediately behind it to the south; the streets are regular, conveniently wide; the houses built of stone; and everything wearing the appearance of ease, competence, and great solidity. The house of Mr. BAINE, in which I was lodged, was, in every respect, as nice an affair of the kind as I ever set my eyes on; outside, inside, and all about it, as complete as anything of the sort that I ever beheld. But the great curiosity here, and the thing upon which the people pride themselves, and most justly, is what they call the "SHAWS-WATER," of which I must speak a little, though my account must be very inadequate. For a good while I declined going to see this affair; but, at last, I did go, and I rejoice that I did; for I have seldom seen anything in my life that afforded me more pleasure. GREENOCK lies on a little flat, to the north of very high rocky hills, which stretch round behind it nearly from water to water. No fresh water stream or river comes near it; and though it had public pumps or wells, it often experienced very great inconvenience from the want of fresh water. On the high land about six miles to the south of it, there was a little stream or bourne (as we call those runs of water which are occasionally dry), which come out of one of the still loftier hills to the south. After going in a northerly direction for some distance, it took a turn to the west, and went down a deep ravine into the Firth of CLYDE, not approaching anywhere to within six miles of GREENOCK. In finding its way to the ravine it passed along a flat at the back of the GREENOCK hills. By the means of dams, the water, proceeding from this bourne, was formed into a lake; at six miles, observe, from GREENOCK, but between the lake and GREENOCK, was a chain of lofty hills, beginning at the east and terminating towards the west. Here was the water, but the difficulty was to get it to GREENOCK. After various schemes about tunnels to go under the hills, and steam-pumping, and God knows what besides, Mr. THOM, a native I believe of the Isle of BUTE, made a proposition for carrying the water to GREENOCK by an aqueduct, which he finally accomplished, at a comparatively trifling expense, and in a manner so clever, as to be worthy of the admiration of every beholder; and there are now two hundred and sixty acres of water in the grand reservoir, with three other subsidizing reservoirs, of greater or lesser extent; the whole amounting to 396 acres; and there is all this water brought to the side of the high hills behind GREENOCK; and there it comes tumbling down in various aqueducts; not only supplying the town with water amply at all times, but furnishing the means of turning flour-mills, cotton-mills, or any thing of the sort, at the cheapest possible rate. Four large mills for corn, or flax, or both, are already put in motion by this water; they are building now, and they say that here are the means of working forty of the largest mills that can exist. The reservoir or lake, is six hundred feet above the level of the sea; the aqueduct takes the water from the tail of the ravine, which is very deep, and carries it along the end of the high hills at the back of GREENOCK; gets it creeping about in all directions, till it finally brings it to its desired spot, always by a fall of six feet in the space of a mile. To guard against the consequences of melted snow, or torrents of rain, there are self-opening and self-shutting sluices; and, therefore, though the aqueduct is only six feet wide at the bottom and twelve feet wide at the top, its banks are never disturbed. They say, that the people were wholly incredulous as to the practicability of effecting this thing; that scarcely anybody believed that the water could ever be brought to GREENOCK; and that, on the day on which the aqueduct was opened for the water to proceed, not less than ten thousand persons were assembled to witness the result of this brilliant experiment. Mr. THOM, who did me the honour to accompany me and Mr. BAINE, in riding round the lake, is a man of too much sense and too much merit to set any value upon an empty title; but if George the Fourth had made him a baronet, instead of COUTTS, TROTTER, WALTER SCOTT or Parson BATE DUDLEY, he would, at any rate, have, in some degree, diminished the disgust with which men now view that hackneyed hereditary honour.

After going to the Scotch church, on Sunday the 21st, and there beholding a very decent service, and hearing, from three verses of St. PAUL's 2nd Epistle to TIMOTHY, beginning at the 14th, a very able sermon in defence of the doctrine of the Trinity; after dining, on the Monday, with Mr. BAINE, the chief magistrate, in company with his colleague, and several other gentlemen of the place; I set off (after another lecture that evening) the next day for this place. I cannot, however, take leave of GREENOCK without observing on the contrast which it formed with all the other sea-ports that I had ever seen in my life. Captain COBB, with whom I crossed the Atlantic the last time, used to be everlastingly pestering me with his praises of GREENOCK; about its solidity, cleanliness, and the good manners of the people. As I was going to the church, the sight brought COBB to my mind. All the people seemed to be in the streets; all going away to their different churches; no noise of any sort; no dirtily-dressed person; and not a soul to be seen who did not seem seriously in the business for which the day was set apart. COBB used to say, that it was like a Connecticut sea-port; and I dare say it is; for the religion is the same, and I dare say that the manners of the people are very much alike.

Sir MICHAEL SHAW STEWART is the landowner in and around GREENOCK; he has a very beautiful place a little way from the town, and down by the side of the Firth; there are many farms in a little valley going from his house round to GREENOCK; these farms are small, but the people appear to be very comfortably off, and, though living amongst these rocky hills, twenty times as numerous as in the fine fat lands in the Lothians. The deciduous trees do not grow large; I saw no oaks at all; but Sir MICHAEL STEWART has some very fine woods of fir and larch upon the hills round about his house; the ever-greens flourish here surprisingly; I never saw the *Portugal laurel* and the *arbutus* in greater perfection. The horse-chestnut, the lime, the plane, the sycamore, and the ash, all seem to flourish as well as in any part of England. Ayrshire comes down, in one part, very near to GREENOCK. The cows are of the *Ayrshire-breed,* white and red, with a large portion of red; small head and neck, fine tail, straight back; in short, the Durham cows precisely, only upon a small scale. From these cows comes cheese, in great abundance and very fine. They say that it is the only county in Scotland that produces cheese. I should like very much to have half-a-dozen of these cows; but to get them from such a distance is next to impossible, without an enormous expense; and, perhaps, they would degenerate after all.

In the scourging days of CASTLEREAGH (who soon afterwards cut his own throat and killed himself, at NORTH CRAY, in Kent, and who was carried to his grave amidst the exulting shouts of the people of London and Westminster); in those scourging days, the scourge reached even GREENOCK; corruption in her fury hunted out victims amongst the public-spirited men, even in this pious and quiet town;

one of whom, deeming accusation to be a sentence of death, and giving himself up as a condemned man, even before he was tried for high-treason, actually *shaved his head*, that the executioner might not be able to hold it up by the hair! The jury saved him: he lived to see the end of CASTLEREAGH, and to shake by the hand one who risked so much in defending the conduct of him and his countrymen upon that occasion: Ah! foolish and base villains of the LONDON and EDINBURGH press! If you forget these things, the reformers of Scotland do not. To the grateful recollection of these acts of mine, I owe the reception that I have met with. Relying upon this recollection, I set at nought all your instigations to Scotch hostility: the result has shown the innate virtue of this people; and also shown the soundness of my judgement.

STATESMAN VANSITTART, who began his brilliant career as Commissioner of Scotch Herrings, first started, it seems, from this nice town of GREENOCK, which is famous for its fisheries; and, what is curious enough, the Scotch have by no means forgotten the statesman, and the small manoeuvring which was played off by him, while he was in Scotland; the nice little contrivances to get himself the *freedom of the city of* EDINBURGH, and all the other pretty means by which the base creatures of OLD GEORGE ROSE assisted to get him puffed up, in order that there might be a pretence for giving him parcels of our money. The history of this VANSITTART is all that will be needed by our children who are now being born, to enable them to judge of the state of degradation of their fathers. This man did what they call *study the law*; carried a *bag* (made for holding briefs) to the *quarter-sessions* of READING in Berkshire, of which county he is a native; having marched in all possible ways, in the same line and direction as ADDINGTON, and having started with him from pretty nearly the same spot. The law not being a profitable trade with our VAN, he took to *politics*; and we shall, by-and-by, see him taking to *piety*. His first stroke by way of getting on in the world was a *pamphlet*, written by him *in praise of the* PITT-SYSTEM *of finance*; and the object of which was to induce the nation to believe that the war did not at all impoverish them; and that THE DEBT which Pitt's monstrous loans were creating, presented no subject of *alarm* to the mind of any sensible man, excepting the circumstance, that "*the sinking fund might pay it off too soon!*"[2] No wonder that VAN is a peer, and a law-maker in his own right; from such hopeful beginnings what was not naturally to be expected? VAN's promotion began, as matter of course; and there being great scarcity in England, in the years 1800 and 1801, VAN was, in the former year, made "*Commissioner of Scotch Herrings*," and as such came to Scotland under the patronage of old GEORGE ROSE, then a secretary of the Treasury, and a sinecure placeman to the tune of 3000*l*. a year, with another sinecure place for his son WILLIAM, to the tune of two thousand pounds a year, or thereabouts; which sinecures his sons GEORGE and WILLIAM still have, while the weavers of PAISLEY are covered with rags and are half starved. VAN having executed his commission, went back to England, slavered over with the praises of the base part of the Scotch, and well loaded with the contempt of every Scotchman of sense and independence. The salary of the "Commissioner of Scotch Herrings" continued till he got another post, the name of which I have forgotten, but which, doubtless, he will be *desired to tell some of us* one of these days. PITT went out of office in 1801 to let in ADDINGTON, to make the peace of AMIENS for him; and VAN (great in finance) became under his countryman, ADDINGTON, a *secretary of the Treasury*. There was VAN, now in his element: *taxing, funding, loaning, and Exchequer-billing*. Oh! what a time for VAN! His glory, however, was too great to be uninterrupted. PITT, tired of being out of place, and his tax-eating crew sighing to be again at the honey-pot, turned out ADDINGTON; away went poor VAN, but well-provided for by a *retired allowance*. PITT lived but a short time after this: the Whig Ministry that succeeded him lasted but fifteen months; the old Duke of PORTLAND became Prime Minister; and PERCEVAL, the real Minister, was placed in the post of *Chancellor of the Exchequer*; and back went VAN into his post of Secretary of the Treasury. PERCEVAL having been put an end to in the year 1812, the wise LIVERPOOL became Prime Minister, and VAN, *Chancellor of the Exchequer*; in which post he remained, until succeeded by "*Prosperity* ROBINSON," in the year 1823, when the King did himself the honour, an honour quite worthy of such a king, to clap a coronet on the head of VAN, and put him in the house of hereditary lawgivers, under the title of "BARON BEXLEY," of BEXLEY, in the county of KENT; where VAN, they say, is now in the habit of *singing hymns* in his groves, on one bank of the pretty little river CRAY, having in full view, at the same time, on the other bank (at scarcely a stone's throw distance) the house in which CASTLEREAGH cut his own throat!

Curious progress! beginning with the curing of Scotch herrings, and ending in a peerage! Curious literary progress! beginning with a pamphlet expressing fears that the national debt would be paid off too soon, and ending with the circulating of Bibles and the singing of hymns! But VAN had merits as a *statesman*, to be sure? yes, that he had; for, in 1811, he proposed a resolution, which the 658 adopted, stating, that a "*one-pound note and a shilling were equal in value to a guinea in gold.*" In 1819 he supported PEEL's Bill, and the doctrines on which it was founded, and which declared that the one-pound note *had been worth only fourteen shillings in gold in 1811!*[3] In 1822, VAN brought in a Bill (which was passed by the clever 658) to *issue small notes again*, in violation of the bill of 1819! This was VAN's last and greatest act of all; for it produced the TERRIBLE PANIC of 1825 and 1826, which has been ruining families, undermining property, and producing unspeakable misery, from that day to this. Devil take the King, I say, then, if he had not made VAN a peer! Neither Johnathan WILDE, nor any of his DESCENDANTS, ever merited a HALTER better than VAN merited a peerage!

But what is most curious in the history of VAN, is, that while a nation, whose money matters VAN held the management of, was growing *poor*, VAN was growing *rich*! This is something very wonderful: that he should be growing rich while the nation was growing poor. In human life, generally, we find, that all belonging to the same concern become rich or become poor together. If the farmer become poor, you soon see his servants and his stock of every description exhibiting symptoms of his diminished means. If the tradesman become poor, you see all his work-people worse clad and worse fed. All being under the influence of the *same cause*, all experience a *similar effect*. Just the contrary with VAN, who is said to be worth *half a million of money*, and who, having the linnet, the lark, and all the harmonious finches, to join him in the day, and the nightingale's melody to assist him by night, sings his hymns in some of the sweetest groves with which God has ever had the goodness to garnish the earth; just the contrary with VAN, I repeat, who has thus been rising into enormous wealth, while the industrious millions, of whose money he has so long had the fingering, have been sinking into misery; and while that DEBT which he (pious man!) was *afraid* would be paid off *too soon*, swelled up, *during his financial career, from three hundred and forty to eight hundred millions of sovereigns!* Wonderful thing! Strange spectacle! Prodigious cause, which could produce effects so opposite at one and the same time.

However, leaving the "feelosofers" to account for this, I cannot dismiss VAN without talking of something *practical.* How it was that VAN *got* his money it is impossible for me, *precisely*, to say: how much was brought to him by the daughter of old EDEN, who was, also, nearly all his life, a placeman and a pensioner at the same time; about these matters I will not speak, because I cannot speak with certainty; but I know these things; namely that VAN had little or nothing thirty years ago; that he now has a town house, a country house, and a peerage; and that he is said to be worth a very large parcel of money, besides those estates in land which we know him to have; and I know that, though his salaries were large enough and a great deal too large, they could not have been much larger than the amount of his annual spending during the said thirty years. Now, then, I put it to any *reasonable* man, whether we ought to be deemed impertinent and troublesome, if we were to ask VAN, in this day of our need, to *help us a little*; to give us a lift; I mean, to give us a little of his money! I am aware that it will be said by his friends, that he *owes us nothing*; that all he has has been *honestly gotten*; and that if *we*, sinful creatures as we are, cannot account for his having got rich while we have been getting poor, it is because we are unable to comprehend how effective piety is in the producing of riches. Those friends of VAN will refer us to the history of GIL BLAS, giving an account of the prodigious prosperity of DON MANUEL ORDONNEZ, who was a keeper of the great poor-house of the city of VALLADOLID, and who "was so pious a man that he *got rich* in taking care of the concerns of the *poor.*" I am aware of all this; I am aware that there is nothing to oppose to these observations of the friends of VAN; but still I must be permitted to say, that I can see no harm in respectively applying to VAN to spread a little of his money about amongst us as well as his Bibles. We ask for bread, and he gives us a book; which, as far as the belly is concerned, is much about the same thing as giving us a stone. In short, not to mince the matter any longer, I am for making a *regular* application to VAN for some of his money. Poh! for the coronet and the robes! let him keep them; but, for some of his money I am for making a regular application, either in the way of a *gift* or of a *loan*; and, if I be in Parliament, and if no other man propose it, I, WILLIAM COBBETT, am the man to do the thing. The French republicans (sad dogs!) had what they called *des emprunts forcés*; that is to say, *forced loans*. Nay, in one or two instances, they had *dons forcés*; that is to say *forced gifts*. God forbid that I should propose an imitation of these sad fellows; I shall tread in the steps (as far as I have any influence) of the "*heaven-born*" minister, PITT; and shall propose, in the case of VAN, nothing more than "*a voluntary loan*," or, "*a voluntary contribution*," not forgetting to remind VAN that he was one of the great literary defenders of these two methods of obtaining supplies for the relief and safety of the nation! And thus I, *for the present*, take my leave of VAN, giving him my positive assurance, that, if he and I live till I have been in Parliament a month, he shall again hear from me, who have not had my eye off him for a month at a time, during the last thirty years.

There is a neighbour of VAN, who was brother secretary of the Treasury along with GEORGE ROSE, and who is now a noble peer under the name of FARNBOROUGH, in which parish (near Bromley in Kent) my Lord CHARLEY LONG has his mansion and park and some of his estates. I dare say he would be glad of an opportunity of lending the poor nation a little money, or even giving it some, if applied to in a respectful and every way proper manner. I am for no impertinence in these cases; for no disagreeable questioning or alter-cation; but just a simple and respectful appeal to the charity and generosity of the parties. However, enough of these things for the present. I must now get on with my tour; which tour my readers will, I dare say, wish to see at an end, being, as it everlastingly is, inter-rupted by these digressions. Well, then, to get on, we set off from GREENOCK about two o'clock, after having surveyed the SHAWS-WATER, and taken leave of our friends; and after having (which I had nearly forgotten) been to see the straw bonnets and hats of Mr. MUIR. My readers will recollect my numerous writings about this straw-bonnet manufacture, and all the instructions relative to which I have given with so much care and neatness in my little work called "COTTAGE ECONOMY;" they will recollect what infinite pains I took about it; and I can tell them, that it was not only pains that it cost me; but, altogether, more than *three hundred pounds* in the way of expense, without ever having the design or thought of profiting from it myself in any degree whatever, directly or indirectly. I was the originator and the perfecter of the whole thing myself. This manu-facture gives decent and wholesome employment to many persons in the South of England, and converts into beautiful articles of dress the offal produce of our own native fields. Amongst other persons who applied to me for information respecting this matter, were two very simple, but very worth men from the ORKNEY ISLANDS, which are situated to the *north of the North of Scotland*. and about eight hundred miles to the north of London. Whether I deserve, as the mortified, spiteful, and ridiculous reptile, who writes the *Scotsman* newspaper at EDINBURGH, says; whether I deserve, as this beaten reptile says I do, to be deemed an enemy of Scotchmen, let these good fellows of the ORKNEY ISLANDS tell.[4] If they had come from my own native parish, I could not have treated them with more generosity and kindness. The distance from which they came, indeed, was an additional motive to the exercise of kindness towards them. Victuals and drink, at all times of the day, and at the same table with my own family, were at their service. I devoted to them time which I never yet bestowed upon persons of high rank in life. I showed them the various sorts of straw; explained to them the modes of platting, of bleaching, of raising the straw; and set some young women at platting that they might see them at work; gave them specimens of the plat, and of the straw, and of the mode of sewing it together; wrote many letters to them afterwards, and got franks from my Lord FOLKESTONE and other members that the postage might cost them nothing.[5] Before this they used to plat *split-straw*; and, for the making of that poor brittle and coarse stuff, *they used to import the straw from England*! *They now raise their own straw*; and about two thousand of them, in those most northern parts; in those little islands almost in the *Frozen Ocean*, now gain comfortable livings at their own little homes, by a manufacture which surpasses everything of the kind ever seen in Great Britain. Let these people say what I deserve at the hands of Scotchmen. I wonder, by-the-by, who is the *landowner* in the ORKNEYS; what proud leather-headed fool it is, and whether he has not yet discovered that it is his duty to come to me and thank me for this great benefit done to his islands; if the haughty and stupid and insolent aristocracy think it wise, tacitly, to discourage the progress of so clear a benefit to the country, merely because it cannot be encouraged without adding to my celebrity, and without creating public gratitude towards me; if they think that, by this conduct of theirs, they can prevent the people from duly estimating my services and for being grateful for them; if the stupid things think this, will they NOW open their eyes, or will they be blind still? Will they still persevere in showing their insolent spite; after what they have now seen? I think they will. To the mortification of their proud stomachs, let them know these things that the *people*, the *millions*, everywhere say, "If any *other* man had done this good to the country, he would have been applauded to the skies by the aristocracy, and loaded with riches at our expense;" that, even this base and malignant hostility (which is everywhere perceived and understood) has made the people rally round me with ten times the zeal that they otherwise would have done; and let them, for their comfort, take this, that ninety-nine men out of every hundred, in the whole island of Great Britain, are firmly convinced that the reform will not be worth one straw *unless I be in Parliament*! There, mass of stupid pride, take that, get it down into your stomach, or chew it about and spit it out again, just which you please. If I had the power to destroy you (speaking with some exceptions), I should have as perfect a right to do it as a man has to kill a viper that is just about to stick its teeth into his flesh, and, if I were not to do it, as I certainly should not do it, the forebearance would be an act of generosity and not of justice. Ah! turn up your upper lip, and draw up your nostrils, now, do! Be supercilious asses to the last. But, remember, that you have an account to settle with the people, who may possibly be less disposed to forebearance than I am; and whose demands, they being just and legal, no man will have a right, even to endeavour to control. Remember *that*; and now listen, if you like, or let it alone if you don't, to the account of my progress in my tour, which will be much better employment for you than the endeavour to hatch addle-headed schemes for driving the working-people from the land of their birth, and for raising by steam-engines corn and cattle which there will be nobody to eat.

After viewing Mr. MUIR's great parcels of bonnets and hats, we came on through PORT-GLASGOW to PAISLEY, a distance of about sixteen miles. At first, and until after we pass PORT-GLASGOW, the Firth of CLYDE is close upon our left, with high and almost perpendicular rocks, covered on the top with scrubby underwood, on our right. Then gradually wheeling round to our right, we come into a country perfectly flat, stretching all round to a great distance. The land is a sort of fenny or moorish land, but apparently bearing fine crops of corn, though we saw here none of these noble fields of turnips which we saw in the counties of Berwick, Haddington and EDINBURGH, that is to say, in the Lothians. The cows are still of the AYRSHIRE breed, and very fine. We arrived at PAISLEY about five o'clock, and I lectured at seven, in a large church: I did the same the two succeeding evenings. On the 24th, I went, in consequence of an invitation which that gentleman gave me in person at GLASGOW, to dine with Mr. SPIERS, at his beautiful seat, near the CLYDE at

ELDERSLIE; where I saw some as beautiful trees as I ever saw in the whole course of my life; and a great many of them, too; in short, as well-wooded a park as is to be seen in all England, and as well arranged and as neatly kept; the pastures of this park as fine as can possibly be conceived; scores of oxen fatting, and hundreds of the little black-faced sheep, which I perceived, get the foot-rot sometimes, when brought upon these fat lands. Mr. SPIERS, who is called the father of the county of RENFREW, who is said to be the *oldest reformer* in the kingdom, having commenced his career in that way in 1778, who was ten years a member of Parliament for this county, who is a brother-in-law of Lord DUNDAS, I believe a nephew-in-law of Lord FITZWILLIAM, and who, of course, has had ten thousand tugs at him to withdraw him from his reforming principles,[6] has, nevertheless, the surprisingly great merit of having been able to resist the power of all those tugs; as a complete proof of which, I mention for the satisfaction of my readers, and for the mortification of those toad-eating, spiteful devils, the hired scribblers of the *Scotsman*, and JACK WALTER and the she-proprietors of the bloody old *Times*, the fact, so honourable to me, as well as to all the other parties concerned in it; that Mr. SPIERS (the greatest land-proprietor in the county of Renfrew) came to PAISLEY to be chairman of a dinner, given to me there, on the 26. of October, accompanied by his son-in-law, Mr. BONTINE, who is a candidate for the county (against Sir MICHAEL SHAW STEWART), whose address I shall by-and-by insert, who is a young man of great promise, and who is, I am glad to say, likely to succeed: this venerable and universally-respected gentleman, accompanied, besides, by his eldest and second sons, did me and the reformers of PAISLEY the very great honour of presiding at a dinner, which was conducted in a manner worthy of the good sense and public spirit of the parties, and which, after short, neat, and pertinent speeches from the gentlemen whom I have named, and from others, and particularly from Mr. SPIER's eldest son, who discovered in this little specimen, quite enough to convince me of his capacity to be greatly useful to his country. After these things, this dinner terminated at a very early hour, without a single man appearing to have partaken of anything stronger than water. Here I, in fact, took my leave of the people of PAISLEY, amidst marks of friendship, such, indeed, as I have everywhere experienced, and such as would, if there were no other ties, bind me fast, to the last hours of my life, to the service of my grateful, kind, and generous countrymen.

Dalzell House, near Hamilton, 28. Oct. 1832
The day before the dinner took place I went to see the beautiful manufacture of silk, carried on by Mr. FULTON and Son. I never like to see these machines, lest I should be tempted to endeavour to understand them. I constantly resist all the natural desire which people, out of kindness, have to explain them to me. It is also wonderful that as in the case of the sun and the moon and the stars, I am quite satisfied with witnessing the effects. This silk affair, however, afforded one very pleasing circumstance. It was all put in motion by a wheel, turned by three men; and there was a great number of young women and girls employed at the work, and all very neatly and nicely dressed. The things they make are beautiful beyond description. I went afterwards to see the weaving of shawls and of waistcoat-stuff at Mr. BISSETT's the means and operation relating to which, appeared still more wonderful. In these fabrics our countrymen now surpass, not only all the rest of Europe, but those of India too; and I understand that PAISLEY surpasses all the rest of the kingdom in this respect. A blessed *Government* it must be to produce a state of things in which a *barrack*, furnished with well-fed, well-clothed, and well-armed soldiers, is established for the purpose of keeping in a state of obedience to the laws, these ingenious and indefatigably industrious people, who, while the soldiers are well fed, well clad, and well lodged, have not half a sufficiency of food of the very coarsest kind; have their bodies half covered with rags; scarcely know what a knife, fork, and plate mean; and have, in many cases, nothing but a mere whisp of straw to sleep upon! Blessed state of things! Better that the country should be abandoned; better that it should become a desert, than that such a state of things should be suffered to exist; better that destruction should come upon the whole of us, than that the makers of these beautiful goods should thus be compelled to live like hogs and dogs, while those whose bodies are decorated by these goods are wallowing in luxury, proceeding from deductions made from the earnings of these indefatigable people. On the same day when I expected to go and see Mr. DUNCAN HENDERSON, who, from his attachment to me, or rather to my writings, had taken so much pains to cultivate my *corn*,[1] I was informed, that I had to see his widow, for that he had died on the day of my first arrival at GLASGOW. As a mark of my respect for the memory of so worthy a man, a man of so much public spirit, and so justly beloved, I went to see Mrs. HENDERSON, at which she was very

much pleased; and she showed me a letter, written by myself to her late husband, on which she had set so much value as to have it framed and hung up as a picture. Not to see him, and still more to find that he was dead, really cast a damp over my pleasures at PAISLEY; though at no place where I have ever been in my life was I ever received with more cordiality, nor was my reception anywhere ever accompanied with circumstances better calculated to leave lasting impressions of gratitude on my mind; amongst which circumstances I must by no means overlook the hospitable, the cordial, the brother-like, and sister-like manner in which I was received and lodged by Mr. and Mrs. ARCHIBALD STEWART, of whom I took my leave yesterday morning (Saturday the 27th), and came to this place by the way of Glasgow, stopped again at Mr. BELL's, being taken up by him and brought to HAMILTON where (again in a church) I lectured last night. I forgot to mention, that, even on the day of the dinner, I went out, in the middle of the day, and lectured at a very nice little manufacturing town called JOHNSTONE; and I will be bound to say, that a more soul-stirring sermon never came from that pulpit before. I did not *melt* the hearts of my audience, but I made them pretty hot, when I described the manner in which my Lady SUTHERLAND *had swept the people off the land in the North.* "What!" exclaimed I, "have we not a right to *be* upon the land of our birth? Are we to be told, that we are bound in duty to come out and venture our lives in defence of that land against a foreign enemy, and yet, that we can be swept off from it when the landowners please?" Faith, my Lady SUTHERLAND would have had some new thoughts come into her head, if she could have witnessed the indignant and enraged looks of my hearers.

This noon-lecture at JOHNSTONE was to make up for the idle time in the evening that was to be passed at the dinner. So that, here have I been in Scotland twenty days, and I have lectured every day except the Sundays, and on each of the Sundays I have written a *Register*. Having travelled, besides, the better part of two hundred miles during the same time, slept in seven different beds! "What! the Lord ADVOCATE[2] and ABERCROMBIE and the POTTERS and SHUTTLE-WORTH and their mountebank, and CHARLEY PEARSON and *Sergeant* WILDE and Lord MELBOURNE and the tallow-man and brewer privy-councillors; "what!" will they all exclaim, "will this devil of ours never die and never be ill!" and old daddy BURDETT, that poor decrepit patriot, will exclaim, "What! and is he then actually to come and pull me along by the ears, *'gout'* or *no gout*, and perhaps through 'a heavy fall of snow';[3] is this never-eating, never-drinking, never-sleeping, never-resting, inflexible, hard-hearted dog, to come and remind me of what I used to say about the regiment and the room;[4] about Lady LOUISA PAGET and Mrs. FOX and her daughters; and about *'hired sheriffs, Parliaments and kings;'* is he to come at last, in reality, and drag me as a badger is dragged out of his hole, and remind me of what I used to teach about *'the necessity of pulling down great families;'* and, above all things, is he to come and drive me out to face the cheated people of WESTMINSTER, or compel me to help him *'to tear the leaves out of the accursed Red Book?'* "

From GLASGOW to HAMILTON (near which is the famous palace of the Duke of that name), the road runs along not far from the CLYDE, and we enter, in fact, into what is called *"the vale of the Clyde,"* which has in it everything that can be imagined that is beautiful. Corn-fields, pastures, *orchards,* woods, beautiful in their own form as well as in the variety and fine growth of the trees. Dr. DREAD-DEVIL[5] (who wrote in the same room that I write in when I am at *Bolt-Court*) said, that there were *no trees* in Scotland, or at least something pretty nearly amounting to that. I wonder how they managed it to take him about without letting him see trees. I suppose that lick-spittle BOSWELL, or Mrs. PIOZZI, tied a bandage over his eyes, when he went over the country which I have been over. I shall sweep away all this bundle of lies. I have no whim and no prejudice to gratify;[6] it is my business to speak of things as I find them. On the 1st of November, I am to go to LANARK, which is at the *"falls of the Clyde."* I defer my account of this vale till I have been thither, and until I have seen both banks of this beautiful river. How surprised my readers will be to hear of Scotch orchards, one single orchard being worth from five hundred to a thousand pounds a year; and that, too, an orchard not exceeding ten or twelve English acres, in extent; and how indignant they will be when they are told that the present Reform Bill, brought in by a native Scotchman, GIVES FEWER MEMBERS TO ALL SCOTLAND, than are given to a population in England NOT EXCEEDING THAT OF EDINBURGH ALONE, and not anything like that of Glasgow alone!

But to remark on these matters, and to prove to Englishmen, that this treatment of Scotland is as injurious to England as it is to Scotland herself, must be put off to my next, which will be dated from I cannot tell where.

New Lanark, 1. November, 1832.

Here I am upon the most interesting spot of earth that I ever set my foot upon in the course of my long and rambling life. But, before I proceed to give an account of what I have seen on the two banks of the river CLYDE, I must go back again, as in reality I did, from DALZELL HOUSE to GLASGOW, on Monday, the 29. October, to attend at a public dinner there given to me; and at which place on the 30. and 31., I gave lectures for the benefit of two classes of the working people. I must therefore quit the CLYDE for the present, and go back to GLASGOW, where I remained from the 29. to the 31. inclusive, and where the transactions were such as not to pass without full notice in this my account of Scotland. I shall probably not have room for my notices relative to the country, the scenery, the orchards, and other things on the banks of the CLYDE, until my next; but, at any rate, I must do full justice to the *political part* of these my CALEDONIAN adventures; this, after all, being the matter of the greatest importance; the sense, the steadiness, and the courage of the Scotch; their adherence to what they once get firmly into their heads; these being well known to the whole world, it is of vast importance that all my readers, *and particularly my* Lord GREY, know the true state of their minds with regard to me; for though his lordship may possibly smile at that, and draw up his nose, and turn up his upper lip, it were as well if he did not do it, and if he paid attention to the facts which I am about to put on record, and which facts it is impossible for me to misstate, putting them here upon paper which is to be read by thousands upon thousands of witnesses.

In my last I mentioned that I lectured at HAMILTON on Saturday, the 27., went that night and slept at DALZELL HOUSE, whence I dated the close of the last number of this acount; as that lecturing belongs to the part which this number is to embrace, I shall notice some particulars belonging to it, before I come back to GLASGOW, and give an account of what took place there. These particulars are very interesting, and will show my readers all over the kingdom the nature of the struggle going on in Scotland. The lecturing place was in what is called the BURGHER church; that is to say, the dissenting church. Here is an established church in Scotland; an established *Presbyterian church*; the priests of which have the ancient Catholic churches (where such remain); and which priests are paid by what are called TIENDS (which is only another word for tithes or tenths); but these TIENDS are *not a tenth part of the produce* as in England.

They are an annual allowance of a certain quantity of corn from each estate. This is not rendered in kind, however, but in money, according to the market-price at the time when the payment becomes due. For instance, the priest is to be paid for so many boles of wheat, on account of such an estate, on a certain day of the year; so on throughout his parish. This mode of payment renders it a great stretch of disinterestedness to induce the priest sincerely to pray for plenty; for the scantier the crop, the higher the price; and the higher the price, the higher is his pay. This is putting disinterestedness and piety to a very severe trial. In the great towns, there is an assessment on the rental for the payment of the priests. The patronage of the livings is in *the principal proprietor of the parish*; so that one of these great lords has the appointing of a dozen or two of priests.

This is called the established church of Scotland. But there is the seceding church; that is to say, there is, in every considerable place, a large part of the people that have *seceded*, or *drawn off*, from this established church. They do not differ from the other in their creed, or in their mode of worship; but each congregation insists on the right of nominating its own minister, and also insists on the minister being maintained by voluntary contributions, and not by compulsory assessments, or by TIENDS. So that here are *two churches*, one of which is pretty nearly as extensive and as firmly established as the other; and, as the seceders have generally the most able and most diligent ministers, they are daily gaining ground over the established church.

It will easily be conceived that the established church, exclusively under the patronage of the nobility, and trembling for the stability of the TIENDS and the compulsory assessments, are not *very warm friends of any change at all,* particularly of that very great change, the absolute necessity of which is the great burden of all my lecturings. Parsons have noses as keen as that of a crow: they smell danger at a greater distance than any part of God's creatures. It is said that the *Bald-Eagles,* in North America, they being in CANADA, will smell a dead horse upon the borders of the Gulf of MEXICO; but, wonderful as this may appear, my belief is that the noses of parsons are still finer than those of these *Bald-Eagles.* No wonder, then, that I have everywhere found the established churches shut against me, while the seceding churches have, wherever necessary, flung open their doors for my reception. This was the case at HAMILTON, where the fine-nosed gentry carried their hostility a little farther than merely shutting the doors of their church. They spread about the assertion that I was an *infidel*, and did everything in their power to prevent people from attending the lecture, in which, however, they by no means succeeded; and I had a very numerous audience, considering the size of the place. Having heard of what had been going on, I began by observing, that I had written and printed a hundred volumes; that I challenged the *Kirk* to set a hundred of its priests, each to take a volume, and to find, in the whole hundred, if they could, one single sentence hostile to religion or morality. I then related to them, that the Government itself, once took a paper of my writing, had a *million* of copies printed, at a cost to the public of between three and four thousand pounds; copies of which it sent by the post to every parish in the whole kingdom, with *directions to have it read from the pulpits!*[1] And read from the pulpits it was; and that, therefore, it was rather hard that the *Kirk* should represent me as an *infidel!* After having prefaced a little further, I proceeded with my lecture, striking my opponents in a very *tender part*, of which, however, I was not fully aware, until I afterwards learned the following particulars; namely, that the registration of votes for this borough (which has been hooked on to that of FALKIRK and another or two) showed that about a hundred and twenty pensioners resided in this little borough of HAMILTON; that a Mr. AUGUSTUS MURRAY, a son of Lord DUNMORE, and a nephew of the Duke of HAMILTON (the great lord of the country here, who has a mansion in the town, and a monstrous palace in a park just by it), is the "*Whig candidate*" for this bunch of boroughs, *against* Mr. GILLON, the present member and the radical candidate, whose friends had invited me to lecture at HAMILTON. Besides all this. Mr. AUGUSTUS MURRAY is either the brother or the nephew of Lady AUGUSTA MURRAY, the mother of the children of the Duke of SUSSEX; the monstrous pension of which lady I have so strongly remarked upon on so many occasions. It is very curious that the party whom I met at my friend's house at HAMILTON, all went to see the very fine and noble palace recently erected by the Duke; and some of them told me, that he wished me to go, if I chose, and have the palace and other things shown to me. It is very curious, I say, that I should take it into my head not to go, notwithstanding importunities so very pressing, that it was hardly good manners to resist them. I did resist, however, to the great astonishment, and not entirely the satisfaction of friends whom I was naturally extremely anxious not to displease. I saw there was danger of some atrocious newspaper lie arising out of my appearance at that palace. Besides, there would have been a species of meanness, even in putting my head under the roof of a man whose power it is one of the professed objects of my labours to curtail. The circumstances which I have above related as to Mr. MURRAY, will, when the paper shall reach the eyes of my friends who were of the party on that day, convince them, I trust, that my refusal to joint them on their visit to the palace was founded on good reason, and did not arise from perverseness or caprice.

From HAMILTON I went, as before related, to sleep at DALZELL HOUSE, stayed there on Sunday, and on Monday morning, the 29. of October, went back to GLASGOW to the dinner. This dinner is a matter of great importance; not as it concerns me, but as it shows the temper in which the people of Scotland now are. I shall insert a report of it, as given in the *Glasgow Chronicle* of the 31. of October. Every one will know how impossible it is to be accurate, in a report made under such circumstances and to such an extent. The report, therefore, must not be taken as at all unfair, because it omitted to mention the most material part of what I stated relative to the calumnies of BURDETT and his most infamous crew of newspaper hirelings. After stating the circumstances under which I received the money from him, I proceeded thus: "The ruffian miser sees it continually put forth, as he himself put it forth; that I went *off* to America, to carry away his money and defraud him of it.[2] The miser knows, that he gave it to me to clear off a debt owed to Mr. SWANN, a paper-maker, and an acquaintance of his own, and that Mr. SWANN went and received the money, and not I; the villainous miser knows, that I had to borrow money of WILLIAM CLEMENT, the proprietor of the *Morning Chronicle* (who then published the *Register*), in order to carry me and my family to America; the miser knows that he spread the story, in order to prevent me from ever again showing my face in England; the vile lady-and-child[3] miser knows, that I voluntarily came back again to face him and his demand; the wretched miser knows, that the Government having stripped me of everything, my own friend, Mr. TIMOTHY BROWN (whom he first introduced to me), made me a bankrupt, and carried the bankruptcy through at his own expense; the grinding miser knows, that Mr. BROWN wrote to him, 'You say that COBBETT owes you money, come then AND SWEAR TO YOUR DEBT:' the wretched miser knows, that he did not dare to come and swear to his debt; the miser knows, that in 1824, when a subscription was proposed to be begun for the purpose of putting me into Parliament, and when he was afraid of seeing me upon the same boards with him, that he then wrote to his crony, RICHARD GURNEY, of NORWICH, to *say that he would subscribe five hundred pounds*, and that he authorised GURNEY to show the letter to my friends in Norfolk;[1] the ruffian miser knows, that, when, in 1826, a subscription was proposed to put me in for PRESTON, he wrote to Colonel JOHNSTONE, the member for BOSTON, telling him that he would subscribe for that purpose, and that he afterwards repeated this to Colonel JOHNSTONE verbally, and told the COLONEL to name the sum he should subscribe; let the execrable miser choose, then, between the baseness of tendering his money to put a rogue into Parliament, the baseness of having made the tender without an intention to fulfil it, the baseness of hiding himself from taking a part in the atrocious lies published by the hirelings, while he is underhandedly assisting the hirelings to circulate those lies. The conclusion is, either his charge against me is utterly false, and he is the foulest of all calumniators; or he has been, twice under his own hand-writing, offering his money to put a rogue into Parliament. Let the ruffian miser choose between the two."

With regard to the rest of the proceedings at the dinner, they will speak for themselves. Every one concerned in them not only makes allowances for little inaccuracies, but must feel wonder that a report at such length, and so accurate, could possibly be made and published in so short a space of time. As to what BROUGHAM and MELBOURNE and *prosperity* ROBINSON and the EDINBURGH REVIEWERS and such-like people may think of this dinner, it is, perhaps, of very little importance; but it is quite necessary that *my Lord* GREY view it in its true light. *He* ought to see, and he will see, that we did not meet here for the purpose of eating and drinking; that it was a meeting held for the purpose of declaring to the whole nation what was the feeling of this great and opulent city, with regard to those principles which I am so well known to entertain, and those great measures of which I am regarded as the champion. In this light it is that my Lord GREY will view the thing. It was not to honour me personally, nor to honour me at all; it was to do honour to the political principles which I have so long been maintaining. It would be childlishness to view this matter in any other light. Viewed in this light, every incident, however trifling in itself, becomes matter of importance. Here, then, in a city consisting of two hundred thousand

people, distinguished at once for everything that is elegant, and
everything that is opulent: literary institutions, arts and sciences,
navigation, commerce, manufactures, and all in the highest perfection; the emporium of Scotland, surrounded in every direction by
towns and villages, all animated with the same spirit; and here, in
this great city, under the name of a convivial meeting, it is sent forth
to the world, that the political principals of COBBETT are the pre-
dominant political principals of Scotland! This is the light in which
every man of sense will view it. The low and filthy wretches at
MANCHESTER have actually been sending down pamphlets from their
mountebank to Glasgow, and writing pressing letters to their friends
at that city, to circulate the pamphlets about, "in order to show up
COBBETT!" The proceedings at this dinner constitute the answer to
the despicable reptiles, whom, if I live but a few years longer, I will
hunt off the face of this earth. I will make them, and the tallow-man
privy-councillor, know what it is to employ a mountebank-player to
do that which they were too great cowards to do themselves. I shall be
back with them pretty quickly now; and I will make them feel the
consequences of sending pamphlets to GLASGOW. So much for the
dinner at GLASGOW. I wished very much to get off for England
immediately after that dinner was over; but the working people had
been excluded from the lectures by the prices necessary to keep the
theatre from being a scene of confusion. They very much wished that
I would lecture to them upon terms different from those on which
admission had been given at the theatre. There were two bodies of
them, the *Trades* and the *Manufacturers*. I, at once, very gladly
offered to preach to them for nothing; and it was fixed that I should
do it to the *Trades* in the theatre, on 30. of October, and to the
Manufacturers in a church, on the 31. of October; and this I did. The
delegates of the *Trades* delivered to me, upon the stage, an address; to
which I, upon the spot, gave an answer, which I had written before.
These two papers I here insert, deeming them to be of sufficient
importance to justify this application of space that they will occupy.
The address was prefaced by a very handsome and eloquent speech
from the delegate who handed it to me. I do not know what
BROUGHAM and his gang of reviewers may think of this matter; but I
know that if I were a minister, every bone in my body would rattle at
the bare thought of attempting to carry on a system held in
detestation by millions of men, of whom these delegates are a fair
specimen.

MR. WILLIAM COBBETT

Respected Sir, — We, the undersigned delegates from various shops, factories and districts, in behalf of a great portion of the operatives of Glasgow, are desirous of expressing our heartfelt gratification at meeting with a person whose voluminous political writings, the produce of half a century, have done so much towards keeping the public mind in wholesome agitation, enabling us to form a just estimate of the men and measures which have so long misdirected the magnificent resources of a mighty nation.

We rejoice to behold speedily approaching the inevitable doom of those enormous impositions, in the exposure of which you have been such a valuable instrument. And we are proud to think that a man originally a labourer for his daily bread[5] should be thus fated to rise on the ruin of the aristocratic caste by the mere force of his own industry and talent, proving that the mind, when vigorously exerted and directed aright, is all-powerful in overcoming the fallacious systems imposed upon the many by the greedy and ambitious few.

Notwithstanding the epithets which you have so unsparingly bestowed on persons whose conduct you could not approve, and however much you may have wounded the national pride of Scotland by so liberally slandering her name and people, the operatives of Glasgow regard these ebullitions as the effects of a strong dislike to the iniquitous measures and false theories of political economy associated with the parties you addressed, and that you must have drawn the character of Scotland and Scotchmen from the cringing *booing* place-and-pension hunters, who, in bye-past parliaments, presumed to represent our much-abused country; and we sincerely hope that you are now happily undeceived.

We also sincerely trust that a place for you in the ensuing Parliament will be secured, whereby you will be the more effectually enabled to apply those gigantic powers which you have hitherto displayed in your writings; and you will, by a consistent, steady, and undeviating perseverence, prove that neither wealth nor place, but the reduction of that astonishingly iniquitous Government which has so long degraded us, is the great object of your life — that you will ever bear in mind the ruinous condition of the working classes, the justice and necessity of extending to them the elective franchise; and that you will loudly call for immediate amelioration, by the increasing of our means of comfort, and removing every obstacle to the free exercise of our industry.

The operatives of Glasgow are the more immediately interested in the removal of the stamp duties on newspapers, having one of their own, the cheapness and wide circulation of which they deem of the highest importance; and also a law to limit the time of working in public factories, and in every other department where children are employed. They consider it equally necessary to afford workmen opportunities of acquiring useful knowledge, and they therefore press these matters upon your attention as they would upon the attention of all those who assume the functions of legislation.[6]

That you may long enjoy sound bodily health, and unimpaired mental vigour, for the great struggle in which you are about to be engaged, is the sincere wish of,

Respected Sir, your friends and admirers

[There follow approximately forty names of the delegates from the various Trade organisations.]

MR. COBBETT'S ANSWER.

Gentlemen, — It has been the boast of the present Prime Minister, that *"he would stand by his order:"* it is my boast, that I have always firmly stood by mine, which is that, as you truly observe, of those who labour for their daily bread. The other order, not being able to endure the thoughts of acknowledging the superior talents and wisdom of our order, and not being able to corrupt me, have been, for now pretty nearly thirty years, endeavouring to cast me, by some means or other, into the shade, if not to effect my destruction; and (most curious to behold!) they have gone on, sometimes adopting measures, sometimes rejecting measures, seemingly for the sole purpose of opposing my principles and of falsifying my predictions; till, at last, they have made it a question, whether their order shall, or shall not, continue to exist; while I have gone on increasing in influence, and while my order is as firmly established as the foundations of the earth itself.

Be assured, gentlemen, that this journey to Scotland was not at all necessary to convince me of the intelligence and virtues of Scotchmen, against whom, in general, I never had a prejudice in my life, and, therefore, had none to be removed. In speaking of the perverse and renegado *pretended philosophers*, who, like similar reptiles in the distant provinces of the Roman Empire, have gone to the seat of government to sell their own country and help to enslave ours, I have been obliged to designate them by naming the part of the kingdom from which they came; but I have invariably said, at the same time, that I imputed not their disposition to the people of Scotland, whose oppressions, whenever I shall have the power, I deem it my duty to remove to the utmost of that power; and, in some measure, my journey to Scotland, by the great knowledge that it has enabled me to acquire, will assist me in the performance of that duty.

With regard to an extension of the suffrage, the abolition of the stamp-duties, the rescuing of children from the hardships to which the wants of their parents induce them to expose them; with regard to all of these, I not only heartily concur with you in opinion; but am already bound, by a most solemn pledge, to the people of Oldham, to do my utmost in accordance with that opinion.

Gentlemen, be pleased to receive, and to communicate to the working people of Glasgow, with every mark of my respect and regard, my sincere thanks for this address, compared to which, a patent of nobility from the King would be regarded by me as some dirty, toad-eating ballad, put in competition with the Bible.

I am, Gentlemen,

Your faithful friend, and most obedient servant,

Wm. Cobbett.

Glasgow, 30. Oct. 1832.

The next evening I gave a lecture to the manufacturers at the Tolcross church, in the eastern district. Upon this occasion also an address was delivered to me, before the audience, previous to the beginning of the lecture. This address was also preceded by a very clever speech, from the gentleman who presented it; for gentlemen these are, if we be to judge from their understandings and their talents. The ADDRESS was as follows. After which came the lecture to a very numerous audience.

TO MR. WILLIAM COBBETT

Sir, — The inhabitants of the east district of the barony parish of Glasgow, and other villages adjacent, having themselves, according to their different circumstances and abilities, long and arduously struggled in the cause of radical reform; and who, through many years of protracted suffering and deeply-felt degradations, have, from the strength and acumen of your many writings, which they have been in the practice of consulting with a studious avidity, been led to look up to you as the mighty champion, the undaunted and unshaken advocate of that great and glorious cause. And, Sir, with feelings deepened by an interest and pleasure which they want words to express, they congratulate themselves on the event of your visit to Scotland, your progress to, and stay in, the important city of Glasgow; but in a particular manner in your appearance here this evening, to give a satisfaction of heart, and a triumph to the recollection of an anxious and intelligent community.

And now, Sir, as they hold that through your agency, by the strength of that mighty weapon which you have long wielded, and do still so indefatigably wield, the enemy has been made to bow his head, that one step has been gained on the road to national emancipation, they do hope, nay are assured, that in life your labours of love shall not cease until the whole is accomplished. That the sphere of your usefulness may be extended by soon having a seat in the legislature of our country; and that you may live and enjoy the blessing of health until your soul being satisfied with the success of your work, your spirit may rejoice together with the spirits of an emancipated people, when they shall raise the song of triumph over the broken chains of oppression, and the grave of tyranny, is the fervent and sincere prayer of, Sir, your ardent friends and admirers.

The radical reformers of the east district of the barony parish of Glasgow, &c.

(Signed in their name and behalf by)

[There follow fourteen names.]

To describe the enthusiasm of these worthy fellows is quite impossible; men, boys, women, girls, children six or seven years old, all squeezed about me, stretching out their hands begging to touch mine. The men who conducted the business, scolded them and wanted to keep them off; but I said, "Let them alone, let them do what they like: they won't take any piece of me away." Upon these occasions it always occurs to me to think how quietly the base POTTERS and SHUTTLEWORTH and haughty BAXTER and the tallow-man privy-councillor and the brewer and old bawling BURDETT; how quietly and uninterruptedly they would get along in the same place! They got me into the vestry: one brought a Bible, which his wife had desired him to bring to me, that I might write my name in it, on the blank leaf, that she might have it to show her grand-children: another brought one of my own grammars for the same purpose; another brought another book. I was quite astonished myself to find that my name and all about me were so well known amongst these people. One blessed me for the *"Protestant Reformation,"* another for my *"Advice to Young Men."* Ah! poor deluded creatures! Poor enthusiastic creatures!" BROUGHAM and his EDINBURGH *Reviewers* will exclaim. Oh, no! my bucks! That won't do; for this is the country of *"antalluct."* If, indeed, it had been in SUSSEX, or KENT, or HAMPSHIRE, or WILTSHIRE, where I had been saying that fire was a good thing, then, indeed, you might have said that it was chopsticks applauding a brother chopstick; but this was in the country of *"antalluct."* Therefore, no shuffling, if you please. I knew very well, that I had the *Scotchies* on my side as well as the *chopsticks*; but I had not the proof to produce without coming here: I was sure that it was so; but I wanted the means of making others sure of it, too; and I have now done the job: I have now blowed up MALTHUS and the whole crew: I have been into the accursed *"boothies:"* I have sent my account of them over the world; I have brought it back to be read in Scotland, while I am here and publicly exhibiting myself with that description having been read by the people of Scotland. I have shown, I have proved, the docrines of MALTHUS and the EDINBURGH crew to be damnable doctrines: I have proved to the chopsticks of England, that they ought to perish to the last man to maintain the poor-law of *Elizabeth* unimpaired. I have now produced practical proof of the object and tendencies of STURGES BOURNE's BILLS: in short, I have blowed the hellish conspiracy against justice and humanity into the air. I am thinking *whether* the *"feelosofers"* will now go to find out that *happiness and independence* which arise from an absence of poor-laws! What do they think of *Ireland*? I really should not wonder to see Dr. BLACK turn to Ireland *now*, and to be followed by BROUGHAM and all his puffing tribe. Ah! Doctor! come and join me before I get out of Scotland, and you shall hear some of the execrations which your countrymen pour out upon the *Malthusian "feelosofers."* They do hate you all from the bottom of their souls. Come and tell them that you are a *Malthusian*. Let the

"*all jaw and no judgement;*"[7] let him come and tell the people in the
eastern district of GLASGOW, that he is "*prepared to defend, to their
full extent, all the principles and propositions*" of the pensioned
parson MALTHUS; let him come and say that to the people of the
eastern district of GLASGOW; let the jawing fellow do it on a wet day;
then let him see how long it will take for the waters of the CLYDE to
wash from him the dirt with which, in five minutes, he would be
covered.

Scotland; the *happy state of Scotland arising from the absence of
poor-laws*; Scotland being thus snatched from them, and their being
hardly base enough to refer to the happy state of Ireland, I should
not wonder if they were to go to AUSTRIA, or, in case of failure there,
to POLAND or RUSSIA; or, which would cut the thing short, at once to
the infernal regions themselves. The base and lazy villains must endeavour to keep their doctrine up; by preaching this doctrine they
get placed and pensioned and provided for by the detestable oligarchy of England: the scrawling ruffians must keep up the doctrine;
or, awful to think of! they must . . . go to work! The vulgar-minded,
the lazy, the unfeeling villains, who seem as if they could drink hot
blood rather than suffer sweat to come through their skins, must
keep up this doctrine; must continue to feed the landed tyrants with
the hope of being able to reduce English labourers to lodge in
"*boothies*," and to feed upon oats, barley and peas; they must keep
this hope alive; they must continue to make the land-fellows in England hope that they shall be able to sweep the people off the land, or
to make them live upon the food of horses and of hogs; the ruffian
slaves must keep this hope alive, or they themselves must rake
kennels, empty privies, or crack stones.

On Tuesday evening, after having been at the lecture before mentioned, I went to see the Royal Exchange by *candle-light*. When I
was there before there was an immense crowd in every part of the
building, so that I could have no fair view of it. I wished to be able to
notice it in a rather particular manner; because their "*exchanges*"
are the subject of boast with LEEDS, MANCHESTER, LIVERPOOL,
BRISTOL, and other great commercial places. I have never viewed
any of them in a particular manner, having no very good opinion of
the politics of the persons generally assembled in them. Here the
case is different: every thing that I have met with here (laying aside
the constant kindness and politeness with which I myself have been
treated) has had a tendency to create in my mind a great respect for

the persons that usually assemble in this place; and from that feeling
I am now induced to give a hasty account of it, thinking that it may
be entertaining to my readers, if not *useful* besides in enabling them,
from this specimen, to judge of the style and manner, as well as of the
magnitude and opulence of this city of GLASGOW, which, observe,
has, by the gracious goodness of the pro-consuls of Scotland, *two*
TRINITY-HOUSE pensioners, while NEWBIGGIN (consisting of a
hundred and twenty-five souls) has *eighty-five* of those pensioners.

This edifice is placed between two of the principal streets of the
city, *Queen-street* and *Buchanan-street*, with its front to the former,
looking eastward, having a noble *Corinthian* portico, which faces
and is seen from the whole length of INGRAM-STREET; another very
fine street, terminated to the west by this grand portico of the
Exchange. The portico is formed of two rows of pillars, eight
advanced in front, and four farther back on the flanks. Above, and
immediately behind the portico, rises a cupola or lantern, built of
the same fine white stone as the Exchange building is. The cupola or
lantern is also of the *Corinthian* order of architecture, and is
supported by about a dozen columns, with a vane surmounting the
whole. Here is a place intended for a clock, which, being to be
lighted by gas, is to show the time at night as well as by day. Round
the other three sides of the Exchange are numerous columns of the
same order, of course; and at the western end of it, separated by a
broad and finely-paved street (there being the same on each side of
the Exchange) stands the Royal Bank of Scotland, which is also built
with the same fine stone, having a portico with six columns of the
Ionic order, and capacious enough to hold ten thousand bales of
paper money; while on all sides you see splendid shops and places of
business; all, in their several degrees, bearing the outward and visible
signs of great solidarity and opulence within.

As to the inside of the Exchange, after passing under the lofty
portico, you pass through a grand entrance-hall into an oval-shaped
saloon, having a cupola above for the purpose of light. You then
enter into the GREAT ROOM, or, as they call it, the NEWS-ROOM,
which is about a hundred and twenty, or a hundred and thirty feet in
length, I suppose, and about sixty or seventy feet broad. The floor
above is supported by several lofty pillars, most judiciously arranged,
in two rows, running the whole length of the room, each pillar consisting of *one single stone.* Thus there is a grand *promenade* in the
middle of the room; while the two sides, each of which has three

large and elegant fire-places, are fitted up with highly-finished mahogany tables, for the subscribers, merchants, and strangers, to read newspapers, magazines, and other periodical publications. They say that here are a hundred newspapers taken in; and, amongst the rest, I cast my eye, without seeming to know it, upon a little octavo weekly publication, in the fate of which I felt somewhat interested, but which, in an account of a building so magnificent as this, the reader will consider as too unimportant to be named.[8] This splendid room is lighted by several brilliant gas-chandeliers, pendent in a row from the middle of the ceiling, which is arched, and very beautiful as to its decorations. The height of the middle of this arch from the floor may be thirty or forty feet.

Very much to the credit, and strongly bespeaking the character of the directors and proprietors of this establishment, and, indeed, bespeaking the character of the city itself, this NEWS-ROOM, which is opened about seven in the morning, and is not closed till ten at night, is quite free for the admission of all strangers gratuitously, without even an introduction by a subscriber, as is the case in all the news-rooms which I have seen in England. The subscribers are about fourteen or fifteen hundred in number, who pay, I am told, not forty shillings a year a piece, which, one would suppose impossible to be sufficient to remunerate those who erected the building and who sustain the establishment. The construction of the building reflects the highest credit on the architect, who is a Mr. HAMILTON, somewhat famous, however, in his other undertakings of a similar sort, both private and public. The principal projector and promoter was Mr. DAVID BELL, who is said to have devoted that attention to it, a share of which, doubtless (and a largish share) he will devote to a very different object when he shall have exchanged his present state of "single blessedness" for a state of vastly greater blessedness, because that will be *double!*

A gentleman who appeared to be a West India Merchant, told me, that the grand room up-stairs was devoted entirely to the exhibiting of samples of all the sugar imported into the *Clyde*; there being, however, a variety of other rooms for other mercantile purposes. This affair, which, Royal Bank and all together, is said to have cost not more than fifty thousand pounds, would, if it had been an undertaking conducted under the auspices of the jobbers of the city of London, have cost half a million of money. Those vagabond jobbers, who make me pay church-rates to two churches without letting me have a church to go to, would have spent more than fifty thousand pounds in eating and drinking success to the undertaking; and would have voted themselves, and their wives, another hundred thousand to pay the expenses of *"summer excursions,"* in order to produce a renovation of their faculties, impaired by the extent of their guttling and guzzling, undergone in projecting and executing the job; in short, they would have made a loan, and plunged the city deeper in debt than it is now; and that is quite deep enough. The city debt and the "national debt" will both go together; their destruction will overwhelm and extinguish a set of vermin as vile as any that ever were destroyed by water or by fire.

Below the ground-floor of the Exchange, are, a coffee-house, private rooms, a larder most beautifully and abundantly furnished, all kept in the neatest and nicest manner. After coming from the lecture, as I mentioned before, I went down into these appartments with some friends, where we were furnished with tea, and other things, according to our fancy; amongst which were oysters, which are very abundant both here and at EDINBURGH, small and white, and as good as I ever tasted in London.[9] A friend asked me, upon this occasion, whether "I did not think that this would be a good place for the collective, who might come down and gorge and guzzle here below, while the law-making was going on above, instead of coming rattling down-stairs to give their votes at the risk of their drunken necks." I answered that those beastly and infamous scenes were *"bygone;"* for that, if a reformed Parliament were base enough, and insolent enough, to attempt to pass laws, and say "AYE" and "NO," while picking their teeth and belching out brandy and water; if a reformed Parliament were to consist of men base and insolent enough to sit and make laws in the midst of a cook-shop and a tap-house, I trusted that the people would know what was due to themselves, and that they would soon convince the *reformed* Parliament that it stood in need of further reforming.

Thus I quit this very elegant building; and, for the present, GLASGOW itself; for though I am to go back to it again for one night, it will only be to give a FAREWELL LECTURE, and then set off into Ayrshire, on my way to England. I am here, at the famous NEW LANARK, which is near the celebrated "FALLS OF THE CLYDE." I saw a book once of views of the CLYDE. Nothing upon paper can give any one an idea of the reality in this case. But to give anything like a true account of what I have now seen; to do anything approaching to justice to the waters, the woods, the verdant hills, the numerous and most beautiful orchards of apples and pears and plums, that I have seen on the banks of this river, and on those of the CAULDER and AVEN, which empty themselves into it; and of the *glens* (as they are called) which lead from the hills down to these rivers; to do anything approaching towards justice to all these, will demand time, one moment of which I have not now at my command, having to lecture at the borough of LANARK to-night, and having to set off for GLASGOW early in the morning.

WM. COBBETT.[10]

New Milns, 5. November, 1832.[1]

I got here yesterday, lectured here last night, am to go to KILMARNOCK to-morrow, to DUMFRIES next day, and the day after to CARLISLE. I shall have to say a great deal about this place, very near to which is Loudon castle; and, of course, the Marquis of HASTINGS is here the chief lord of the country. I have no time to say anything at all as *to* this place; but I will just say, that I wish BROUGHAM and the *"feelosofers"* had seen me come in yesterday, and heard me make the church ring last night with a description of the conduct and future intentions of the Whigs, and had heard me urge the necessity of introducing the English poor-law into Scotland. That is all at present.

New Milns, Sunday, 4. November 1832.

At the close of the last letter, I informed my readers that I had arrived in this little and most beautifully-situated manufacturing town, which is an ancient borough of the county of AYR, and of which I have to say a good deal by-and-by, after I have gone back, in order to do something like justice to the banks of the CLYDE, and after I have pursued my rout from GLASGOW to this place.

The CLYDE, the firth, the harbours, and commerce of which I have spoken sufficiently, takes its rise in the lofty hills which divide the counties of PEEBLES and DUMFRIES from the county of LANARK. Like other great rivers, it has tributary streams falling into it; but it becomes a great river soon after it has tumbled over the celebrated falls of LANARK. No man living has ever beheld, in my opinion, a river, the banks of which presented a greater number and a greater variety of views, or more beautiful views, than those which are pre-

sented to the eye on the banks of the CLYDE. Some persons delight
most in level pastures on the banks of rivers; some in woods of trees of
various hues; some in hills rising up here and there nearer to, or more
distant from, the banks, some of the hills clothed with woods and
others with verdure; others (delighting more in utility than show)
seek on the sides of rivers for an inter-mixture of corn-fields,
pastures, and orchards; others (having a taste for the wilder works of
nature) want to see deep banks, some of them three or four hundred
feet high, with woods clinging to their sides down to the water's edge;
while there are others (caring nothing about sterility so that they
have the romantic) that are not satisifed unless they see the waters
come foaming and tumbling down rocks thirty or forty feet high,
with perpendicular sides, as if cleft by a convulsion of nature, and
these side rocks crowned at the top with every variety of trees, over
the tips of which you, from the opposite bank, see the verdant land
covered with cattle and with sheep, or the arable land with corn or
with turnips, the finest that the eyes of man ever beheld. Such are
some of the various tastes of various persons: let them all come to the
banks of the CLYDE, and each will find that which will gratify, as far
as this matter goes, every wish of his heart.

I do not by any means exaggerate in any one particular. In
Scotland or out of Scotland, justice to my subject as well as to my
readers would bid me say this; but I am not sure that I should say it if
I were not sure that I shall be out of Scotland before it can possibly be
read. To be sure, the kind of treatment that I received from every
soul that I came near, gentle or simple, on the banks of this river, was
extremely well calculated to make everything appear to me *"couleur
de rose;"* and, if I had been forty years younger, it might well have
apologized (considering who were some of the persons from whom I
received it) for a very considerable degree of exaggeration; but any
description that I can give is very far short of the reality. I have
always taken great delight in viewing the earth in almost all its
shapes, and in contemplating its various productions. Born in a very
beautiful valley,[2] lying in the midst of the wildest heaths in the world,
but which heaths are continually presenting to the eye of the traveller
little beautiful spots, I contracted the habit, when a child, of
comparing one of these beauties with another, and the habit has
stuck to me throughout my whole life. In NOVA SCOTIA and in the
United States of AMERICA, how often have I stood to admire the
water-falls in the rocky *creeks*, with lofty banks, trees growing out of

the interstices in the rocks! How often have I wished that every soul in England were there to see the same! These creeks, as they call them, are cross rivers, falling into the great river; some of them mere little streams; others, such as we would call rivers; just thus it is with the tributary streams of the CLYDE, with this difference, that, in America, the surrounding country consists of endless woods; whereas on the banks of these Scotch creeks you see the green hills or the corn-fields over the tips of the trees that cover the lofty banks. These creeks have all their *falls* upon a smaller scale. The CLYDE itself has three grand *falls*; the first in going up the river, a little nearer GLASGOW than the borough of LANARK; the second about three miles farther up; and the third about a mile above that; and beyond that the river, comparatively insignificant in size, winds gently through a moory tract of land lying at the foot of the mountains. The first of these falls brings the water down sixty feet from the bed above; the second about eighty feet; the third not so much. The middle falls are just above the manufacturing village of NEW LANARK; the vast and various machinery of which is put in motion by the waters, taken in a most curious manner out of the river, and applied to these purposes. This NEW LANARK, of which we have heard so much as connected with the name of Mr. OWEN, stands upon a little flat, which nature has made on one bank of the river, on which the manufacturing buildings stand, and also dwelling-houses for the work-people. This village is about a mile and a half from the town of LANARK. At one end of it is a beautiful park, which, together with its mansion, are occupied by Messrs. WALKERS, who are managers of this manufacturing concern on account of a company called the "NEW LANARK Company." This house and park were the residence of *Lord Justice Clerk*. Mr. QUEEN who was made Lord BRACKSFIELD (the name of this seat), after his famous works with regard to MUIR, PALMER, GERRALD, and MARGAROT, those parliamentary reformers who were transported by the sentence of this man. In this house, which looks down into the CLYDE, at about two hundred yards distance, and is in every respect as beautiful a spot as can well be imagined, I was lodged in the very same room which contained the present imperial slaughterer of the Poles,[3] and the present Lord CHANCELLOR, who, *in his way*, is full as great a man as the other, and entitled to full as much admiration. In going from the town of LANARK, down to the new village, you come to a spot, as you descend the hill, where you have a full view of the great falls of the CLYDE, with the accompanying rocks and woods which form the banks of the river. At the same time you see the green hills, and the cattle and sheep feeding on them, at the summits of the banks on each side, and over the tops of the trees. The fine buildings of the factories are just under you; and *this,* all taken together, is by far the most beautiful sight that my eyes ever beheld.

We went up to the very edge of the falls, stood upon the tips of the rocks and looked down upon the smoking water. In the crevices near the tops of the rocks, the jackdaws have discovered inaccessible places for depositing their nests; and here I saw such multitudes of that bird, such as I had never seen before. There were thousands upon thousands of them skimming about over a sort of bay, formed by the twirling water after it comes down the falls. I could see that their mouths were open, but the noise of the water prevented me from hearing their chattering, for which I was very sorry, as the same noise necessarily prevented them from hearing an invitation which I gave them, to come up and take possession of Lord HOLLAND's new church in "ADDISON ROAD," near *"Cato Cottage"* and *"Homer Villa,"* in the sensible parish of KENSINGTON. On the side of the rising hill, on one side of these falls, is the seat of Lady MARY ROSS, sister of the Duke of LEINSTER, who has very kindly had paths made in her woods, for the convenience of persons coming to see the falls. On the other side are the remains of an old castle (rising up amongst the trees) called COREHOUSE CASTLE, near to which is the seat of a Mr. CRANSTOUN, a Lord of Session, who has now the title of Lord COREHOUSE.

After having been to the falls we came back through the manufacturing village. All is here arranged with great skill; and everything that you behold, dwelling places of the people (about fourteen hundred in number); their dresses; their *skins*; all bespoke cleanliness and well being; all savoured of the Quaker.[1] I have never been into any manufacturing place without reluctance, and I positively refused to go into any of them here, alleging, that I had no understanding of the matter, that the wondrous things that are performed in these places, only serve, when I behold them, to withdraw my mind from things which I do understand. Mr. BELL prevailed upon me, during my first visit to the CLYDE, to stop at a manufacturing village, belonging to Messrs. MONTEITH, at a place called BLANTYRE. Here the water-wheels were wonderful to behold; but they afforded nothing interesting to me, who thought a great deal more about the condition of the people, which appeared to be very good here also, than I did about the cause of the movement, or about the mechanical effects of the machines. Being at NEW LANARK, however, I was rather curious to know whether there was any reality in what we had heard about the effects of the Owen "*feelosofy*." I had always understod that he had been the author of his own great fortune, and the founder of this village; but I found, that the establishment had been founded by a Mr. DALE, who had had two or three daughters with great fortunes; that Mr. OWEN had got one of these daughters, and one of these fortunes; that Mrs. OWEN had been dead for some years; that the concern had long been in other hands; that the only part of it which was ever of his invention was a large building,[5] in which the "*feelosofical*" working-people were intended to eat and drink in common; that they never did this; that there had been a place at some distance from LANARK, fixed upon for the execution of the "OWEN PLAN;" that a large space had been surrounded with a high stone wall for the purpose; that the scheme had been abandoned; and that the wall had been taken down, and sold as *old stones!* The building in NEW LANARK, which OWEN had erected for the "*feelosofers*" to carry on their community of eating and drinking, is used as a *school-room*; and here I saw boys in one place, and girls in another place, under masters appointed for the purpose, carrying on what is called "education." There was one boy pointing with a stick to something stuck up upon the wall, and then all the rest of the boys began bawling out what it was. In one large room they were all *singing out something* at the word of command, just like the tribe of little things in *Bolt-court*,[6] who there stun the whole neighbourhood with singing "*God save the King*," "*the Apostles creed*," and the "*Pence table*," and the fellow who leads the lazy life in the teaching of whom, ought to be sent to raking the kennel, or filling a dung-cart. In another great apartment of this house, there were eighteen boys and eighteen girls, the boys dressed in Highland dresses, without shoes on, naked from three inches above the knee, down to the foot, a tartan plaid close round the body, in their shirt sleeves, their shirt collars open, each having a girl by the arm, duly proportioned in point of size, the girls without caps, and without shoes and stockings; and there were these eighteen couples, marching, arm in arm, in regular files, with a lock-step, slow march, to the sound of a fiddle, which a fellow, big enough to carry a quarter of wheat or to dig ten rods of ground in a day, was playing in the corner of the room with an immense music book lying open before him. There was another man who was commanding officer of the marching couples, who, after having given us a march in quick step as well as slow step, were disposed of in dancing order, a business that they seemed to perform with great regularity and elegance; and it is quite impossible to see the half-naked lads of twelve or thirteen, putting their arms round the waists of the thinly-clad girls of the same age, without clearly perceiving the manifest tendency of this mode of education to prevent "*premature marriages*" and to "*check population*."

It is difficult to determine, whether, when people are huddled together in this unnatural state, this sort of soldiership discipline may or may not be necessary to effect the purposes of schooling; but I should think it a very strange thing, if a man, calculated to produce effect by his learning, could ever come to perfection from a beginning like this. It is altogether a thing that I abhor. I do not say that it may not be useful when people are thus unnaturally congregated; and, above all things, I am not disposed to bestow censure on the *motives* of the parties promoting this mode of education; for the sacrifices which they make, in order to give success to their schemes, clearly prove that their motives are benevolent; but I am not the less convinced that it is a melancholy thing to behold; that it is the reverse of *domestic life*; that it reverses the order of nature; that it makes minds a fiction;[7] and, which is amongst the greatest of its evils, it fashions the rising generation to habits of *implicit submission*, which is only another term for civil and political slavery.[8] However, the consolation is, that it is impossible that it should ever become anything like general in this nation. The order of the world demands that nine-tenths of the people should be employed on, and in the affairs of, *the land*; being so employed, they must be scattered about widely: and there must be *homes* and domestic life for the far greater part of the rising generation. When men contract a fondness for anything which has a great deal of novelty and strangeness in it; when they brood over a contemplation of some wonderful discovery which they think they have made; when they suffer it long to absorb all the powers of their minds; when they have been in this state for a considerable length of time, they really become *mad*,[9] as far as relates to the matter which has thus absorbed all their mental faculties; and they think themselves more wise than the rest of all mankind, in exact proportion to the degree of their madness. It is unfortunate enough when follies of this sort lead only to disappointment and ridicule; but the parties become objects of real compassion when the eccentric folly produces dissipation of fortune and the ruin of families.

From this account of the "OWEN-PLAN" I come to something a great deal more pleasant, the numerous and plentiful and beautiful orchards on the banks of the CLYDE, on its two great tributary rivers, the CAULDER and the AVEN, and on the banks of the numerous *glens*, which terminate when they arrive at one or the other of these rivers. Now I have seen the orchards over the greater part of Devonshire, Somersetshire, Gloucestershire, Herefordshire, and Worcestershire. I have seen the orchards in Pennsylvania, New Jersey, and in that "garden of America," Long Island; and I have never seen finer orchards than on the banks above mentioned; and I have never seen, at one time, a more beautiful show and variety[10] of apples, than I saw on the table of Mr. HAMILTON, of DALZELLL-HOUSE, on 29. of October. The apples, pears, and plums, were gathered in; but there were the trees, and the leaves still upon them; and more clear, and more thriving trees I never saw; and I believe that some of them surpassed, in point of size, any that I had ever seen in my life. At the exquisitely beautiful place of Mr. ARCHIBALD DOUGLAS called MAUDSLIE CASTLE, which is situated in a beautiful flat, washed on one side by the CLYDE, and having a semi-circular wood running round the back of it at a convenient distance; at this place I saw, standing out in the park as ornamental trees, apple-trees, which I thought extended their lateral branches to twenty feet in every direction from the trunk of the tree, which, observe, is a cir-cumference of a hundred and twenty feet, forming a shade quite sufficient for fifty oxen to lie down in. These trees were straight in the trunks, and their top shoots perfectly vigorous and clean. I *may* have seen larger trees in Herefordshire and Long Island; but I do not think that I ever did see any so fine, taking trunk, branches, and cleanness, altogether. But these fine orchards are *general*, all the way up the CLYDE, from very near GLASGOW to the falls of that river. Mr. PRENTICE, the editor of the *Glasgow Chronicle*, has the good sense to have a pretty considerable farm, at six or seven miles from GLASGOW. About three English acres of his land form a garden and orchard, the trees of which are about six years old, very fine, quite free from canker, bearing very fine fruit. The cherry-trees are very fine also; the plum-trees are fine; and an orchard is not a mere matter of ornament or of pleasure here, but of prodigious profit;

under the apple and pear-trees are gooseberry or currant-bushes, very well managed in general; and these orchards very frequently yield *more than a hundred pounds sterling in one year from an English acre of land*! Like other things, the fruit here has fallen in price since the time of the PANIC, in spite of the *"cherished* one-pound notes," as Sir JOHN SINCLAIR calls them. Money has not grown up *"like grass under the cow's mouth,"* as Mr. ATTWOOD says it ought; and therefore the pecuniary produce of orchards, like that of fields and manufactories, has been greatly diminished. But these orchards are always a source of very considerable income. I think that my friend Mr. M'GAVIN, of HAMILTON, told me that his orchard, which is less than an English acre, has yielded him eighty pounds a year, clear money; and it is no uncommon thing for the proprietor of ten or a dozen acres, to sell the fruit by auction upon the tree, for something approaching a hundred pounds an acre. In our apple counties no man thinks of anything but fruit to make *cider* and *perry*: here, the whole is table-fruit; and, as I said before, I have never seen so great a variety of fine apples in England, at one time, as I saw upon the table of Mr. HAMILTON, of DALZELL-HOUSE. This orcharding is a real *business*; it is conducted in a very excellent manner; a cultivation of the land generally takes place amongst the trees; the trees are kept in a very nice state; I saw scarcely any canker; no cotton-blight;[11] and in very few orchards did I see any moss, though I did see it in some.

Amongst other pleasing things belonging to these orchards, Mr. STEWART (the proprietor of some very fine orchards) has some American trees, sent to him by me, which are just beginning to bear, and he gave me a very fine apple which had been gathered from one of them this year. "Cast your bread upon the waters," says the precept, "and have patience to wait to see it return." I sent from England to Long Island, to Mr. JESSE PLATT, to send me some *cuttings* of apple-trees; they came to me at KENSINGTON; Mr. M'GAVIN, at HAMILTON (four hundred miles from KENSINGTON), got some of the cuttings after they came from Long Island; he put some of them upon some of the branches of his trees: and he showed me a bough which had proceeded from this cutting, from which he gathered forty pounds of weight of fine apples last year! What a deal have I done in my life-time to produce real and solid good for my country! and how different has been the tendency of my pursuits to that of the pursuits of the noisy, canting, jawing, popularity-hunting, newspaper-puffing fellow, BROUGHAM, who, or whose partisans, cannot point to one single *good thing* that he has ever accomplished![12]

Mr. HAMILTON, of DALZELL, took me and Mr. BELL to LANARK, as I have before mentioned, on the 1st of November; on our return to GLASGOW on the 2nd, he was kind enough, in pursuance of previous invitation, to take us to Sir HENRY STEUART's, at ALLANTON. I had met Sir HENRY STEUART at DALZELL-HOUSE, on the previous Sunday; and he had done me the honour to present me (in my character of brother tree-planter) with a copy of his book on the removing and planting of trees. This book is not to be read in a hurry, being full of principles and science; but before I got to ALLANTON, in spite of the *dinnering* and other hubbubing, I contrived to find time to read some part of the book. Sir HENRY STEUART lives in a very ancient family mansion, in the midst of his own moderately-sized estate. He found the spot around the house destitute of trees, and, therefore, destitute of beauty; and he has actually, by his own mechanical operations, made it as pretty a landscape as can possibly be imagined. A run of water, or rather a soak, that came down as a sort of swamp, he has turned into a very beautiful lake; and, as to the trees, he has brought them, *of all sizes*, from the size of your leg to the size of your body, and a great deal bigger, and placed them about upon the ground just where he pleased. Landscape has been his study, and anything in greater perfection than this, as far at any rate as relates to trees, it is impossible to conceive. The trees are not only of the proper sorts, but in their proper places; not only present the greatest possible variety that nature has given them, as to kind, height, and form; but *every tree is in a state of vigorous growth,* having an appearance of having grown from a seed upon the spot; shoots at the tops of them two or three feet long; and not leaving the smallest room to suppose that they had ever been removed at all. How many country mansions are there in England that stand in need of the hand of Sir HENRY STEUART! He showed me trees as big round as my body,[13] which he had caused to be taken up and carried a mile, or thereabouts, and to be planted where I saw them, at an expense of about fifteen shillings apiece. To know how he has done all this, you must read his book, it being impossible for me to give anything like an adequate description of the operation.

From Sir HENRY STEUART's, which lies a few miles distant from the CLYDE, we came back to DALZELL-HOUSE, on our way to

GLASGOW, passing through the estate of Sir JAMES STEWART, at COURTNESS; and here I saw some of the prettiest *hedges* that I had ever seen in my life. They are composed of a mixture of beech and whitehorn, with a great predominance of the former. They are about seven feet high from the ground to the top; the base about seven feet wide, and nicely clipped on both sides up to a ridge. The fields, in one part that we went through, were fine pasture: on the side there was a dairy of beautiful AYRSHIRE cows, and over the other hedge a little drove of West Highland cattle, feeding into fat beef. These hedges are very common all over Lanarkshire. Sometimes they are clipped into the shape of a *wall*, lower or higher according to the fancy of the owner, and always in good taste. On our way we were shown the seat of Sir ALEXANDER COCHRANE, and then, passing through the grounds, and close by the house of Lord BELHAVEN, we came to Mr. HAMILTON's at DALZELL, which is, after all the endless variety of pretty country seats on the CLYDE and on the CAULDER, the AVEN, and on all the GLENS which are tributary to these larger waters, the place at which, if I were to be compelled to reside in Scotland, I would choose to reside. In point of beauty, Mr. DOUGLAS's at MAULDSLIE, does, perhaps, exceed all the rest. A Mr. LOCKHART has a most beautiful place, fine woods, trees of great height and girth, where I was shown a Spanish chestnut-tree, twenty-four feet round; another Mr. LOCKHART has a beautiful seat on the CLYDE. In short, it is all such a mass of pretty places, and all with stone-built mansions, of the most solid structure, and in the best possible taste; that one is at a loss to say which one would like best; but, if I were compelled to choose, I would choose Mr. HAMILTON's of DALZELL. The most amiable manners of the parties within might have some sway with me in this decision, but the place itself was just to my taste; the house a very ancient structure, with plenty of room; from the windows of one end you look into a deep *glen*, where the waters come tumbling over rocks, and wash, in the time of high water, the walls of the ancient castle; the trees in this glen, ashes, beeches, oaks, elms, as tall, and nearly as straight as the tulip-trees in the glens in America, with all sorts of native underwood not forgetting an abundance of yews; the bridges across this glen; the walks winding about on each side of it; the orchards and the fruit trees mixed amongst forest trees, seen from the windows of the other parts of the house; the fine low lands and meadows (at the end of the pleasant walks through the orchards), down upon the banks of the

CLYDE, where it runs as smooth as if there were not a rock in the country, and where it is lined with beeches and sycamores and áshes, as large and as lofty as I ever saw: then, on the other side of the house, at the end of half-a-mile of gentle up-hill, through some very fine plantations of larches and of oaks, a farm-house and farm-yard, and pastures with dairy cows feeding and Highland cattle fatting: all these put together made me think this the place, of all the places in Scotland, that I should like to live at. There is nothing to be called a view from the house itself; but, on a part of the estate, where this bank of the CLYDE becomes steep and lofty again, there is a view of the CLYDE and of the grand palace and park of the Duke of HAMILTON; there is a view here, to behold which all strangers are taken to see. I did not think it equal to the view at LANARK; but it is very fine, very grand, and is the boast of the CLYDE.

Well, then, should I not like to *live here* better than amidst the really barren heaths and sands of Surrey, with only here and there a little dip of ground on which it is worth while to bestow labour? Oh! that is quite another matter. To *live* here is a proposition not to be decided on without consulting the heart as well as the eye. That philosophy was quite sound which said that "our last best country ever is at home;" and mind, where you do not find this feeling implanted in the breast, nature has not done her work well. Where there is not this feeling, there will be but a very feeble love of country; for we go on, first, from our own family and neighbours and parish to our own counties; then to our own country at large; and, observe as long as you will, you will find that he who is not more attached to the spot on which he was born than to any other spot of his country, will very easily bring himself to like any other country as well as his own. Hence it is that we always find the patriot-passion most strongly implanted in the hearts of the common people; and if it had not been more strongly implanted in those hearts than in those of the renegado pretended *higher* orders and *feelosofers*, who have gone from Scotland to England, Scotland would, at this day, have been wholly abandoned, instead of presenting, as it does, such a mass of public-spirited men, resolved upon a restoration of their rights.

It is curious, that, the substratum of the land here is just that sort of *red stone* which is everywhere the substratum in Devonshire, Somersetshire, Herefordshire, Worcestershire, and Gloucestershire, which are the counties of orchards. Sometimes here is white stone beneath; but, generally speaking, it is *red*; and the top soil is very frequently red also; and here is iron stone frequently found near the top of the ground; and coals are everywhere at no great distance, precisely as it is in the vicinity of Ross in Herefordshire; and the rocky glens here, precisely resemble those in the forest of DEAN, and on the banks of the WYE. I believe that this vein of red ground and stone runs the whole length of the island, for I have traced it from Devonshire to COVENTRY with my own eyes. I find it here upon the CLYDE; and, I dare say, it winds about till it comes out somewhere or other at the north end of the island. Wherever apples will grow well, HOPS will generally grow. In a *Register*, written last summer, I observed, that, if it were not for this grinding and taxing system of Government, people would grow their own hops all over the kingdom; that God had given them to us, to grow spontaneously; and that I had seen them growing in the hedges from the Isle of Wight to Lancashire, and that I made no doubt, that they were to be found in the Highlands of Scotland.[14] During the time that I was on the CLYDE, Mr. HAMILTON took me to see the *"wild cattle"* of the Duke of HAMILTON, which are kept, *like deer*, on a part of the estate on the banks of the AVEN;[15] which cattle, when of full size, are about the size of Devonshire cattle; they are all over white, except the ears and the nose, which are black; they are wild, just like deer, fed in the winter as deer are fed, caught as deer are caught, or shot as deer are shot. They form a sort of heir-loom in the family; and are kept, as if they were such, in the exclusive possession of the family. In our way to see these cattle, we stopped at the house of Lady RUTHVEN, which is situated within thirty or forty yards of the top of one of the banks of the AVEN. These banks are two or three hundred feet high, set with trees as thickly as possible, beeches, birches, and ashes, all growing beautifully up out of the interstices of the rocks, upon a bed of which the river comes rattling over below. On the side of the bank on which Lady RUTHVEN's house stands, a beautiful garden has been made by moulding the bank into the form of steps resembling stairs. A little distance above this garden the river takes a wind; a little distance below the garden you see the river passing under two bridges at some distance from each other, over which two roads pass, both of which, I believe, are turnpikes: so that this is one of the prettiest spots that man ever set his eyes on; and as if Providence had designed that nothing should be wanting, there were, within the house, some very polite and obliging ladies, one of whom, was, I was told, Miss Stirling a cousin of Mrs. HALSEY, or HOLSEY, of HENLEY-PARK, in the county of Surrey; and a portrait of which Miss Stirling I, if I were forty years younger, should certainly attempt to draw, however impossible it might be for me to come up to the original.[16] In this garden we found *some hops growing,* a branch of which I gathered and dried, and have now very carefully packed up to take to London, along with a variety of apples, which I intend to exhibit at *Bolt-court,* to the astonishment, I dare say, of nine tenths even of the Scotchmen that are living in London, of whom I never yet met one who seemed to know anything at all about his own country, and who did not seem to assent to the sententious and dogmatic lies of old Dr. JOHNSON, who, from the remissness of Scotchmen themselves, has been suffered to misrepresent their country, and to propagate mischievous error concerning it, from one end to the other of the world. Mr. HAMILTON told me, with regard to *hops,* that their growing upon the banks of the CLYDE, was by no means a new discovery; for that his father had a whole piece of ground *in hops* sixty years ago; that this piece of ground is now an orchard, and is called the *"hop-garden orchard."*

There are, besides coal-mines, innumerable iron works on the banks of the CLYDE as you approach towards GLASGOW. We went over the bridge, called BOTHWELL-BRIDGE, where the famous battle was fought in 1679, between the *Covenanters* and the army of Charles 1.,[17] under the Duke of Monmouth, or, rather, between the Covenanters and the English troops and the Royal *Scotch troops united.* And this has always been the way with Scotland and Ireland: always kept down by domestic defection; always like the distant Roman provinces. But it was Cromwell who was the great *destroyer.* He must have been in reality, what BURKE calls an "architect of ruin;" for, everywhere in Scotland as well as England, when they show you a disfigured and partly-demolished edifice, they ascribe the mischief to CROMWELL. Like the devil, old NOLL, as the cavaliers used to call him, seems to have been *everywhere* and in all places at one and the same time. The Scotch of the present day, as well as the Irish, seem to think that he was the devil for the time being. But, the Scotch sent forth a worse devil than CROMWELL, of whom they do not seem to entertain a just degree of abhorrence; namely, that surprisingly wicked old vagabond, BURNETT, who was born here, near one of these beautiful banks of the CLYDE, and after whom they name one of their plums, of which they grow a great abundance. This crafty fellow did more mischief by his quiet scheme, than CROMWELL ever did by his bayonets, bullets and cannon.

While I acknowledge, with great gratitude, the politeness, the kindness, the unaffected hospitality, with which I was everywhere received, by persons of fortune and fashion in Scotland, and particularly on the banks of the CLYDE, I am not stupid beast enough to ascribe their conduct towards me to any merit that they thought me to possess. It is possible, indeed, that, in some of the instances my manners (so different from what the atrocious villains of the press had taught them to expect) might have excited feelings of rather a friendly character;[18] but I ascribe their treatment of me to their natural good disposition and their polite education; and their manifest desire to see me, I ascribe solely to that *curiosity* which must naturally have been excited in their minds, to see a man whose name the accursed newspapers, hired and bribed by the accursed corruption, had made to reach the ears of every human being in the kingdom; and in which man, this band of incomparable villains, hired and paid by this incomparable feeder of villainy, had made all the world believe that there was something more than mortal.[19] While, therefore, I shall always be proud of the attention shown me by gentlemen so respectable, and by ladies so amiable, I would have it understood that I am not coxcomb enough to ascribe it to any other than the true cause.

Before I quit the CLYDE, to which the readers will say I cling, as Adam is said to have clung to Paradise, there is something which I have to mention, of which I am still more proud than of the things I have just treated of; something that rouses the politician again, drives away the waterfalls and the trees and the orchards, and which would, were it not a shame, make me forget even the Scotch ladies amongst the rest! I mentioned before that Mr. HAMILTON took me and Mr. BELL to LANARK, on the 1. of November, and that I was to lecture in the town of LANARK in the evening of that day; to do which I had received an invitation from my readers in that town, to which invitation I had given my answer that I would do it. As we were going to LANARK from Mr. DOUGLAS's at MAULDSLIE CASTLE, we saw, out in the middle of a field, near a cottage, a blue flag flying at the top of a long pole. When we got near enough to see what was upon it, we saw that there was a GRIDIRON[20] *painted in colours of gold*, with these words over it: "COBBETT TRIUMPHANT;" and on the other side, "PERSEVERANCE, PUBLIC VIRTUE, JUSTICE TO THE WORKING PEOPLE." And, which added prodigiously to the interest of the thing, this flag had been made for the purpose of a reform jubilee, at LANARK, and had been carried at that jubilee long before my coming to Scotland! Now, I will not bid the grovelling, the envious, the mercenary, the bribed, the base, the bloody villains of the London press to look at this; but I will bid *Lord Grey* to look at it, as something very well worthy of his attention. I will beg him not to try to make up a laugh, as he did, in the Court of King's Bench, while four thousand people were muttering out "shame, shame," at my description of the shearing of the heads of two girls in Sussex by one of STURGES BOURNE's hired overseers; I will beg him not to try to muster up a laugh at the history and description of this flag; but seriously to consider, what will finally be the consequences, if he and the *sergeant* WILDE *Ministry* persevere in obstinately pursuing the conduct of their predecessors, in turning a deaf ear to every thing proposed by me! Let him seriously consider this; let him consider whether the question between Whig and Tory, be not now a mere trifle, compared with the question, *whether my principles shall prevail, or whether they shall not*: whether, in other words, the MANCHESTER *propositions are to be adopted or rejected.* But, to do justice to these good people of the town of LANARK, I must insert the ADDRESS, which was read to me by the chairman of the committee before I began my lecture, in the presence of the audience assembled in the church, and which address was as follows: delivered to me in writing after it had been read:

"TO WILLIAM COBBETT, ESQ.

Sir, — We, your readers in Lanark and its vicinity, take the liberty to express ourselves highly gratified by your visit to this place. We have long considered you the most enlightened political writer of the present day; the most honest exposer of the heartless insolence and specious cheatery of public men. You have associated yourself with our best feelings as haters of corruption, with our highest aspirations as lovers of our country, and above all with our most anxious hopes connected with the labouring people. With esteem never interrupted, we have accompanied you through many years of intellectual labour and excitement, and with pleasure indescribable we are now beginning to taste the result; a result rendered greatly more important to your fame, because of the unjust and disgraceful persecution to which you have been subjected, and the immeasurable magnitude of the THING's power. Sir, we are deeply grateful to you for your exertions in the good cause; we are proud that there is at least one fearless, one independent man in England. We rejoice that your character and merits are now becoming rightly understood and duly appreciated; that your triumph over baseness and misrepresentation will speedily be complete, and that consequently your power of putting to rights the affairs of this great country will be increased a thousand fold.

(Signed in their behalf,)

JAMES HARPER."

BROUGHAM and DICK POTTER, and such-like people will exclaim, "Poh! what's that? Those poor souls at LANARK are quite in a state of seclusion from the world." Very true, BROUGHAM and DICK; but how the devil did they come to hear of me in this their state of seclusion? These two, one a sort of simply spiteful simpleton; and the other a sort of giddy-headed gormandiser of praise, that feeds on newspaper-puffs, as a magpie is said to delight most in sucking rotten eggs; this couple will come to a sort of puzzle upon reading these strange proceedings in Scotland. In England, indeed, amongst the stack-burners and the thrashing-machine breakers, they will think it natural enough that I should have partisans; but in the country of "*antalluct*," they will think the devil is got into the people." I will send them down some of my friend the mountebank's pamphlets," says DICK. "No," says BROUGHAM, "send them down some of my *Penny Magazines*."[21]

Let these fools alone, my LORD GREY, and think a little for your-self about it. Look well at this little ADDRESS from these people at LANARK; and ask yourself what, except their own sincere conviction, could have made them act and speak thus? Ask yourself what power I could have, to have influenced them to do this? What means I, whom they had never seen before, and were, in all probability, never to see again, could have had to induce them to do this deliberate act, which cost them some pains, and which, in fact, cost them some little money? No! You will not reason: you have present power in your hands. You will curl up your lip and draw up your nostrils, just as they did when NOAH was actually stepping into the ark.

Before I quit LANARKSHIRE, it is right for me to observe, which I do with great pleasure, that the working people are treated much better here than in the LOTHIANS; that the farms are smaller, the occupations numerous, the proprietorships not a few; that the farm-servants are frequently in the farm-houses, and that the *"boothie" system* is by no means so prevalent. Though, mind, small farms have been moulded into large ones within the last thirty or forty years; cottages have been swept away in very great numbers; the people have been huddled together in great masses; and that every one of these masses has to exist under the continual scowl of a barrack.[22] As to *agriculture*, LANARKSHIRE is a very fine county altogether; it has a due mixture of orchards, woods, corn-fields and pastures. Its cows are generally of the AYRSHIRE breed; its neat-cattle, the West Highlanders, and Highland sheep. Near to GLASGOW and PAISLEY, butter and milk are the chief products of the soil. The county is famous for its *breed of horses*; and they are, indeed, very fine horses, whether for riding or for draught. These horses, as is the custom all over Scotland, go single in a cart, and draw a ton weight very well, on a good road. They are not *heavy*, and yet they are stout. They are very much prized all over Scotland; and many of them are taken into England. Now, bidding adieu to LANARKSHIRE for the present, and returning to my departure from GLASGOW, on my way home, which departure I mentioned in my last *Register*, I must here publicly bid farewell to Mr. HAMILTON, of DALZELL, which I do with every sentiment of gratitude for his great kindness to me, and with the most fervent prayers, that, at an age not less than that of his venerable father,[23] he may terminate a life, the happiness of which may meet with as little interruption as any that ever was experienced by any human being.

On Saturday, the 3. of November, I set off from GLASGOW towards England, in a post-chaise, accompanied by my friends, Mr. BELL and Mr. TURNER, who took their leave of me at an inn on the road, about fourteen miles from GLASGOW, where I changed horses. In quitting GLASGOW we almost immediately entered Renfrewshire, and passed across it into Ayrshire. A chain of hills intervenes and divides the two counties. For several miles from GLASGOW the land is exceedingly good, naturally, besides the goodness which it derives from its nearness to so populous a city,[24] and from its nearness also to PAISLEY, which we leave a little to our right. After this flat and fine land, we go over about seven or eight miles of high country, not under the plough, except here and there; having some bits of heath and furze here and there and some moory parts very full of rushes. This is not, however, by any means a *barren* country. There is grass to the tops of the hills; and these hills, even to their tops, have numerous *herds of cows* feeding upon them. Sometimes so few as ten in a herd; but, very frequently as many as *fifty*. KINGSWELL, the little place where we changed horses, is in AYRSHIRE, so famous for its beautiful breed of milking cows, and for the making of that cheese which is so highly prized all over Scotland, and all along the English border, under the name of DUNLOP-CHEESE, DUNLOP being a little village, about six miles to the right of KINGSWELL, and being in the middle of these extensive hills, which are *pastures* resembling our *downs* in the west of England; but on a bed of rock instead of a bed of *chalk*; none of which latter, by-the-by, is to be seen, I believe, to the north of DUNSTABLE, in Bedfordshire. To see herds of cows instead of flocks of sheep, was a novel sight to me; but this was quite enough to convince me, even before I had made any inquiry at all relative to the *dairies* or the *cheese*, that this is not barren land. From KINGSWELL we soon began to descend into a country of fields and woods; and, coming down a hill towards a river, by the side of a park set with stately trees, we saw a flag flying from a staff on the top of a fine castle, to signify, as I suppose, (after the manner of Duke SMITHSON), that the castle contained at that moment the precious deposit, consisting of its Lord. We were yet a mile and a half from NEW MILNS, that public-spirited manufacturing village, a deputation from which had come on foot, twenty-four miles to GLASGOW, to present that address to me which was published in the *Register*, dated from GLASGOW, and published in London on the 27. of October. The chaise was yet a mile and a half from the village, when the *boys* (always the advanced guard) began to meet us in groups. As we advanced, the groups grew more and more numerous, and the parties composing them continued to increase in size, the *sexes* becoming duplicate at the same time. Arrived at the very first house in the village, the committee, accompanied with three flags, and a tremendously large *gridiron* on a pole, made for the purpose, met us with a request that I would be so kind as to get out of the chaise, and walk in the procession to the inn; a request with which I instantly complied, and on we went preceded by a drum and fife. It was a general holiday in the village, every soul of which seemed to be present, from the oldest person down to the baby in arms. Arrived at the inn, I found the magistrates of the BURGH, who are called bailiffs, assembled, with a great number of burgesses, to present me with the freedom of the BURGH, which they did in due form.

delivering to me the necessary document, and I going through the usual solemnities; the chief bailiff stating, as the grounds of this mark of their respect and attachment, that the people of the BURGH owed their political knowledge to me; that the nation owed the reform, in their opinion, to me more than to any other man, and more than to all other men put together; and that they had more reliance upon my future exertions than upon those of all other men, to make the reform productive of good to the people. Upon receiving the document into my hand, I said, "Gentlemen, I am a freeman of a city, to obtain my freedom of which (which I was compelled to do to be enabled to carry on my business in it) I had to pay fifty pounds, and I would sell it now for a pot of beer, if it were not necessary to protect me against the persecution of those who carry on the government of that city, the rulers of which are amongst the lowest of mankind, who tax me at their pleasure, who now make me pay a new-church-rate and an old-church-rate, and give me no church to go to; who tax me for the purpose of depriving my fellow-citizens of PORTSOKEN WARD of their rights; who expend the resources of the city in guttlings and guzzlings enormous, and who daily add to these oppressions the unspeakable insult of taking my money, for the purpose of purchasing gold boxes and jewel-set swords, to be given to men whom I class amongst the ruiners of my country. For these sufferings (to which I hope the reform of the Parliament will put an end) this mark of approbation from you is a great compensation, especially as I deem it a pledge on your part that you will do your utmost in supporting me, and men like me, in our efforts to obtain redress for those manifold and sore grievances, of which those that I have just mentioned form a part."

I now found that the castle which I had seen with the flag flying upon it, was LOUDON-CASTLE, the seat of the Marquis of HASTINGS: and I further found, that this Marquis had *expressed his desire that I might not be permitted to lecture in the great church of the place,* which led me to observe on divers things connected with this Marquis's relationship to the public affairs, with regard to which I might have been silent, if I had not heard this. How *wise* these people are! What pains they take to get themselves beloved, and to have their unsightly parts kept from people's eyes! Will they *never see?* Puppies and kittens see at nine days old, though born blind. There was some excuse for impudent AYLESFORD,[25] when he and his brutal tenant signed and published a protest against the innkeeper at

MERIDEN, *because he suffered me to be in his inn,* though I was very ill from a horrible cold, and required rest for a day or two; there was, on the score of prudence, some excuse for impudent AYLESFORD, the THING being then unshaken; but now, when there is bank reform and church reform, as well as parliamentary reform, all in agitation! Well, let them go on; let them be blind to the last; let them do nothing that shall make one feel regret, whatever may take place.

It was my intention, agreeably to the notification that had been given, just to harangue the people of this excellent village, in the middle of the day; and then to push on, and lecture at KILMARNOCK (seven miles distant) in the evening. I found, however, that the disappointment would be so great, that I could not depart; and, therefore, I resolved to stay here until Monday, and to go to KILMARNOCK (to which I have just sent a messenger) to-morrow evening; and to stay here and write the *Register* to-day, which, I knew, would be extremely gratifying to these kind and good and sensible people.

Wednesday, Carlisle, 7. Nov. 1832.

In the above part of this letter, which was written at NEW MILNS, I had not time to say anything upon a subject which the greater part of my readers will deem to be of very great interest; namely, the Ayrshire *cows* and *dairies*; and I will, now, speak of that matter, when I get to that part of my journey where I quit this very nice and very valuable county of AYR. From NEW MILNS, after lecturing there to a church crammed full of people on the Saturday night; after writing there on Sunday (which these people excused on the score of *absolute necessity*); after breakfasting with the clergyman of the burgher church, on the Monday morning; after looking at some beautiful cows, and spending as much time as I could in talking with the clever men of the village; after enjoying the surprise of seeing a man who was born upon the *same spot with myself,* and who had strayed from the sand hills of Surrey, and had been here for fifty years, till he had lost every semblance of the Surrey dialect; after passing forty-eight hours, as delightfully as I ever did any forty-eight hours in my life, I set off in a post-chaise, which had come from KILMARNOCK to fetch me. The country to KILMARNOCK, a very fine farming country, and on every side dairies of cows. On our approach to KILMARNOCK, which is a manufacturing town, containing from twenty to thirty thousand souls, and a very beautiful, solid, and opulent place, we were met with three banners flying, and, soon afterwards, a band of music; and in this order were conducted to the *Turf-inn*. I had come on to DUMFRIES (sixty miles) the next day, and to lecture there at night; so that I had not a moment to look round this fine town of KILMARNOCK. After lecturing in a church, I got to bed as soon as I could; breakfasted the next morning in the house of Mr. HUGH CRAIG, who had met me at my approach to the town, and took me in his open chaise, behind the flags and the music; after thus breakfasting, and being delighted with the hospitality; with the manners, and with everything belonging to Mrs. CRAIG, the heartiness of whose welcome was a thing to admire, but not to be described; after this, very sorry not to be able to stay another day, in this nice town, in which I had been treated with such signal distinction, in which a band of music had preceded me, to and from the place of lecturing, and, supposing me, of course, to be fond of music,[1] had remained until a late hour to play tunes at the inn; and in which the people seemed to vie with each other in their eagerness to get at me to shake me by the hand; extremely sorry not to be able to stay another day in this pretty town, and with a firm promise made to myself to come and make due acknowledgement for its kindness, when I come to Scotland again; after all this, ruminating what HUME and sweetly simpering DICK POTTER might, in their wise heads, think of the matter, we set off in a post-chaise to MAUCHLINE, fourteen miles on the DUMFRIES road, there to see the native place of ROBERT BURNS, and to see also, the most ingenious, the most interesting *manufacture of snuff-boxes,* made of the wood of the sycamore, and painted and finished, in all the various shapes and colours that the manufacture exhibits to the eye. Mr. SMITH, the proprietor, most obligingly conducted us through the several departments. Some of the work-people were hewing out the wood, which, from that rough state, we saw passing on from hand to hand, till it became an elegant piece of furniture for the pocket. Some were making drawings upon paper; others making the paintings upon the boxes; and all was so clean and so neat, and every person appearing to be so well off.

At this little town, we waited the arrival of the stagecoach, which took us on at a great rate from MAUCHLINE to CUMNOCK, soon after which we got to DUMFRIES-SHIRE. But, now, let me stop and do justice to this county of AYR, which will always be a great favourite with me. There are some high and mountainous lands in it; but I saw not one acre of real *barren* land. Some moors; but these not large, and yielding peat so good as to be better than inferior coal. On the banks of its rivers there are excellent orchards; indeed, there are orchards, here and there, all along the road. The country is well set with farm-houses; and hardly any of the farms are very large; but the great glory of this country is its cows and its dairies. These cows are so renowned that you find them, here and there, all over the South of Scotland; and, I am told, that they are scattered about Cumberland and Westmoreland too. In my *Register*, dated from PAISLEY, I think I spoke of having seen some of these cows, when I went to take a look at the SHAWS-WATER, at GREENOCK. But, Mr. THOM (not "THORN," as my printers have chosen to print it), who went with me to see the SHAWS water-works, and who appeared to have great understanding in such matters, told me, that those which I so admired were "ugly mongrels;" and this I have really found to be the case; for, when I came to see them at NEW MILNS, I was almost ashamed to remember that I had admired the others. It is a most perfectly shaped DURHAM-cow on a reduced scale; and much more abundant in milk in propor-tion to its size, and perfectly hardy at the same time. The colour is very handsome; being, generally, a deep-red ground, with white dis-tributed in somewhat the form of a branch of a tree. The white colour is prevalent sometimes, and sometimes the animal is pretty nearly quite red all over. Many of these cows will give twenty of our quarts of milk at a time; and the milk is much richer than that of any other cows, except the ALDERNEY; and they are not known in the North. It is the habit here to *let*, or *set*, the cows. That is to say, a farmer gives up the produce of so many cows to another person, who is, of course, a sort of labourer. The farmer finds the house, the sheds, the food of the cows, and every thing necessary for the carrying on of the business; and the renter agrees to give him so many stones of cheese, to be delivered at certain stated periods, and to be of a certain quality, for the use of every cow. A farmer who thus sets his cows, told me, that, this year, he had set his cows for *sixteen stones* of cheese each for the year; but, observe, that, in spite of JOSEPH HUME and his "feelosofers," who have caused the people to expend more than a million of money by their vile and silly Scotch job, to make uniform "*Imperial*" weights and measures;[2] in spite of this foolish and something worse "*Imperial*" weight-and-measure job, which was to make us all regulate our lives and conversations by a standard, founded on the "beating of a pendulum in a heat of sixty degrees, according to FAHRENHEIT's thermometer;" in spite of all this most boggling manner of extracting money from our pockets, to put it into those of *"feelosofical"* jobbers; in spite of all this, the *stone in Ayrshire* consists of sixteen pounds; and each pound consists of twenty-two ounces and a half, in spite of JOSEPH and his jobbing *"feelosofy,"* which is a matter for the serious consideration of JOSEPH's enviable co-operator, DICK POTTER; and may become an interesting theme, or exercise, for the pupils in their reformed Mechanic's Institute.[3] This being the case, the AYRSHIRE sixteen stones amount to three hundred and sixty London pounds of cheese; and this the farmer now sells at nine shillings and fourpence a stone, hard money; for the one-pound *"nots"* do not enhance his price one single farthing, and cannot, as long as the Old Lady[4] is compelled to pay in gold. Thus, then, the farmer receives seven pounds nine and fourpence for each cow. If the cow do not yield so much, the renter is compelled to give the stipulated quantity and quality of cheese. Whatever she may yield more he has for his profit, besides having the whey for his pigs; and, observe, it is but a smallish cow, and is not fed upon rich pasture, generally; and the food, as allowed by the farmer, is very little besides oat-straw, all the winter long. If they have anything better, it must arise from the care and exertion of the renter; he must cut the straw into chaff, and boil it, or do something or another to make it better than raw straw. Yet he makes a living out of this, and generally saves money.

I was so delighted with all these cows, that I was resolved that my country should not be wholly without them; and, therefore, a very kind friend at NEW-MILNS is to send me up a bull and ten cows, three of them three years old last spring, seven of them two years old last spring; all of them to calve by the month of May next, and the bull two years old last spring. If they come safe and sound, as I dare say they will, they will be worth a Kentish, a Sussex, or a Surrey farmer's going fifty miles to see, in the month of June or July next. I have directed them to be caused to rest a week in the neighbourhood of MANCHESTER, and if BARON TOM POTTER have a mind to make it up with me, he will give them a run for a week in the park at PIPKIN-PLACE. The drover has a written direction to take them to some field "near PIPKIN-PLACE, in the parish of PENDLETON;" and I recommend it to the electors of WIGAN,[5] when they shall hear of the arrival of this seeding dairy, to go and candidly and frankly make an estimate of the *"antalluct"* of this young Scotch bull; to question him with regard to the principles now proper to be acted upon by a member of Parliament; to ask him for an explanation of his ideas relative to the measures necessary for the relief and deliverance of a nation; to ask him what he thinks of the *Whig-war*, of the "*church-reform*," of the "expansion of the currency;" and ask him to show how it is possible for the working man to be benefited by "the improved system of banking," now carried on at the sign of the Three Golden Balls. Then I advise them to put exactly the same questions to DICK POTTER. If the bull talk less nonsense than DICK; discover the possession of less brains than DICK discover; then the electors of WIGAN, if no third candidate offer, will, in duty to their country, their neighbours, and their children, be bound, by every thing sacred amongst men, to reject DICK, and to elect the bull; and upon my soul (and I should not be afraid to take my oath to the fact) I believe that the bull would talk the less nonsense of the two. Oh! I would go a thousand miles to see the looks of these Scotchies, especially at NEW MILNS, while DICK, or TOM, or SHUTTLEWORTH, or BAXTER, was making a speech to them. To see their looks at them, and to hear them exclaim, "*Ah, gude Gode!*" Ah, DICK! I would find other guess-men than JOSEPH HUME; if you were to come to Scotland yourself, instead of sending your dirty pamphlets to GLASGOW; and let JOSEPH HUME take care, or he will get properly chastised for posting down to MANCHESTER to keep you in countenance. I can tell him, that his countrymen[6] look at him with a very suspicious eye; and that this last movement of his, intended to prop you up in your slanders against me, will only tend to swell into certainty that which before was only suspicion.

I leave AYRSHIRE behind me, with a great deal of satisfaction at having seen it. It is a nice country; not rich, but good and solid; and it is well studded over with comfortable farm-houses, and the accursed "boothies" do not offend the sight. It wants, particularly in the manufacturing towns, what all Scotland wants; namely the English poor-laws, and all the laws of England; but this is a large subject, and of vital importance. There are many matters of interesting moment to be discussed and settled; but here I, at any rate, mean to make my stand; I mean, let what else will be done or left undone, to fight to the last inch with all the legal means in my power, to cause STURGES BOURNE's Bills to be repealed, and to establish, beyond all question, the RIGHT of every man and woman, to be upon, to remain upon, and to have a sufficient living out of the land of the country in which they were born. I mean, and I am

resolved to make this the first point of all, if I be intrusted with the
representation of any part of the people; and I would pledge my life,
that BROUGHAM and his *Poor-law* Commission will shrink into
nothingness at the approach of the discussion of the subject.

We reached DUMFRIES about five o'clock in the evening of
Tuesday, the 6. and I lectured at the Theatre at half after seven;
and, considering that the people have been frightened half to death
about the cholera morbus (of which disease great numbers have
actually died here), the attendance was wonderfully good. Poor
BURNS, the poet, died in this town, an *exciseman*, after having
written so well against that species of taxation, and that particular
sort of office. Oh! *Sobriety!* how manifold are thy blessings! how great
thy enjoyments! how complete the protection which thou givest to
talent; and how feeble is talent unless it has that protection![7] I was
very happy to hear that his widow, who still lives in this town, is
amply provided for; and my intention was to go to her, to tell her my
name, and to say, that I came to offer her my respects as a mark of
my admiration of the talents of her late husband, one single page of
whose writings is worth more than a whole cart load that has been
written by WALTER SCOTT.

I was prevented from putting this intention into execution by the
necessity under which I was of being at ANNAN, to breakfast at ten
o'clock, and *lecture there at twelve*; after which I had seventeen miles
to come to *this city*, in which I am *to lecture to-night at half-past
seven!* One would need lead a sober life to be engaged in *"carryings-
on"* like this! But I must make haste along now, for the fellows "up at
Lunnon" have got into a war to keep *our pensioner* upon his throne;
and most likely, contrary to the wishes of their *"allies"* and to the
wishes of *our pensioner's* subjects also.[8] Faith! I must get along; but it
is now six o'clock and I must go and shave and dress for the play.

Carlisle, 8. Nov., 1832.

I had not time, last night, to speak of the country from AYRSHIRE,
across DUMFRIESSHIRE, to DUMFRIES, from DUMFRIES to ANNAN,
and from ANNAN to the river that divides Scotland from England. I
have not time to do it now: I must, therefore, leave what I have
further to say of Scotland, until the next letter, which will, *possibly,*
be written in *Bolt-court.* It is hard to say, much less to swear, what
one will do in such case; but my project is, to go hence on Saturday

morning, lecture at PENRITH on Saturday night, go on Sunday and sleep amongst the "pig-styes of APPLEBY" (which are to send no more members to Parliament), taking a look at BROUGHAM-HALL in my way, having painted its owner in his true colours at PENRITH; on Monday to lecture at DARLINGTON, on Tuesday at STOCKTON, on Wednesday at BRADFORD, passing through sensible LEEDS, and leaving it to choose between the nominee of the Duke of NEWCASTLE[9] and the nominee of BROUGHAM, the placeman-son of ZACHARY MACAULAY,[10] ZACHARY himself being in our pay. Leaving *sensible* LEEDS to this its alternative, and quitting BRADFORD on Thursday morning; lecture, if they like, at ROCHDALE, on Thursday night; go to OLDHAM on Friday; to MANCHESTER on Saturday, the 17.; to BRUMMAGEM on the Sunday, the 18.; and *to London on Monday, the 19.* There to behold DENMAN on the bench, with a big wig hanging down his shoulders; *Sergeant* WILDE, "our right and entirely beloved THOMAS WILDE," a "right honourable privy-councillor," one of the body which Lord COKE calls "*honourable, noble, venerable,* and *reverend.*" There to behold CHARLEY PEARSON . . . I have not yet heard what; but surely, CHARLEY is not to be over-looked! Oh, how I sigh for the sight; how I do long to know what CHARLEY is to be! If there had been a *setting-in,* as the women call it, of peers in the month of May last, CHARLEY, people about *Fleet-street* said, was to have been one of the batch; and, at any rate, the thing will never be complete till CHARLEY be in it some way or another. Here I must break off, having, by these enchanting thoughts, been led along till I have almost written the eyes out of my head; and I must not do that quite; for I may possibly be charged with the duty of reading cart-loads of papers; for loan-maker BARING said, that the great towns would send "*pushing men, who would read every paper that was before the House.*"

WM. COBBETT

I must not omit to notice a letter which I received from BARRHEAD, to which I was obliged to return an answer, saying that I could not go, as I had fixed, immoveably, on the line of march which I had to pursue. The letter is of no consequence now; but I publish it as a mark of my respect for the gentlemen from whom it came; and I hereby assure them that, if I return to Scotland next year, which it is my present intention to do,[11] I will go and thank them in person for the honour which they have done me.

"Barrhead, 30. Oct., 1832.

Sir, — At a public meeting of the inhabitants of this village, held on Friday evening last, it was proposed by some of your admirers, and unanimously agreed to, that you should be invited to lecture here at your earliest convenience. A committee was then formed to correspond with you, and learn *at what time* and upon *what terms* you could come.

We think we may get the burgher church here for your lecture, which we can secure after hearing from you. The lecture would require to be in the evening, to suit the inhabitants, as they are nearly all connected with public works.

I am, sir, for the committee, your truly,

James Lambert."

Oldham, 16. November, 1832.

In the last letter I mentioned that I must postpone, until the present letter, my account of the county of DUMFRIES, across which we go from AYRSHIRE to get into Cumberland. Dumfriesshire is much about like Ayrshire in point of land and productions; it is hilly occasionally, and has some fine farms on the flats, some of which are large; but generally they are small; the cottages numerous, built of stone, and made white by whitewashing, which gives a very pretty appearance to the country, though there are, generally speaking, very few trees. We cross several very pretty rivers; the orchards are by no means bad, and the apple-trees very clean; the land is moory, and affords peat in several instances; a large part of the land is in pasture; dairy work and the fattening of hogs seem to be the principal uses of the land. The hogs are of the white lop-eared breed. Hams, bacon and butter, are the principal products of the county. The woods are very fine in some parts, especially from SANQUEHAR to THORNHILL, which consists, in great part, of the estate of the Duke of BUCCLEUCH. I suppose that Dr. JOHNSON did not travel this way, for here is a beautiful river, and immense woods on both sides of it for nine or ten miles at the least; this river, which is called the NITH, goes all the way to the town of DUMFRIES; and after dividing Dumfriesshire from Kirkcudbrightshire for a few miles, falls into the SOLWAY FIRTH. Leaving at a great distance to my left the lofty hills, celebrated by BURNS, now crowned with snow, while the valleys below are covered with grass and dairies of fine cows, I got on to the town of Dumfries.

From DUMFRIES to the town of ANNAN (sixteen miles), is a very fine farming country; here and there a peat-moor, with large stacks of peat; that being the fuel of the country, and it being exceedingly good fuel, a man telling me that it boiled a pot quicker than coals, and produced less ashes. Here the cattle are of the Galloway breed, and the dairies are very numerous. Fine large valleys of corn-fields; hanging woods on the sides of the hills like those of Surrey; sometimes hills consisting partly of furze, and partly of broom, with a good deal of grassland between them; the cottages very numerous, and the people, particularly the children, looking very well. At eight miles from DUMFRIES, the SOLWAY FIRTH, with the sun shining beautifully upon it, presents itself to our right. Here we go through a long scattering village, which it would drive BROUGHAM and MALTHUS half-mad to behold; for, here the *little Scotchies* seem absolutely to swarm. What is to be done to prevent these Scotch women from breeding? Nothing short of *"clearing the estates"* A LA SUTHERLAND; a mode of proceeding so much eulogised by the ignorant and brutal scoundrels of the *Edinburgh Review,* and by their London echo Dr. BLACK. At thirteen miles from DUMFRIES we come to an estate, where something in the *"clearing way"* appears to have been put in practice, some years ago, by the Marquis of QUEENSBERRY, who is, it seems, the principal lord of this beautiful country called ANNAN-DALE; and who, having seen some remarks published respecting his *"clearing"* works, published in the *Carlisle Journal,* prosecuted the editor, criminally, and got him *fined and imprisoned*! Well, then, the account of the *"clearing"* was libellous, I suppose; but, though libellous, it might be *true*; for the truth could not be given in evidence to justify the publication.[1] Now, I should like to have a report of that trial, and the account of that sentence, which would give me some account of the clearing work; and would enable me to get at *positive evidence* respecting the *"clearing"* work, of which the miscreant *Edinburgh Review* has been the eulogist. I am determined, if I be in Parliament, that this question of ABSOLUTE RIGHT *to exclusive proprietorship of land*, shall be brought to the test, and submitted to a solemn decision. It is to establish this absolute and exclusive right, that all the monsters who are endeavouring to destroy the POOR-LAW, are labouring; and, if we do not beat the monsters at this game; if we do not teach them to repent of the hour, or rather teach the greedy and insolent tyrants who employ them, to repent of the hour when they attempted to establish this ABSOLUTE RIGHT on which they proceed to clear the lands: if we do not teach them to repent of this; if we do not teach them that the doctrine which gives all men a *common right in the land*; if we do not teach them that this doctrine, though it implies a total destruction of civil society; if we do not teach them that this doctrine, horribly unjust as it is, is still *less unjust* than the doctrine which says that a man *has NO RIGHT to be upon, and to have a living out of, the land of his birth*; if we do not teach them this, and make them give way in time, events will teach it them with a vengence.

At about four miles from ANNAN, we leave the famous parish of GRETNA, about a mile to our left, a spot so dear, doubtless, to the *"feelosofer"* WAKEFIELD, who, with brass of extraordinary thickness, is now writing and publishing pamphlets, describing the innumerable hordes of villains said by him to be assembled in London, and insisting on vigorous measures to keep the *"lower orders"* in subjection. We have now fine land and fine farming, fine dairies and everything else fine, with here and there a piece of moor and peat land, all the way to the river that divides Cumberland from the county of DUMFRIES. At ANNAN we were very hospitably received, and met several gentlemen of the town, at breakfast, at the house of Mr. NELSON. At noon I lectured at the Assembly Room to a very respectable audience, and thus took my farewell of lecturing in Scotland. At the end of ten miles, or thereabouts, we pass over the river ESK, over a very fine bridge, into Cumberland, having about seven miles still to go to reach CARLISLE.

It is curious that, the moment we get into England, at this point, all becomes sterile and ugly, and continues on heathy and moory, for several miles so that one would think, that it was England and not Scotland, that is the beggarly country. The land, however, soon begins to be inclosed and to be better in quality.

Daventry (Northamptonshire), 21. Nov. 1832.

At OLDHAM I found that all was settled to my perfect satisfaction. After writing in the morning, making a speech out of doors at noon, and another in the evening, by candlelight, I set off in a post-coach for MANCHESTER; slept there that night; met the electors, and addressed them in the Riding-school the next evening, which was Saturday; came to BIRMINGHAM by the coach on the Sunday; lectured at BIRMINGHAM on the Monday evening; came by the coach to COVENTRY yesterday in the afternoon; lectured at COVENTRY last night; and, by the coach, came to DAVENTRY this morning; intending to get to London to-night. Thus I began this speeching and lecturing work at COVENTRY; and at COVENTRY I ended it. But I cannot even suspend, for a short time, the movements of my pen upon the subject, without expressing my satisfaction at having seen this part of my country, and more especially this part of my countrymen. My friend Mr. MARTIN, of BIRMINGHAM, I found full of delight at finding that Scotland was so good and so fine a country. He, like almost all the rest of us, had formed his opinion of Scotland, from the sayings and sarcasms of ignorant or prejudiced men. He had just been reading my description of the banks of the CLYDE; and when he came to me at the inn, he seemed full of surprise at what he had read. "Why," said I, "you are not *sorry*, are you, that it is so fine a country?" "No!" exclaimed he, "but very glad indeed; and I am glad that *you* went to see it with your own eyes; for, we should never have got the truth from anybody else: either they do not see, or they do not know how to describe what they have seen." This was very much the truth: I do see, and I know how to describe that which I have seen; and gratitude for excessive kindness received out of the question, I must have been the basest dog that ever lived, not excepting a Scotch "*feelosofer*," or an Irish "*reporther*," if I had not endeavoured to do something like justice to the country, and to the people of Scotland.[2]

HIGHLANDS OF SCOTLAND[1]

The reader has been told that I only went to the foot of the HIGHLANDS, therefore he knows that I can know nothing about them in detail; but I saw quite enough to convince me, that I had always been greatly deceived with regard to the value of even this part of Scotland, which has always been called "*barren*;" and barren, meant, in my view of the matter, land capable of producing *nothing at all* that was of any use. I was born at FARNHAM in Surrey; and ARTHUR YOUNG, in his survey of England, says, that from FARNHAM in Surrey to ALTON in Hampshire is "*a space containing the finest ten miles in the kingdom.*" It is very fine. It is a narrow valley, down

the middle of which beautiful meadows are watered by the
occasional overflowings of the little river WEY, which afterwards
passes through GODALMING and GUILDFORD, and falls into the
Thames at WEYBRIDGE. At FARNHAM this river is a very small affair,
which, if in America, would not be entitled to be called even a *creek*,
but must be content to be called a *run*. Contemptible as it is,
however, in point of magnitude, it was, about threescore years ago,
quite broad enough, and deep enough, to have spared the borough-
mongers and tax-eaters a monstrous deal of trouble, I, from one of
the bathing places in it, having, about that time ago, been pulled out
by the foot, which happened to stick up above the water, and to
enable a brother-swimmer a great deal older than myself to preseve
this everlasting torment to the *"higher orders."*

This little river, which I used to think beyond all comparison the
greatest in the world, does, however, cause there to be some of the
prettiest meadows under the sun; and these continue along from a
mile and a half on the east end of FARNHAM to the town of ALTON in
Hampshire. On the south side of the river the ground rises very
steeply from very nearly the edge of the meadows, and is generally
clothed with very pretty woods, intermixd with hop-gardens: on the
other side it rises more slowly, now and then spreading off into a
level; and on this side, for the whole of the ten miles, there are the
finest hop-gardens in the world, intercepted by very fine-corn-fields,
bounded, generally, by beautiful hedges. Therefore, I don't know
that YOUNG was wrong; and I don't know, that it was necessary for
him to tell the whole story about my country; and, indeed, if he went
from London to CHERTSEY and did not put his spectacles on (he was
very weak-sighted all his life, and blind several years before he died);
if he did not put his spectacles on as he was going from CHERTSEY to
GUILDFORD, and then went to FARNHAM over the HOG'S-BACK,
looking right forward at the Bishop of WINCHESTER's park, and not
turning an eye, even to the right or left, his unmixed praises of the
vale of FARNHAM are perfectly accountable. He was not bound to
know that the town of FARNHAM, and the little valley there was a
mere *little strip*; that, if, when he was in the middle of the town, he
had gone off due north, or due south, he would have traversed, in
either direction, full *twelve miles*, compared to which the
HIGHLANDS of Scotland are the land of CANAAN. There is barrenness, indeed: there it is that you see sterling sterility. It is a bed of
sand, every grain of which will go through an hour-glass, and upon

which a blade of grass will grow no more than it would upon the iron plate of this American stove[2] by which I am now writing; and my real opinion is, that this tract of country, partly in Surrey, partly in Berkshire, partly in Hampshire, running, in one place, a good stretch into Sussex, contains a greater quantity of real barren land than is to be found in the HIGHLANDS of Scotland, all put together. Nothing but heath will vegetate upon this unadulterated sand, and even that will but just live upon it. Rabbits will not stay upon it, except upon the skirts, where they have fields to go into to feed. Its native inhabitants are a little sort of lizards, that we use to call "effets," meaning *efts*. This is real barrenness. Now, the Highlands of Scotland consist of rocky mountains, or rocky lands; and of deep glens, or ravines; all rocky; everywhere a heap of rocks; but *grass* will grow amongst rocks; and I can readily believe that which I was told, that some of the best pasture was on the tops of the highest mountains. This is very different from the sand heaths; for though there are little spots in them which will bear grass, you sometimes go for miles without seeing any of these spots. In so immense a tract of land as that which lies between WOKINGHAM in Berkshire and PETERSFIELD in Hampshire, there are certainly numerous very pretty dips; and in these the land is generally extraordinarily good; and, in cases where the sterility is not so complete, where the commons are greenish, and studded round with cottages and little gardens and fields, most assuredly the sight is the prettiest, and the life the happiest, in the world; because the soil is warm, the spring and the singing birds come early, the ground is dry; the air excellent, and the sand-hills, so convenient for boys to roll down, the finest places in the world for the breeding and rearing of Members of Parliament, and Prime Ministers:[3] but, as to produce of food, acre for acre, taking in the whole space that I have described, and leaving out the valley of the WEY, I am very certain that this spot is inferior to the HIGHLANDS of Scotland.

For, now, just look at the produce of these HIGHLANDS. In the first place they produce everything of the bread kind that is eaten by the inhabitants. It is oats, of which this bread kind is made, to be sure: but it suffices; and that is enough for our argument. In the next place, these HIGHLANDS send out of themselves every year, as I was assured, a hundred and fifty thousand head of horned cattle and four hundred thousand sheep, all bred and reared in those HIGHLANDS. Without, however, binding oneself to *numbers*, the fact is notorious that the quantities of both are prodigious. Now, though the HIGHLANDS do not, like the sand-hills of Surrey, breed Members of Parliament, &c., they are certainly a great deal more productive than the sand-heaths of which I have been speaking; and all that we have heard about this barrenness of the HIGHLANDS of Scotland has been most monstrous exaggeration. The Island is good to the very northernmost point of it: one part is good for one thing; another part is good for another thing; but there is in reality nothing bad belonging to it: God made it to be the happiest and greatest country in the world; and nothing but parliaments, such as we have seen for many years past, could have steeped it in that misery, that trouble and that peril, in which we now behold it.

I do not like to conclude without saying *something* relative to the treatment of the people of the county of SUTHERLAND, which is the most northerly county of the HIGHLANDS. It is a very large county: the county of CAITHNESS is equally northern, but, at any rate, *Sutherlandshire* lies at the north end of the Island. My readers will recollect what was said at the time about the "CLEARING" of this county by the Countess of that name, and by her husband, the Marquis of STAFFORD. I wish to possess authentic information relative to that CLEARING affair; for, though it took place twenty years ago, it may be just necessary minutely to inquire into it now. It may be quite proper to inquire into *the means that were used to effect the* CLEARING; and if any one will have the goodness to point out to me the authentic sources of information on the subject, I shall be extremely obliged to him.

And, now I, for the present, take my leave of Scotland with expressing a hope, that, going from, and returning to, that very identical room, in *Bolt Court,* from which Dr. JOHNSON went, and to which he returned to spread over England the belief, that there was not a tree in Scotland, and that all was sterility and worthlessness, I have done something, at any rate to remove the errors which he so largely contributed to plant in the minds of Englishmen, relative to Scotland. I never do things by halves; never depend upon mere idea when I can present objects to the eyes. While I am writing this up-stairs, I have to exhibit below, a beautiful sample of apples, which I have brought from the banks of the CLYDE, and a cheese of excellent flavour, and of half a hundred weight, which I brought from the county of AYR: I could not bring Scotland itself to London; but I have brought indubitable proofs, that all that we have been told about its sterility has been either sheer falsehood or monstrous exaggeration. To do these things would, under any circumstances, have been the duty of any Englishman, having seen that which I saw, and being possessed of the same capacity and the same means. But, seeing the kindness with which I was received and treated in Scotland; and seeing the generosity which every one seemed anxious to display towards me; seeing the mass of prejudice and of calumny that Scotch good sense and Scotch justice set at defiance in my favour; seeing all these, to have neglected to perform this duty, would have marked me out as the most unfeeling and ungrateful of all human beings. I have, I hope, discharged this sacred duty with good effect: at any rate, I have discharged it to the utmost of my power; and, when I look towards Scotland, I feel only one draw-back from the happy recollection; and that is, that I may, with regard to the future, have excited in the minds of my most ardent friends there, hopes and expectations that I may either want the occasion, or want the capacity, to realise. However, of one thing I am quite sure; that, in whatever degree I may be found wanting, in a still greater degree they will be found indulgent and generous.

WM. COBBETT.

Bolt-court, Fleet-street, 7. Jan. 1833.

APPENDIX A

Extracts from some of the speeches delivered at the dinner given in Cobbett's honour at Glasgow, as reported in the *Glasgow Chronicle* of 31 October 1832.

THE CHAIRMAN (Archibald J. Hamilton of Dalziell):

'I rise to propose the health of the most extraordinary man of any age, or of any country—the most voluminous, and at the same time the most clear, concise, entertaining and instructive writer that ever has lived. . . . I shall mention an anecdote to show the power of his writings: a few days ago I had a visit from a friend, who is an officer in the household of his present Majesty, and, as you may suppose, he is no radical. . . . He told me that it was lately asked of the Dean of Carlisle, one of the most accomplished scholars in the English church, what he considered to be the finest specimen of the English language in print, and the Dean at once replied that a late essay by Mr. Cobbett, upon what subject I forget, was to his mind the finest thing in the whole language, and what he would first show a foreigner (great applause). . . . So little truth is there, indeed, in the old axiom of "large head, little wit," that the very reverse of it is now admitted to be the fact. For it is not a little curious that nearly all the leading men in this empire, and at all sides too, are men of large stature. (A laugh.) Look at those giants of reform and conservation, the Dukes of Sussex and Cumberland . . . look at Mr. O'Connell, the giant of Ireland . . . and now look at our guest, Mr. Cobbett, the giant of the people of Britain, the colossus of the English language. (Immense cheering.) I beg leave to propose his health, with long life and prosperity to him.' The toast was then drunk, amidst the most deafening and long-continued applause.

MR. COBBETT, in rising to return thanks was received with three rounds of applause. After thanking them for the great honour they had now done him he would trouble them with a few facts relative to himself. . . . He disregarded the quarter of a century of calumny which had been heaped upon him (cheers); he had often been advised to prosecute the villains who had spoken falsely of him; but he said he had in his hands a pen, and the liberty of the press, and he would continue to wield it. (Cheers.) . . . All the fraud, meanness, and malignity, which could be invented or executed, had been put in action to induce Scotsmen to give him a bad reception. . . . Now, however, instead of crying out to throw him (Mr. C.) into a ditch, or on Scotsmen to pay him the debt they owed him, they were beginning to callumniate his entertainers, and anticipating every dinner at which he had the high honour to be present, they reprobated the very thought of it—said they were fools, and destitute of sense or principle, who would attend it because he was present. (Cries of "Hear.") . . . He would, however show the world . . . the grounds on which he had been accused. The first charge was that of inconsistency. . . . For twenty-six years he had steadily advocated the cause of Parliamentary Reform. (Cheers.) That's at least pretty fair. For twenty-nine years he had been predicting the evil consequences of funding, of borrowing, and of paper-money. . . . It was again said that he was fond of money; very fond indeed, when he might have rolled in it in 1803; again when the Whigs came to power in 1806, and again in 1817: at all these times he might have had as much as he could ask in a reasonable way. . . . The Government considered what was best[1]—whether to expend millions on hirelings to write him down, or to give him 100,000*l* to keep him silent. All these offers have been published . . . but they were invariably refused. He should not ask them, however, to ascribe this so much to disinterestedness as to foresight: he saw the flowery path, but he saw thorns at the end of it: he saw that the system would go to pieces and bring disgrace on all who had been connected with it. He had spoken to his wife of it many times. (Cheers.) Five or six years ago, a gentleman came to Kensington and said to Mrs. C., "See what Huskisson is now², and Cobbett might have been equal to him; God only knows what he might have been. (Cheers.) When he was told this, he said, "Nancy, what might we have been? We might have had, so far as I know, a coronet and a coach and four, and you and I might have been lolling in a coach, you in diamonds, and I drowned in money (a laugh); but loaded with the contempt of the people. I might have been Mr. Huskisson and you Mrs. Huskisson." But she did not like this. She bristled up, and said that she would have no name but her own name. . . . '

THE CHAIRMAN gave the health of a lady, who, if her husband had been a scoundrel, might have been a Duchess of Botley, or somewhere else— "Mrs. Cobbett." (Great applause.)

MR. COBBETT— "She was born in Kent, and her mother was born at Stirling. (Cheers.) Her father was born at Berwick (cheers); and she will be much gratified at receiving her title from you." (Cheers.)

THE CHAIRMAN gave "Lord Grey, and his Majesty's other reforming Ministers," which was drunk with immense applause.

MR. COBBETT said he had perfect confidence in Earl Grey, but he was so much hampered by some of his colleagues that he was very much afraid he could not carry his whole intentions into effect.

THE CHAIRMAN gave 'The Duke of Hamilton, and a speedy day of reckoning for the Manchester yeomanry and magistrates."

MR. COBBETT reminded the meeting that there was one other person concerned in the Manchester massacre— Lord Sidmouth. (Cheers.) An honest Parliament would have called him to account before now, but an honest Parliament will yet do it. (Cheers.)

MR. PRENTICE said he was sure the toast with which he had been intrusted would be drunk with much pleasure and interest. It was of the greatest importance to the country that the electors of Oldham should do their duty by returning Mr. Cobbett to Parliament. (Cheers.) The Reform Bill would very ill fulfil its purpose, if it failed to ensure the return of the man who, above all others, was instrumental in bringing it about. (Cheers.) . . . He then gave "The Independent Electors of

Oldham, and may they do their duty by returning Mr. Cobbett to Parliament." (Great applause.)

MR. COBBETT, in reply, stated his election for that place to be secure. He had pledged himself, if returned, to bring to justice those who figured in the Manchester Massacre (cheers); but he never could have presumed to do this if he had not been half a lawyer. Without this his *Register* would have been barren indeed.

MR. WM. LANG gave "The Independent Electors of Manchester who have promised their support to Mr. Cobbett."

MR. COBBETT returned thanks. The constituency being large, the committee had not, when he came through, had time to canvass the whole; but his belief was, that he should be returned for Manchester as well as Oldham, or no one would be returned at all. (Cheers.)

Note. Up to that point, some twenty-six toasts had been given and replied to. The following toasts were then given from the chair: 'A speedy and complete reform of the abuses in the established church.' 'The Lord Advocate and the independence of the Scottish bar.' 'The French nation, and may it soon reap the good fruits of the glorious three days of July.' 'The Poles, the bravest of the brave; and may they soon break their tyrants' chains.' 'The speedy abolition of slavery.' 'The abolition of all monopolies in trade, commerce, and law.' 'The Belgians.'

MR. TURNER proposed the health of Mr. McGregor and the Kelvinhaugh band, which had kindly attended at the dinner. (Great applause.)

The reporter concluded his account by recording that 'The company broke up at half-past ten, highly gratified with the evening's proceedings. The dinner did great credit to Mr. Fleck.'

APPENDIX B

COBBETT'S SCOTOPHOBIA

Cobbett's prejudice against the Scots which was, for all his later protestations, persistent and frequently voiced, was expressed at three different levels. The first, which he had, in all probability, inherited from his forebears, may be described as the popular level. The others, which were superimposed on his original and native prejudice, operated at the political and intellectual levels.

The popular prejudice was a traditional one and was, as its title suggests, common enough amongst Englishmen of his day. Remnants of it survived in the jokes told about Scotsmen in bars and music halls until, in this respect, Irishmen, and later Pakistanis, replaced them. It was, fundamentally, an anti-immigrant sentiment which arose from a belief that hordes of uncouth, impecunious and bare-arsed Scots were swarming out of their barren and starveling country in order to batten off the English.

Cobbett declared that it had originated with 'those greedy Scotch minions' who had come south with James I. He accordingly praised 'that honest Englishman', Guy Fawkes, who had bravely told the king and his Scotch council that he had wished 'to blow the Scotch beggars back to their mountains again'. Doctor Johnson, who was never more than light-heartedly Scotophobic, expressed it better when he declared, 'Sir, it is not so much to be lamented that Old England is lost, as that the Scotch have found it.'

Cobbett was never so elegant when it came to voicing this particular prejudice. He had started his writing career in the United States, where the second of his published works had been a pamphlet called *A Bone to Gnaw for the Democrats*. This was primarily an attack on Thomas Jefferson and his

'democratical and French-loving followers', but the occasion
for it had been a work recently published in Philadelphia
called *The Political Progress of Britain*. It was a work which,
when first published anonymously in England, had exposed its
author, a Scot called James Thompson Callendar, to the
danger of being prosecuted for his seditious and anti-
Hanoverian sentiments. He had fled to America and had there
published an enlarged edition of the work in which he described the tyranny he had been subjected to and the perils he
had escaped from.

To this, Cobbett replied: 'What are his adventures in
Scotland, and his "narrow escape", to us, who live on this side
of the Atlantic? . . . Is it any thing to us whether he prefers
Charley to George or George to Charley, any more than
whether he used to eat his burgoo with his fingers or with a
horn spoon? . . . Just as if we cared whether his posteriors were
covered with a pair of breeches or a kelt, or whether he was
literally sans-culotte? . . . He is like a cur baying at the moon.'

Vulgarly vigorous stuff, and he was writing in a similar vein
at the popular level thirty-five years later, shortly before he
toured Scotland where, for the first time in his life, he thought
it necessary to assure his audiences that he entertained not the
slightest prejudice against their race. Those of them who had
read his *Political Register* might have remembered such a
passage as this, written eighteen months earlier. 'Base and
degraded indeed are we if we suffer in silence those beggarly
burgoo-eaters to swagger over us, while they are sucking our
blood. . . . These vagabonds have contributed largely towards
the ruin of England; they have been sucking its blood ever
since James 1 . . . but ever since George 111 mounted the
throne, they have been eating up our very flesh. . . . They will
not work; they depend on the taxes in all countries whither
they go. . . . Even those who employ them hate them.'

This theme of the Scot who became unwilling to work and
reverted to parasitism once he had crossed the Tweed was one
that Cobbett kept coming back to. It is true that he sometimes
threw in a phrase which suggested that he was not prepared to
condemn the entire race out of hand. Nevertheless there must
have been at least some amongst the audiences he flattered and
coaxed when he was actually in Scotland who remained scepti-

cal. Too much of what he had written demonstrated that he was more inclined to generalise than to particularise when it came to lambasting the Scots.

There is, for example, the following well-known passage from *Rural Rides*. In the summer of 1822 Cobbett had paused to watch the haymakers at work near St Albans, a sight which had caused him to write: 'It is curious to observe how the different labours are divided as to *nations*. The mowers are all *English*; the haymakers all *Irish*. Scotchmen toil hard enough in Scotland; but when they go from home it is not to *work*, if you please. They are found in gardens, especially in gentlemen's gardens. Tying up flowers, picking dead leaves off exotics, peeping into melon-frames, publishing the banns of marriage between the "male" and "female" flowers, tap-tapping against a wall with a hammer that weighs half an ounce. They have backs as straight and shoulders as square as heroes of Waterloo; and who can blame them? The digging, the mowing, the carrying of loads; all the break-back and sweat-extracting work they leave to be performed by those who have less *prudence* than they have.'

Again, there was one of his many arguments with John Black, one of those 'renegado' Scots who had settled in England, where he had become editor of the *Morning Chronicle*. He was, like Cobbett, self-educated, which should have persuaded Cobbett not to refer to him facetiously as 'Docter'. He was also a Radical, which was why Cobbett ought to have agreed with him. But 'Dr.' Black had, amongst other things, 'published more than a hundred articles within these four years in which he represented the invasion of the Irish as being ruinous to England. What monstrous impudence! The Irish come to help do the work; the Scotch to help to eat the taxes; or to tramp "aboot mon" with a pack and a licence, or in other words, to cheat. . . . This tricky and greedy set . . . have been the principal inventors and executors of all that has been damnable to England.'

Cobbett was hardly less sweeping or less prejudiced when writing about the political and intellectual activities of the Scots in England. Those who are old enough will remember that a common complaint made against the Americans when their troops were stationed in Britain during Hitler's War was that 'they were over here and over-paid'. Cobbett would have complained, if the phrase had occurred to him, that the Scots were 'over here and over-powerful'. Indeed there was some truth in his argument that, wherever one looked, whether in politics, the armed forces, the colonies, India or Threadneedle Street, one could always find a great many Scotsmen in positions of influence and power.

He had been saying as much ever since 1805, when he had, with considerable gusto, written about the downfall of Henry Dundas, first Viscount Melville. Before his impeachment that 'uncrowned king of Scotland' had spread his patronage widely amongst his countrymen, who had prospered accordingly. Melville had consequently come close to persuading the English that he was offering them as spoil to his countrymen.

Cobbett continued to protest about the positions of power occupied by the Scots. Melville had been dead twenty years when he wrote about the 'Scottish faction who ruled England and disposed of its riches at pleasure. . . . To them have been given the army, the navy, the colonies. They have it all. First the faction of the BUTES, then that of the DUNDASES, have engrossed every-thing where money is to be got; while their country pays next to nothing in taxes. To the BUTE faction we owe the loss of America; to the DUNDAS faction we owe the indelible disgraces of the last war against that country. DRUMMOND, COCHRANE, ROSS; it was all Scotch. Look at the navy list; look at the governorship of the colonies; look at the East Indies and the West . . . look at Newfoundland, Nova Scotia, New Brunswick, Canada; look at it all, and you will find it all Scotch; every-thing that has power, every-thing that has emolument, is Scotch.'

He added, hopefully (it was 1831, and Reform was in the making) — 'Reform will change this; reform will destroy the accursed system out of which it has sprung; it will restore meat and bread to the English working people, and it will reduce the straight-backed Scotch idlers to work or to starve. *It cannot do otherwise.*'

But Reform was seven years into the future when he tackled a similar theme in 1825: 'The *navy* will, like *India,* soon be a Scotch thing altogether. . . . This miserable Northern corner of the island, the whole of which is *not worth so much as the county of Kent,* and does not *pay so much clear into the King's Exchequer,* is fast getting possession of all the ships and all the good things of the *"English Navy".* . . . Fine talk about "our country" indeed. I look upon the Scotch . . . as being far less my countrymen than the Yankees are.'

As readers will have noted, Cobbett greatly resented the example Scottish landowners and farmers were setting to their counterparts in England. Their large mechanised farms were, perhaps, the most efficient in Europe, but they established a pattern which, when copied in England, would finally destroy that country's ancient agrarian civilisation and turn a once prosperous peasantry into a landless and urbanised proletariat.

But what Cobbett resented more than the presence and the power of the Scots in England was their intellectual domination of the English. It was, indeed, a time when Scottish philosophers, political economists, historians, authors and reviewers appeared to dictate to the English in all matters of policy, thought and taste. Cobbett would have been disinclined to allow any Scot to dictate to him, even when he agreed with him. But there was remarkably little in the philosophies of Adam Smith, David Hume, Henry Brougham, Francis Jeffrey, or John Ramsay McCulloch, Cobbett could agree with.

These were the hated *'feelosofers'* he held collectively responsible for Malthus and Bentham, for the industrialisation of England and the emigration of Englishmen, for high taxes and paper money, for dear food and low wages, for depriving the poor of their rights under England's ancient Poor Laws and for forcing 'hedukashion' on them. Their theories had persuaded the English to glorify commerce and give predominance to wealth. They had, from the days of Bishop Burnet onwards, corrupted, enfeebled and impoverished the political, social, economic and intellectual life of England.

It was that Edinburgh-born Whig, Bishop Burnet, who had helped found the Bank of England and the 'vile paper-money and funding system' that went with it. 'Bear in mind,' Cobbett wrote,' that the paper-money system is the *Scotch-system.* It was invented by BURNET, and improved upon by LAW. It once, under LAW, reduced the people of France nearly to famine, and totally ruined the state for years. It has been more destructive to this kingdom than the sword, pestilence and famine altogether; but it is still eulogised by the Scotch *feeloso-fers*, those enterprising sons of the barren North, who sally forth to *instruct* (and devour) the gulls o'th'Sooth.'

John Law of Lauriston had, indeed, come close to ruining France's finances, and had thereby done something to prepare the way for the French Revolution. If a single Scottish *feeloso-fer* could do so much to the French, how much more, Cobbett suggested, could the present horde of Scottish *feelosofers* do to the English. He quoted, with approval, the epitaph on Law that had been published in *Le Mercure de France* after his death:

> Ci git cet Ecossais célèbre,
> Ce calculateur sans égal,
> Qui par les règles de l'algèbre
> A mis la France à l'hôpital.

Walter Scott's trashy novels were filling the heads of young girls in England with a great deal of historical nonsense. As for that more serious Scottish historian, George Chalmers, he had dared to deny Cobbett's theory (which put paid to Malthus), that England had supported a larger population in the Middle Ages than it did in the second decade of the nineteenth century. How dared a Scot interfere in that manner with the history of the English. 'No people here "mon, teel the Scotch cam to sevelize" us! Impudent, lying beggars. Their stinking "*kelts*" ought to be taken up, and the brazen and insolent vagabonds whipped back to their heaths and rocks.'

But the *feelosofers* he probably hated most of all — Malthus apart — were the Edinburgh Reviewers. They were supporters of 'that miserable queer old coxcomb', Jeremy Bentham. They subscribed to the pernicious theories of 'the barbarous and impious Malthus'. They were 'eulogists and under-strappers of the Whig-oligarchy'. But, worst of all, they had produced Brougham. Brougham and he had fallen out when they were both, in their different ways, advising Caroline of Brunswick at the time of the Bill of Pains and Penalties. Brougham wanted to force 'hedukashion' on the English and had founded The Society for the Diffusion of Useful Knowledge and, in conjunc-tion with another Scot, Dr. George Birkbeck, the Mechanics'

Institutes for that purpose. Above all Brougham had, as Grey's Lord Chancellor, introduced that Bill to reform the English Poor Law which Cobbett would spend his last years combating. 'It was a Scotchman of the name of BROUGHAM who proposed this bill to the House of Lords; and he said that such a bill was necessary to prevent the poor from SWALLOWING UP THE LORDS' ESTATES . . . the half-drunk, half-mad Scotch vagabond had the impudence and insolence to deny that the working people, when in distress, had a right to relief out of the land.'

It was not surprising that, a couple of years earlier, Cobbett had written an open letter to 'that nasty palaverer' Brougham to mark a certain anniversary. 'It is now about five-and-twenty years since you and I had a first skirmish, you being then a very desperate *Edinburgh Reviewer*, just arrived in London in a Berwick smack, freighted to the very choking of the hold with adventurers come to get pickings out of the "loons o'th'Sooth. You have carried on your botheration pretty well (since then).'

Another Edinburgh magazine Cobbett had little regard for was *Blackwood's*. But he was not above making use of an article by that 'base liar', William Blackwood in order to score off 'Dr' Black. That article had shown that, on the proposed basis of giving the vote in the towns to every £10 householder, the city of Glasgow would contain some 8000 electors. But statistics showed that there were 2850 public houses and 1425 brothels in the city whose rental value would be £10 a year or more. This meant that, out of the 8000 householders enfranchised, '4,275 would be ale and brothel housekeepers'.

Cobbett used these statistics in a *Register* article headed 'Scotch Morality' — 'My readers will recollect that I have frequently reprobated Dr. BLACK's assertion that the misery and crimes of the working people of England arose, not from their hard lives and ill-treatment, but from their *want of education*; and that it was the *better education* of the Scotch that made them *more prudent* and *more moral*. I always denied . . . that the Scotch were more prudent and more moral. . . . Now I do not cite the liar Blackwood, as *proof* of the correctness of my opinion; but his statement, if it be only a quarter part true, shows that Dr. BLACK knew very little about the morals of his own country, and shows, that the silly stuff about *"education"* has, at any rate, no good effect.'

Cobbett's Scotophobia — if that it was — had been increased by other provacations than those provided by the Butes, the Dundases and the *feelosofers*. In 1803, when he was possibly no more prejudiced against the Scots than was customary for an Englishman, he had been attacked, unjustifiably as he thought, by a good number of Scots over the Lutz Affair. That was a complex case revolving around what had actually happened at the Battle of Alexandria in 1801. That famous victory, the first the British army had won against the French, had been the cause for great celebration, not least in Scotland. For a Scot, General Abercromby, had been in command; a famous Scottish regiment, the 42nd, had been credited with having repulsed the counter attack by the 21st demi-brigade, known as 'The Invincibles' which feat had made victory possible; and Sergeant Sinclair of that regiment had been acclaimed as the hero of that encounter, he having captured the standard of the Invincibles after having cut down the French ensign carrying it.

The Scots have always been particularly proud of the valour of their soldiers. The Scottish papers were full of Abercromby, the 42nd and Sergeant Sinclair. The Highland Society, under the chairmanship of the Duke of Atholl, recorded its pleasure at the news that the 42nd had 'nobly maintained the hereditary glory of the Caledonian name' and resolved to pay by subscription for a medal to be struck and given to every soldier in the regiment in addition to a silver cup (to the value of 100 guineas) for the officer's mess, which cup would have on it an engraving depicting Sergeant Sinclair cutting down the French ensign and seizing the standard.

Cobbett, quite by chance, came across evidence which proved that the popular version of what had happened at Alexandria was incorrect. Far from the 42nd having turned the tide of battle, the regiment had been in full retreat in front of the Invincibles and would have been destroyed had not General Stuart, commanding the Foreign Brigade in reserve, ordered the Queen's German Regiment forward to recover the position. But not only had it been the Queen's Germans who had routed the Invincibles; it had also been a private of that regiment, an Alsatian called Antoine Lutz, and not Sergeant Sinclair who had captured the standard, killed the French ensign and a

French dragoon into the bargain, and brought his trophy back to the British lines.

Cobbett discovered all this only after careful investigation. He brought Lutz before the Cabinet and succeeded in convincing them of the true facts, which he later published in a series of *Register* articles. Those articles, as was to be expected, outraged the Scots. A retired officer of the 42nd called on the Attorney General to lay a suit for seditious libel against Cobbett for so defaming the Highlanders. Within a short while a pamphlet was published in Edinburgh and London under the title *Invincible Standard. Falsehood and Magnanimity Exposed in a Vindication of the Forty-Second Highland Regiment Against the Pretensions of Mr. William Cobbett and the claims of Anthony Lutz.*

What was more surprising was that the London newspapers also attacked him for his 'un-British behaviour'. The *Morning Chronicle* wrote, 'It does not show much *English spirit* to insinuate that the *foreign corps* had a greater share in the victory of the 21st than any of our *native* troops.' *The Pilot* inveighed against 'the sneering malevolence of an *anti-British* mind'. Cobbett, puzzled by these attacks, refrained from horse-whipping the editor of *The Pilot* as he had initially proposed to do, and instead replied, quite mildly that 'there is but one wreath of invincible laurel; before I can restore it to LUTZ, I must take it from the brow of the Highlander'.

It would be fair to say that, from then on, it was war between Cobbett and the Scots. Twenty-eight years later, infuriated because Brougham had claimed the title of Father of Reform which he thought his own, Cobbett wrote: 'The old readers of the *Register* will recollect the affair of the "INVINCIBLE STANDARD", which, if I see any more Scotch puffs, I will, one of these days, republish entire to the eternal shame of the Scotch braggarts. I am the only Englishman that I know of, besides Doctor JOHNSON (and it is curious, that this part of my paper is written *in the very room in which he used to sit*, in Bolt-Court, while he was exposing the frauds of this bragging race); with the exception of him, I am the only Englishman that ever laid on well and truly at this at once crawling and climbing race of men.'

A year later he was in Scotland and assuring the Scots that

they were the most honest, industrious and estimable of nations. Whether all the years previous to that had proved him a Scotophobe, and whether the year he visited Scotland proved him a humbug is a matter for individual judgement. It is worth adding, however, that his last article, dictated from his deathbed, contained another jibe against that 'villainous Scotch *feelosofer*' Lord Brougham.

APPENDIX C

THE NEWSPAPERS ON COBBETT

Readers of the *Tour* will need little persuading to believe that Cobbett had an almost excessively good conceit of himself in general coupled with an exalted belief in his own political importance. Not even his harshest critics had ever underestimated his powers as a political writer and propagandist, although all of them had deplored his use of those powers. But there had been times during his long career in politics when the Establishment had, quite correctly, believed he could safely be ignored. There had been others when it had been necessary to write him down, and a few when it became essential to attempt to silence him, either by buying him off, or by sending him to prison.

The newspapers had long been hostile to him, as, indeed, he was to them. By 1831, however, it had become clear that Cobbett could neither be written down nor silenced. The newspapers, for the most part, continued to blackguard or ridicule him and the government had attempted to silence him through the courts by trying him for sedition. By the time Cobbett had won his case he had become one of the most talked-about, one of the most reviled, and one of the most applauded men in England. In so far as the Whig establishment was concerned he was to be feared. In so far as the Radical Reformers, the Political Unions and the majority of working-class activists were concerned he was the most important man in the kingdom. But for the Moderate Reformers and the Tories, he was the man who could, in the coming election, split the vote, to the detriment of the first and the advantage of the others.

These last sentiments were reflected in articles about his acquittal published in the middle-class but Reformist paper, the *Examiner*, and in the High Tory *Standard*. Both rejoiced that he should so signally have humbled the Whigs—he had subpoenaed the best part of the Cabinet—but whereas the first considered that this had been a great victory for that freedom of the press which all Reformers demanded, the other went on to question why and how Cobbett had become such a dangerous force in the land.

All that related to Cobbett, rather than to the principles of a free press, was contained in the *Examiner's* opening paragraph. 'As we predicted, the effect of the prosecution of Cobbett is likely to settle the policy of Ministers with respect to the liberty of the press. They have caught their Tartar, and he is victorious and free again. *The affair has been, in fact, a trial of the Government more than of Cobbett, and it has been defeated—defeated in the darling object of vengeance. Extraordinary efforts were not wanting to procure a conviction, but they failed.*'

The *Standard* dug deeper.

The manner in which Mr. Cobbett's trial has terminated furnishes a fertile topic of discussion amongst our contemporaries. . . . In the particular case it is necessary to divest our minds of the most tenacious prejudices, for antipathies are much more adhesive than predilections; and, as Tories, we have the strongest possible reason to dislike Mr. Cobbett. We believe him to be the real author of very nearly every great calamity of our time. That the ingenious, but wholly groundless reasoning of his *Paper Against Gold* produced that panic amongst statesmen to which we owe the scourge of the Currency Bill of 1819 seems scarcely questionable; that Mr. Cobbett was truly the efficient incendiary in producing the Queen Caroline sedition, seems to have been made out by sufficient proof; that the series of falsehoods and slanders published under the name of the *Protestant Reformation*, furnished the whole armoury of sophistry by which the Popish Association excited themselves and their country to that determined aggression before which this Protestant nation was compelled to give way, is indeed confessed by a vote of the Popish Association itself. Last of all, the Reform mania, which now 'frightens the isle from its propriety,' is indisputably the work of Mr. Cobbett, and we had almost said of him alone. . . . Reform, whatever shape it take, will be, in the first instance, a reform *made by Mr. Cobbett*—in the end, *a reform* modelled after his will.

The writer, realising, perhaps, that he was raising bogies with which to frighten timid Tories, went on to explain himself.

> We know that we shall be exposed to the censure of friends, and to the ridicule of opponents, for ascribing so much to the power of a person, who is scarcely popular with any party. Our opinion, however, is drawn from sufficient premises: to name but one of which is perhaps enough. . . . We have always found Mr. Cobbett *the author* of every project advanced against the church and the aristocracy, and the author also of every feasible argument employed in support of such project. The speeches of Lord Grey, Lord Brougham, Lord Durham, Sir James Graham, Mr. Thomas Macaulay, &c. &c. &c. have been years ago embodied . . . in the pages of Mr. Cobbett's *Register*. The *Times* has not a thought that is not stolen from Mr. Cobbett's mint, and other more respectable journals are, we are aware, as deeply indebted to the same instructor, though they do not repay the loan with such base ingratitude. That Mr. Cobbett is not popular with any considerable party in the country is no argument against the extent to which the influence of his writings has prevailed. We of the Tory party hate him as our most formidable enemy; and the Whigs and the Radicals stand to him in a relation as little favourable to the existence of friendship. *They owe too much to acknowledge their obligation.*

But the acquittal in the sedition trial had been as much a defeat for the Whigs as it had been a victory for Cobbett, and so that honest Tory, the *Standard* columnist, added: 'Much as we dislike Mr. Cobbett, we are not sorry for the manner in which his trial has terminated.' The article then went on to exult over the blow Cobbett had struck for the freedom of the press, for when it comes to such matters, there has never been any distinction between Jew and Gentile, Tory, Whig and Radical, in Fleet Street.

A great deal more could be quoted from the London newspapers of that time, all of which would show that, whether fearfully, reluctantly, or otherwise, his political and personal importance were accepted as self-evident. But, when he crossed the Tweed, with the editor of the *Scotsman* reminding its readers of 'that national debt of revenge' the Scots owed

Cobbett, it was the manner in which the Scottish newspapers reported him that became relevant. He had been preceded, it should be remembered, by the scurrilous pamphlet distributed by the Potters in Glasgow, and a paragraph in Colonel Torrens's *Globe* which ran: 'Cobbett, who has by this time, we suppose, commenced his lectures at Edinburgh, has been (doubtless) receiving an overflow of that sort of tribute to which his frequent scurrilous abuse of Scotland and Scotsmen has so naturally advanced a claim.'

Neither the *Caledonian Mercury* nor the *Glasgow Chronicle* was inclined to agree with either the *Scotsman* or the *Globe*. They, and especially the *Chronicle*, gave Cobbett, as the reader wil have noticed, what would nowadays be described as an exceptionally good press. The *Fife Herald* was, perhaps, slightly more cautious, but it published a long and interesting article on Cobbett's Edinburgh visit:

> In last week's paper we gave a few notices of Mr. Cobbett, and an abstract of his four lectures in the Edinburgh Theatre. His concluding lecture to the working classes, took place in the Waterloo Rooms, and was preceded by a highly flattering address, numerously signed, presented by Mr. B. Dunn, to which Mr. Cobbett made a characteristic reply. . . . We were led to believe that he meant to proceed northwards as far as Aberdeen; but we perceive that he diverged to Falkirk, on his route to Glasgow, where his first lecture was given on Wednesday the 17th, to a crowded and all-approving audience. Of Mr. Cobbett's leading political theories, some of them sound and others sophistical . . . we may speak at another time. We will only observe for the present, that his powers in enforcing and illustrating any subject, however dry and unattractive, are gigantic and unrivalled.'

After discussing those works which had made Cobbett famous, the writer decided to add some critical and anecdotal comments on their author. 'The egotism which seasons every thing he has written, is quite unique; and as it has led him to bring before the world all the prominent incidents and everyday habits of his life, we scruple not to give publicity to a few private traits of him, picked up by a gentleman in Edinburgh, and imparted to a correspondent here.'

The Edinburgh gentleman had remarked, 'I would certainly very much enjoy a half hour's chat with Mr. Cobbett, but after hearing him lecture for a couple of hours on two seperate nights, the mere ritual of joining hands seemed worth neither his trouble nor mine. If I had put myself the least in the way, I might have got a *congé-d'entrer* from his respectable host. But after hearing how a certain professor fared, I am inclined to hold that it is well I kept aloof.'

That certain professor had certainly been disappointed by his failure to enjoy a prolonged tête-à-tête with Cobbett. Since it was a Sunday morning, with nothing for normal men to do apart from attending Kirk, he had looked forward to a lengthy conversation with the great man. It never eventuated. Sunday was as much of a workday as any other, so far as Cobbett was concerned.

> His host . . . thought himself called on to get up at 5, to see if his guest wanted light or fire, but he was behind hand; his guest had been up by 4, had lighted the fire for himself, and was busy writing. He continued to do so until he joined the breakfast table, where he remained 4 *minutes*, leaving the savant to philosophise with Madame and her young folks. The amanuensis came at 9, and together they kept at it the whole day. He came another 4 minutes to the dinner table, and ate a very spare slice of mutton, without tasting anything else, or anything in the shape of drink. At tea he remained 6 minutes, from the incidental circumstances that news of the proroguing of Parliament . . . was then brought in, and which was treated at some length, as giving a more determinable shape of his future motions in Scotland. He resumed and continued his labours throughout the evening. Those about him say he was quite teeming with ideas. . . . Among those who approached the great journalist here, the first impression of him was akin to that given by Fearon[1] — quite Sir Oracle — but further intercommuning has made that impression give way to a more pleasant one; they now speak of the takingness of his manner, his straight-forward bluntness, *want* of pretension, and that companionable kind of quality, termed by the French, *bonhomie*. He took great delight in the children of the family in which he was an inmate.

Cobbett's financial difficulties were common knowledge, and made much use of by his enemies, who constantly referred to him, erroneously, as an undischarged bankrupt, kept reminding him of the debts he owed Sir Francis Burdett and Sir Thomas Beevor, accused him of manufacturing books merely for the money they would bring in, and insisted that his lecture tours had more of a financial than a political purpose to them.

The *Fife Herald*, in so far as the last charge was concerned, thought otherwise. 'Mr Cobbett went off in a post-chaise to Dunfermline on Monday, and upon my observing that it was a strange place to go to, where little money could be expected, for they had not a place of meeting that would hold above a hundred or two, unless he got some of the churches, he (the correspondent) made me this reply:

> Do you know we are beginning to think that the imputation of sordidness made against Cobbett is not warranted. We (the committee) think he is very little actuated by money considerations, and that he has gone to Dunfermline chiefly because the unionists there had sent to him, saying his coming would do great good. Here he did not seem to bestow a single thought on the money part of the concern. He never asked about the receipts of the night, or in any way evinced the least feeling on the subject. He left all to his committee, who made but one settlement, and one payment ot him, viz. on the Saturday forenoon, being 140*l*., which he put into his pocket without troubling himself to ascertain the amount; nay, if he had had money in view, he had only to say the word, and Saturday would have been a paying day too. The trades were quite prepared for that condition, and he might thereby have added 30*l*. or 40*l*. to his gains. But he had said he was to lecture gratis, and that was enough.

The writer ended by analysing the impact Cobbett's Edinburgh visit had had on the unending war of the Whigs and the Tories. The Tories, he found, had made much of Cobbett, principally because he was 'apt to let a back stroke at the Whigs to which the back strokes of Don Quixote were as nothing'. The Whigs, for their part, had to be cautious, 'although they detest him worse than the arch-enemy'. They were, although more moderately than Cobbett, Reformers, and could not be seen to attack the great Reformer in public. Consequently, 'they pursued that sneaking policy so natural to

them — to hint a fault and hesitate dislike. Of course the Tories
have, throughout the lectures, derived some advantage from
their tactics. I was told by an eye-witness, that the smashing he
gave the Whigs at the Trades Lecture, was terrible. . . . The
Tories, cunning rogues, want him back again. Several of them
were today expressing a strong hope that he would take Edinburgh on his way south.'

Was the *Fife Herald* thinking of the *Scotsman* when it
commented on those Whigs who 'hint a fault and hesitate
dislike'? That comparatively stripling paper-it had been started
as a weekly in 1817 had gone bi-weekly in 1823 — was ardent in
its support for the Whigs, moderate in the sort of Reform it
demanded, and hostile from its earliest days, to Cobbett. He,
in his turn, had always disliked that paper for its association,
through one of its early editors, John Ramsay McCulloch, with
the vile Scottish feelosofers. He insisted on mis-spelling that
famous economist's name, which he rendered as Macculloch,
something quite sufficient to infuriate any Scot. He would not
give him his resounding 'John Ramsay' either, but referred to
him, in a belittling way, as 'Peter'. A passage in *Rural Rides,*
written seven years earlier, reveals how little love there could
have been between them. 'But now, PETER MACCULLOCH;
. . . now, empty Peter, impudent Peter, brazen Peter,
Ricardo-lecture Peter, *Scotch* PETER MACCULLOCH . . . write
no more paragraphs, but go and join your associates, Mr.
Brougham and *Doctor Birkbeck* and the *feelosofer* and *Lord
John Russell* and establish the "LONDON UNIVERSITY" . . . to
"*enlighten*" us, the benighted "loons o'th'Sooth." '

McCulloch had left the *Scotsman* and had, amongst other
things, become an Edinburgh Reviewer, but he had clearly left
a legacy of antipathy towards Cobbett to the *Scotsman.* In a
separate paragraph the paper quite fairly described the
attendance at the first of Cobbett's lectures:

> Last night the celebrated Mr. Cobbett commenced his political
> lectures in the Adelphi Theatre before a very numerous and very
> respectable audience composed of men of all parties and of all
> classes . . . so great was the anxiety to gain admittance that,
> before 6 o'clock, an immense crowd had congregated at the
> various entrances to the theatre, waiting the opening of the doors.

When the doors opened at half past six, the pressure to get in was excessive, and in a very few minutes every part of the house was crowded.

It was with some pleasure that it was able to report that, for the next lecture, 'the "Great Enlightener" had not so over-flowing an audience, although by no means a small one, as on the former night'. Nor, apparently, was it so appreciative an audience.

A few . . . were so foolish as to hiss at the very beginning, and by this . . . only awakened more overpowering plaudits. Others waxed very wroth — we saw it on their faces — at some of his wild mis-statements, which seems to us the climax of folly. We would no more think of wasting indignation on Cobbett for his absurdities than on the Siamese elephant for tossing its trunk.

We laughed most heartily — sometimes at his drollery, sometimes at his ridiculous exaggerations, sometimes at his egotism, and sometimes at his barefaced attempts to flatter and cajole our townsmen. . . . We did not grudge the half crown which procured us so much recreation. We recognise the felicity of O'Connell's description of him as 'a comical miscreant'.

The writer may perhaps, have allowed his Whiggish principles to colour his reporting, but they never prevented him from producing what would nowadays be described as a 'profile' of Cobbett in his old age for which all Cobbett students must be grateful, even though, being a Scot, the writer was unable to distinguish between the soft drawl of Hampshire and the glottal stops of a true Cockney. Cobbett, it would seem, put aitches in, whereas Cockneys, as we all know, take them out.

We witnessed the performance of the London lion yesternight. Cobbett is a stout man about 5 feet ten inches high with a hoary head, a florid complexion, and a remarkably hale appearance. His form is rather clumsy and his gait somewhat slouching. His forehead is phrenologically fine; it is both high and prominent and well developed in all the leading organs. Under it is a pair of small eyes, set very near one another, giving his countenance an expression of craft, and abating a good deal from his otherwise good looks. His mouth is small, and with the aid of his well filled cheeks, gives his face when he laughs an exceedingly comic expression, which reminds us of Jack Emery in his Yorkshire clowns. His speech is plain and distinct, though his *hofficers, harmy* and other such barbarisms betray the Cockney. His voice is clear and agreeable, his manners as a speaker, free, animated, and varied, but never impressive or eloquent. . . . He has considerable powers of mimicry and excels chiefly in lively graphic sketches and touches of humuor.

The contents of the lectures were not exhaustively discussed, and the substance of them the reader has already discovered in the text of the *Tour*. One extract from the *Scotsman's* report, however, reveals how, in Edinburgh at least, the audience reacted.

At the conclusion of his lecture . . . we were more able to detect the fallacy of his observations. On his way northward he had observed between Dunbar and Musselburgh, the finest land he had ever seen, and neither villages nor people in all that extended space. He made some comparison between that part of the country and Suffolk, where there were flourishing villages every three miles; but between Dunbar and Musselburgh the best crops were reared only to be exported, while the natives were left to life like beasts upon oats, barley and pease. (Cries of No, No, and laughter.)

The wheat was sent to other countries, but this should not be the case when he got into Parliament. He would have an Act of Parliament passed to allow the aristocracy to sell the half of their lands, which they would be glad to do, and would have it parcelled out to individuals in small portions, and by this means plenty would flow to all classes. He spoke at some length on this subject, but it only tended to show his extreme ignorance of Scotland and "all that it inhabit'.

Almost three weeks later Cobbett was in Glasgow on the eve of that dinner given in his honour, the speeches at which have been referred to in Appendix A. The *Scotsman's* Glasgow correspondent wrote slightingly about both the dinner and Cobbett, his article appearing in the *Scotsman* of 29 October 1832.

The political excitement having in a considerable degree gone down with us, things have been somewhat stagnant. . . . To revive us a little, however, we have had a visit, as well as you, of the great Lion from the South, who has condescended to show us hyperboreans his teeth, and to growl a bit after his most approved fashion. He has been well lionized here, and is likely to be still further entreated. Nearly a brace of hundreds, a public dinner, and the unequivocal patronage of at least one of our Parliamentary aspirants, are no bad return for three nights' performance of this ancient vender of political cataplasms.

There are certain substances in nature which possess a marvellous property of attracting sticks, straws, and other worthless substances. Our friend Cobbett possesses this faculty in great perfection. Wherever he goes, by a sort of natural attraction, he is immediately surrounded by all those whose more volatile opinions, as well as generous contempt for rigid public virtue, naturally dispose them to welcome one who either supplies to them arguments for their own views, or at least powerfully laughs others out of any which they may chance to possess. However, to say the truth, we have laughed heartily *with*, and sometimes at, the old gentleman. The wight is indeed to be pitied who expected any illumination from William Cobbett; yet he is very entertaining, and occasionally very happy in his sarcasams. Like a skilful coachman, he always applies his whip 'to the raw'. With the morbid parts of our social system, no man is better acquainted, or more skilful and amusing in his demonstrations; although not a bit cleverer than his neighbours at untying any of the Gordian knots of our perplexed politics, he is not afraid to deal with them after a more succint and less laborious fashion. Now, this being more congenial to all those who would rather *act* than *think*, comprehending a respectable minimum of society, it is not to be denied that the advent of the *Great Grumbler* has been hailed with infinite satisfaction by the above description of persons, and with a more chastened delight by the lovers of amusement in general.

This was pretty fustian stuff and paltry abuse. Cobbett might have ignored it had the Scotsman's correspondent not then come on to the subject of the proposed dinner in Cobbett's honour:

We can understand why all men from the Lord Provost downwards, (who, good easy man, it is thought had no *easy* seat of it the first lecture) should have been desirous to hear Cobbett; but speculation is afloat as to the motives and objects of the *minimum*

who are going to honour their idol *with a public dinner*. By some
it is conjectured *electioneering* influences of no small weight are
expected to result from his visit and dinner; by others that the
'Political Union' will incontinently declare against the debt being
held to be *national*; while by others of more sanguine tempera-
ment, it is imagined that in William Cobbett they behold, in so
far at least as the *dead-weight* is concerned, another Peter-the-
Hermit. . . . Whatever may be the occult reasons for bending the
knee at a public board, to the *immediate abolisher* of national
debt, tithes, paper-money, pensions, standing army, corn laws,
malt and all taxes whatsoever—to him, the greatest political
renegado who has ever lived—who has been at once the eulogist
and defamer of Burke, the contemner and worshipper of Tom
Paine, the heartless detractor of Thomas Muir, and the ungrateful libeller of Sir Francis Burdett—the vulgar panderer to English
vulgar pot-house prejudices, and the unceasing detractor of Scotland and its "*antallactual*" people—whatever, we say, may be the
motive for bending the knee to such an honest, patriotic man, it is
a subject of mortification and shame to all of whose character and
talents Glasgow has any reason to be proud.

Cobbett, in his customary impudent manner, re-published
the whole of this in the *Register* under his reply to it, which he
headed 'THE DEVIL Grinding his teeth and Cursing'. It was not
in his character to allow the editor of the *Scotsman* to get away
with publishing such stuff. He had not been exaggerating
when, some four years earlier, he had written, 'When I began
to write, I had attacked no writer. I fell foul of nobody in the
shape of a "literary gentleman". I was as modest as a maid, and
dealt in qualifications and modifications and mitigations to the
best of my poor powers in the line of palavering; but when I
discovered that it was *envy* that was at work in my assailants
. . . I instantly resolved to proceed in the very way in which I
have always proceeded, giving three, four or ten blows for one;
and never, in any case, ceased to pursue the assailant in some
way or other, until he was completely down.' Now, therefore, it
was time for 'three, four, or ten blows' to be delivered at the
editor of the *Scotsman*.

'Reader, you never saw the devil, of course, and, unless you read
the *Scotsman* or the bloody old *Times* newspapers, I dare say you

never will; but, supposing him to be well represented in the caricatures . . . and supposing him to be in a dreadful rage on account of some great disappointment; matter would come out of his mouth something like that which the *Scotsman* of yesterday . . . has belched out in his rage at the kind of treatment that I have met with in Scotland; and particularly at the thought of a *public dinner* being to be given to me at GLASGOW. Read the article, I pray you, and you will see how the wretch writhes; and you will think you hear his vile blood boiling under his dirty skin. A dinner! Ah, why does nobody give him a dinner? He knows very well he is the man that ought to have public dinners given him; that he is the man that ought, in reason and in justice, to be the object of public approbation; and yet his dull-eyed and besotted countrymen cannot perceive it! Well, if I were he, I would let them perish then; I would take no notice of such stupid creatures! But what will the beast say, then, to the dinner at PAISLEY; to the ringing of the bells at FALKIRK; to various other such demonstrations in every town and every village that I have gone near to? Why, he will say that his countrymen are all rogues or madmen. Well, then, why not let them alone. But, seriously speaking about this matter, the hireling fellow would be wholly unworthy of notice, if he were not the tool of the Whig faction, and particularly of JEFFREY and ABERCROMBIE, whom, if I had been a little earlier, I would have blown out of the water, even at EDINBURGH itself. These men clearly see that I have brought into Scotland a mass of information which will finally be their total overthrow. They see that I have put the struggle upon a new footing. That it is no longer Whig-faction against Tory-faction; but both these factions combined against the *phalanx of the people*. They think I am likely to be one of the leaders of that phalanx; and, therefore, rat never sighed for the destruction of cat so sincerely as they sigh for mine. This poor hired reptile puts forth nothing of his own; he is merely a dog set on by his employers; and what he writes is only worth reading as it shows I have stung those employers to the quick. With this preface I insert the article which exhibits the devil grinding his teeth.

One is tempted to believe that, when it came to scurrility and the exchange of insults, there were, indeed, giants in those days. Even the 'poor hired reptile' who was the Glasgow correspondent of the *Scotsman* seems, by present journalistic standards, a man of considerable scope and stature. One could wish, in these degenerate, mealy-mouthed, and near-illiterate times, that there were still journalists with such a talent to abuse, still editors to give them the space in which to exercise that talent, and still readers with the taste, the time and the understanding to appreciate the possibility that, given such conditions, scurrility can be raised to something that is very close to an art form.

NOTES

1. It was Major Cartwright, the true 'father of Reform' who, when asked why he could not be moderately reformist, replied 'Sir, would you have your wife be moderately chaste?' That almost perfect reply is sometimes attributed to Cobbett, as is the title of 'father of Reform'.

DEDICATION   p. 3

1. For Cobbett to congratulate the people of Oldham for their good sense and public virtue in electing him to Parliament was, perhaps, laying it on a little. To assure them that the Scots congratulated them as well was to spread extra butter all round. But, since Cobbett had stood, or had contemplated standing, for a good many different constituencies ever since he had first offered himself to the thoroughly venal electors of Honiton in 1805, he may have thought the people of Oldham deserved his congratulations, if only for their greater perspicacity.

PREFACE   pp. 5 to 7

1. It is one of the joys of Cobbett that he could always succeed in humbugging himself before proceeding to humbug his readers. Far from 'wanting to do justice to everybody', there was scarcely an individual, class, sect or race he had not, at some time or other, blackguarded most unjustly. Hazlitt wrote about him, 'if his blows were straightforward and steadily directed to the same object, no unpopular minister could live before him; instead of which he lays about right and left, impartially and remorselessly, . . . He throws his head into his adversary's stomach, and takes away from him all inclination for the fight, hits fair or foul, strikes at everything, and as you come up to his aid . . . trips up your heels or lays you sprawling, and pummels you when down . . . to his heart's content.'

EDINBURGH   pp. 9 to 36

1. These were the three writers principally associated with the *Anti-Jacobin* of 1797. They had all, at one time, been associates of Cobbett's in his Tory days. Canning and Frere were both accomplished writers of light verse, and Ellis had produced works on the early English poets.

2. Cobbett's attitude towards the aristocracy was always ambiguous. He had an innate respect for ancient lineage he was never wholly able or willing to suppress. On the other hand he came to hate the governing classes, either because they were 'borough-mongers', or else because they failed in their duties as landowners. He reconciled these different sentiments in two ways. If the person in question was no true 'Norman', but an 'upstart'—and, according to Cobbett, all post-Reformation peers fell into that category—he attacked him for pretending to be what he was not. If he was indisputably a 'Norman', he would be attacked with equal ferocity for not living up to his Norman inheritance of '*noblesse oblige*'. Nevertheless Cobbett was never a Leveller and constantly asserted that he had no desire to abolish the House of Lords or to reduce the power and property of the landed aristocracy so long as due regard was paid to the ancient rights of the poor.

3. Cobbett, the one-time Sergeant-Major of the 54th, never lost his interest in army affairs. When he was a Tory he wanted to reform the Army and make it more completely professional. When he was a Radical he wanted to abolish it, and leave the defence of Britain to the Navy and the county levies. He believed a standing army in peacetime was unconstitutional, and a potential instrument for repression. But above all, it was a great burden on the taxpayers. In 1831 he had, with his usual passion for statistics, worked out that there were on the active list four generals to every regiment, and one commissioned officer to every twelve other ranks, this including NCOs, drummers, musicians and servants. They constituted an important part of the 'deadweight' that was crippling the country.

4. 'Chopsticks' was the nickname Cobbett had invented for his beloved farm labourers of the southern counties. It probably had some connection with the cutting and tying of underwood into faggots. No one else, so far as can be ascertained, made use of the word, although Charles Kingsley used a variant, 'chopstraws' in *Alton Locke*.

5. The Special Commissions were appointed to try those arrested

during the agricultural riots of 1830, riots which Cobbett referred to as 'the rural war' but which are more commonly known as the 'Captain Swing' riots. The sentences imposed on the rioters were frequently excessive, considering that no lives were lost. In three of the Southern counties alone, no fewer than 450 were transported, 400 imprisoned and at least three hanged.

6. 'Feelosofer' was, with Cobbett, a term of almost generic abuse to be applied to any author, journalist, economist or politician whose views failed to coincide with his own. Since many of these were, at that time, Scots—Adam Smith, Hume, Chalmers, Birkbeck, McCulloch, Jeffrey, Dundas, Black etc—even such notably un-Scottish 'philosophers' as Bentham, Malthus and Ricardo were made Scots by association and were referred to as 'feelosofers' in the stage-Scots Cobbett so unfortunately adopted.

7. Cobbett constantly complained that he had, over the years, been the first to publish ideas, arguments and theories which politicians of all parties had subsequently claimed as their own. He was, he said, constantly being plagiarised by men who then turned round and blackguarded him for his views. For confirmation of this see Appendix C.

8. It was thought, at that moment, that the Whigs would put Creevey up as a candidate at Oldham in an attempt to keep Cobbett out of Parliament. In the event a Mr Bright stood for the Whigs and came a bad third to Fielden and Cobbett.

9. A plaintiff who was unduly dilatory in bringing his suit could be debarred from his action because of 'lache'. This did not, however, work against the Crown.

10. Since steam power was first used extensively in the North of England and in Scotland, it was there that it was first harnessed to agriculture. At the beginning of the nineteenth century it began to be used to drive threshing machines, which were themselves a Scottish invention, the first one, driven by horses, having been devised by a Mr Menzies of Culterallers in 1740. The Lothians, at that time, and until cheap wheat from the American prairies brought ruin, acted as the agricultural showcase for the whole of Europe. Farmers came there to see all that was 'advanced' and 'progressive' in agriculture. Only Cobbett came to the Lothians to mock at the 'corn weavers' and their 'steam-engine farms'.

11. Malthus advocated nothing more sinful than 'moral restraint' and late marriages as methods of population control. Cobbett preferred to believe that he also supported contraception, prostitution, homosexuality and onanism as alternatives to moral restraint.

12. In 1831 Cobbett had acquired the lease of Normandy Farm at Ash in West Surrey, less than four miles from his birthplace at Farnham. He was thus brought into contact, once more, with the heaths and sandhills he had known as a boy. In spite of his great financial difficulties he was, even whilst in Scotland , busy stocking his new farm.

13. Frederick John Robinson, Viscount Goderich, and later Earl of Ripon, had been unfortunate enough, when Chancellor of the Exchequer in 1825, to invite the Commons to 'contemplate with instructive admiration' the high level of the nation's prosperity. That winter the country was plunged into a deep recession from which it made no very quick recover. Thereafter Cobbett always referred to him as 'Prosperity Robinson'.

14. The light, two-wheeled tumbril or cart, drawn by a single horse, was commoner on Scottish farms than on English ones, where heavy, four-wheeled waggons, drawn by four and even six horses were more common. Experts had already decided that a single horse in shafts exerted more than half the traction exerted by two horses, and so on, *pro rata*.

15. Roxburgh Park is now known as Broxmouth Park. It is still 'very well wooded'.

16. John Gawler (q.v.) was Burdett's second when the latter fought his celebrated duel 'with little PAULL on Wimbledon-common.' Paull, a notoriously quarrelsome man, had fallen out with his fellow candidate Burdett when the two were standing as the Radical candidates for Westminster during the 1806 General Election. Paull, who had already lost the use of his right arm in a duel, had the worst of the encounter, in which both men were wounded, and, because of his gambling losses, committed suicide shortly afterwards.

17. The article in question, headed 'Mr William Eagle and the Election for Norwich' was published in the *Register* of 25 August 1832. It was one of Cobbett's 'puffing' articles referred to in the Introduction. Anyone with a taste for the electioneering literature of those days will find it enjoyable reading.

18. Cobbett, in his later years, spent as much time opposing Poor Law Reform as he spent supporting Parliamentary Reform. The old Poor Law provisions of 5th Elizabeth c.3.(1563) had already been modified, as he thought for the worse, as a consequence of three Bills put forward by Sturges Bourne (q.v.) in 1818. Now, more sweeping reform was contemplated. The burden on the parish rates had become excessive and Benthamite and Malthusian theories were fashionable. In March 1832 a Royal Commission on

the Poor Laws was set up to examine the problem. Cobbett's argument was, basically, that any change in the traditional parish system of poor law relief was a breach of the bargain made by Elizabeth. Before the Reformation, the indigent poor had been entitled, under canon law, to a third of the tithes—or so he argued. When tithes were appropriated to the parsons, Elizabeth substituted relief out of the rates. Both tithes and rates were land-based taxes, and to abolish them, Cobbett argued, was to extinguish the last rights the poor had in the land. The Poor Law reform Cobbett fought until the day of his death was achieved. The abolition of outside relief, and the institution of Union workhouses were some of the results. These were according to the philosophy of the time, rational and well-meant developments, but they left a scar in the folk memory of the poor that still itches.

19. The *Red Book* was one of several Radical publications exposing the political corruption of the times. It listed all the sinecures, pensions and offices enjoyed by the undeserving sprigs of the nobility.

20. Cobbett was, perhaps more than anything else, a 'sound money man'. He attributed most of Britain's ills—a vastly increased National Debt, unprecedented taxes, high food prices, low wages, food hunger—to the inflation that followed Pitt's suspension of cash payments and the great increase in paper money that resulted. It would seem odd, today, to find a Radical leader advocating less government, lower taxes, a balanced Budget and sound money.

21. 'The bloody old *Times*.' Cobbett believed the *Times* to be the most corrupt of all the London newspapers since it gave its support to whatever government was currently in power and took money in various forms for doing so. It was 'bloody' because it had supported the Special Commissions in their task of hanging, transporting and imprisoning the starving agricultural rioters.

22. Cobbett and O'Connell, although theoretically political allies, quarrelled more often than they made it up. When, in 1831, O'Connell, in a speech in Dublin, opposed the extension of English poor-law to Ireland, claiming that it would turn 'the independent and merry Irish' into the 'half-sulky, half-miserable slaves to the poor-law' that Englishmen were, Cobbett became very angry. His reply, published on 11 January 1832 as a supplement to his Manchester Lectures, took the form of a 'Letter to Mr. O'Connell on his Speech against the Proposition for Establishing Poor-laws in Ireland'. It still makes excellent reading, being, in places, extremely funny.

23. Cobbett, in his Tory days, had maintained that Malthus's theories were irrefutable. Now, however, he detested both the theories and their author. The former provided arguments for those politicians who wanted the poor-laws reformed so as to discourage the poor from breeding, and those who wanted to reduce the population by encouraging the poor to emigrate. The latter was a parson, and Cobbett had come to dislike parsons. He was also in receipt of a government pension and Cobbett hated pensioners. So, if a parson, *qua* parson, was 'nasty', a pensioned one was even nastier, and if he belonged, as Malthus did, to the race of 'feelosofers', there could be few things nastier in the whole of the animal kingdom.

24. There were 1.27 English acres to a Scottish one.

25. This was printed as 'berths' in the *Register*.

26. Scottish quarterly dates have always differed from English ones. Nevertheless Cobbett may still have got his dates wrong, since in Scotland, in those days, the Whit term began on 15 May. This may not, however, have applied to farm-servant hirings.

27. This must surely be one of the earliest denunciations of the tied-cottage system.

28. The Law of Settlement was still a governing principle in the giving of, and entitlement to, parish relief. If a pauper had not qualified, either through birth or residence, for settlement, the parish was under no duty to support him, and was entitled to ship him back to the parish where he had last acquired settlement.

29. One of Sturges Bourne's three Bills which had become law in 1818 provided that votes at parish or 'vestry' meetings should be distributed according to the amount of rateable property owned, parishioners being entitled to one vote for every £25 worth of such property. This produced the 'select vestries'. Cobbett objected to them for the obvious reason that the man who paid the most rates had the largest say in deciding the level of the poor rate, and he would have a vested interest in keeping it as low as possible.

30. The First Reform Act did not provide for universal male suffrage. It enfranchised the £10 householder in the towns and the £50 copyholder and tenant in the rural areas. This still left the 'chopsticks' and the majority of factory workers unenfranchised.

31. Cobbett was a pioneer of what are still favoured methods of applying extra-Parliamentary pressure on governments. He encouraged the Radicals to demonstrate peacefully and to exercise their ancient rights of petition on a national scale.

32. Turnpike tolls had long been a matter of concern to Cobbett, largely because he believed that toll owners and gate-keepers were charging the public more than they were legally entitled to charge. He and his sons had laid more than ninety informations against London toll owners, and had succeeded in having their charges reduced on several occasions. In 1823 he was presented with a silver cup and cover 'by the proprietors of the one-horse carts of Kensington and its vicinity as a grateful testimony for his exertions in reducing the turnpike tolls to the amount authorised by law'.

33. In 1807 Francis Jeffrey (q.v.), after admitting that 'Cobbett had more influence than all the other journalists put together', launched a violent attack on him in the *Edinburgh Review*. He called Cobbett a turncoat, ridiculed his new-found Radicalism, and declared that there was not the slightest need for Parliamentary Reform. He changed his mind about Reform, along with most other Whigs, but he and Cobbett were enemies thereafter. There was, therefore, a certain amount of sarcasm in Cobbett's remark. Jeffrey would no more have attended Cobbett's Edinburgh lectures than Cobbett would have welcomed his attendance.

34. Cobbett's version of history was always fiercely partisan. He thought the Reformation had been a disaster for England and the English. Consequently, if there had been no Henry VIII there would have been no Reformation, no dissolution of the monasteries, no changes in landownership, no 'upstart' landowners and married priests to appropriate the tithes to themselves. Elizabeth I, as Henry's daughter, was damned by association. Occasionally, however, Cobbett referred to her almost affectionately as 'Old Betsy', this being whenever he remembered 5 Elizabeth c.3 (1563).

35. Cobbett's Manchester Lectures of 1831 amounted to what would nowadays be called a Party Manifesto, since they outlined, in some detail, the policies the Radicals would press for in Parliament. By urging Radicals to vote only for those candidates who would pledge themselves to those measures, Cobbett was moving away from Burke's concept of the Member of Parliament as a representative, free to exercise his best judgement, towards the modern concept, popular in parties of the Left, of the Member as a delegate mandated to carry out party decisions. The demand for annual Parliaments similarly foreshadows the practice of limiting a Member's freedom of action by obliging him to submit to mandatory re-selection.

36. This was bare-faced humbug. Every number of his *Register* revealed that Cobbett studed the weekly and daily press with great care, especially if these contained attacks on himself to which he would have to reply. Quite apart from this, much of the *Register* consisted of reports and articles extracted from other British and foreign newspapers.

37. The back pages of the *Register* advertised, every week, 'Cobbett's Library'. In so far as the books it listed were concerned, something under twenty were from his own hand. But if to these are added the twelve volumes of *Peter Porcupine's Works*, and the eighty-nine volumes of the *Political Register*, then he was right to boast of his 'hundred volumes'.

38. That account, which appeared the following week in the *Register*, ran, as the reader will observe, to some 40,000 words. When one considers that Cobbett was then close to seventy, that he had spent much of that week travelling, lecturing and sight-seeing, that he had written other, shorter pieces for the next number of the *Register*, and that he proposed to do much the same in the next seven days, one cannot help wondering at the old man's energy.

39. Rioting in such large towns as Bristol and Nottingham had finally persuaded a reluctant House of Lords that the Reform Bill had to be passed or there would be a revolution in England. Cobbett, however, insisted that it had been the 'chopstick' risings during the 'Captain Swing' troubles that had made Reform inevitable. Rural mobs were made up of harder men than the town mobs, and whereas the latter could conveniently be dispersed with a sabre charge or a few volleys of musket fire, farm labourers setting fire to ricks and buildings at night, and going from farm to farm to do so, constituted a threat more difficult to control, and one that a legislature made up, very largely, of landowners, could never afford to ignore.

GLASGOW   pp. 36 to 56

1. Colonel Robert Torrens had acquired the *Globe*, a London evening paper, in 1823, and had amalgamated it with his own paper *The Traveller* under the editorship of Walter Coulson (the 'reporther') (q.v.). Torrens was, in all probability, the first of Britain's newspaper magnates, for he also acquired, at various times, the *Statesman*, the *True Briton*, the *Evening Chronicle*, the *Argus*, and the *Athenaeum*. Cobbett may have been jealous of his influence in political and journalistic circles, but he

but he principally hated him because he was a 'feelosofer' and a
Benthamite.

2. Cobbett had been attacked as a turncoat ever since he had
deserted Pitt in 1803. He had certainly been Tory, Whig,
Radical and Independent in turn, had blackguarded those he
had once praised and praised those he had once blackguarded,
but this, he maintained, demonstrated both his personal honesty
and his political integrity.

3. This was at least half humbug. Richard Ireland was an
Edinburgh bookseller who acted as Cobbett's agent and distri-
butor in that city. The two may never have met, but Cobbett was
too much of a business man not to know who was responsible for
selling the *Register* and his other works in that part of Scotland.

4. A man-of-war 'lying in ordinary' was one that had been taken,
for the time being, out of commission and was moored, with a
skeleton crew, close to a dockyard. Her masts and rigging would
have been removed, and a temporary roof might have been
placed over her to keep out the weather.

5. Political Unions, established to promote the cause of Radical
Reform, were, by now, to be found in many of the towns and
cities in England and Scotland. In 1831, when the agitation for
Reform rose to a climax, a central National Political Union was
set up in London. Some of its members urged that, should the
Lords persist in opposing the Reform Bill, the National Union
should turn itself into a National Assembly and instal a revolutionary government as the French had done in 1791.

6. Cobbett wanted his readers to understand that these were men so
ill-treated that they had not even cleaned themselves up the
previous day in order to go to church.

7. In 1830 Cobbett had moved his business premises from the
Strand to Fleet Street, his offices and shop being established at
No. 11 Bolt-Court. The *Register* of 25 September that year,
informed Cobbett's readers that 'it is curious that *I am now* in
the very house in which Old Dread-Devil Dr Johnson lived and
wrote for so many years'. When Cobbett broke with his family in
1833, he abandoned his Westminster home and lived, when in
London, at Bolt-court.

8. Lady Louisa Paget was the only daughter of the Earl of Uxbridge
who owned rich copper mines in Anglesea and an estate worth
£40,000 a year. She was, none the less, in receipt of government
pensions totalling £600 a year, these being continued in spite of
her two marriages to men of considerable fortune.

9. The 'placeman nursed on sinecurist pap' was John Cam Hob-

house (q.v.) Cobbett nicknamed him 'Little Sancho' because he was a remarkably small man and a constant companion of Burdett, who was a remarkably tall one. This allowed Cobbett to describe him as 'peeping out under Daddy Burdett's arm, like Sancho under the shield of Don Quixote'. Little Sancho's father, Sir Benjamin Hobhouse Bart., had held the largely nominal post of Commissioner of the Board for the Investigation of the Debts of the Nabobs of the Carnatic. His children, therefore, must have been, according to Cobbett, 'nursed on sinecurist pap'. The Hobhouses held shares in Whitbread's brewery, and this, *ipso facto*, turned Little Sancho into the 'brewer privy counsellor'. Cobbett was wrong about Lady Julia Hay. She did, in fact, lose her pension when she married Little Sancho. However, at the time Cobbett wrote, she had six sisters all of whom were pensioned.

10. The house at Holly-Hill in which Lord Cochrane had lived prior to his trial and exile had made him a neighbour of Cobbett's at Botley. The two frequently visited, this being one of the few of Cobbett's friendships which endured. Cobbett was almost certainly right to believe that Cochrane had been wrongly convicted in the De Berenger fraud case, and that he had been the victim of a conspiracy to ruin him led by Croker and his other enemies in the Admiralty, and supported by the Prince Regent and Lord Ellenborough who, as LCJ, delivered a markedly hostile summing-up.

11. The 'tallowman privy counsellor' was Charles Edward Poulett Thomson, later first Baron Sydenham (q.v.) who was the Whig candidate opposing Cobbett at Manchester. His father was the head of the famous firm of Russian merchants, Thomson, Bonar & Co. and as such was responsible for importing Russian tallow.

12. The 'Irish mountebank' was Charles Wilkins (q.v.).

13. Cobbett, when he was in Philadelphia and a High Tory, had roundly abused Thomas Muir (q.v.) in his pamphlet *A Bone to Gnaw for the Democrats, Part Two* (1795). It was somewhat awkward to be reminded of this some forty years later, and above all in Scotland, where Muir was, so far as Scottish Radicals were concerned, a hero and martyr.

14. 'Poor Taffy' was Griffith Jenkins (q.v.).

15. Every government of that period suspected that there was a Jacobinical and revolutionary conspiracy behind each strike and each outbreak of rioting. They all made use of spies and *agents provocateurs* as precautions against a French-style revolution. One of these, Alexander Richmond, had much to do with the

calling of a General Strike in Glasgow in 1820. On the eve of that strike, handbills had been circulated calling on the workers to take up arms. A few weavers and colliers did so, anticipating a general uprising, instead of which they were scattered by cavalry at Bonnymuir. Amongst those hanged for their part in this affair was Alexander Hardie, an ancestor of Keir Hardie. Cobbett had been attacking the government ever since 1817 over its conspiracy theories and its sneaking and un-English use of spies and agents. After Bonnymuir he wrote some of his bitterest articles on these subjects, accusing Liverpool of driving the workers to despair and then using agents to incite them to violence.

16. The 'shuffling fellows' were the Potters, who had once been Cobbett's supporters in Manchester and were now his opponents.

17. Meat in those days came from larger, fatter and more mature animals than any that are slaughtered today. A couple of years earlier Cobbett had described how he had entertained two sportsmen to breakfast at his farm at Barn Elm. The two had eaten, along with a suet pudding and a great many other things, 'about four pounds of solid fat bacon, without a morsel of lean to it, but exquisitely good, rosy as a cherry and transparent as glass'.

18. It was rare for Cobbett to praise any public building built subsequent to the Reformation. Wren's St Pauls was a 'great, ugly, unmeaning mass of stone' and the Prince Regent's Pavilion at Brighton was 'an ugly square box out of which several onion-shaped and turnip-shaped excrescences had sprouted'.

GREENOCK   pp. 56 to 65

1. The Norfolk Petition of 1823 was the first of many such Cobbett helped to organise in the farming counties at that time of great agricultural distress. He came close at that time to forming what has never yet disturbed the pattern of British politics, which is a 'Country' or 'Farmers'' Party. These petitions were presented at county meetings requisitioned by Cobbett, and their demands foreshadowed those outlined later and in greater detail in the Manchester Lectures.

2. This was Normandy Farm at Ash in West Surrey, which he had taken on a long lease the previous year.

3. Cobbett may have been one of the first politicians, but he has by no means been the last to demand that Parliament should keep nine to five office hours. It was not, in his case, as it has been

with others since, that he insisted on Members having no other occupation. He himself had books to write and a newspaper and seed business to run. It was rather that he was accustomed to rising with the sun and going to bed within a short while of its setting, and he believed that no one could attend efficiently to anything who did otherwise. The 'victualler' referred to was Bellamy whose coffee house was contained under the same roof as the Commons. Cobbett insisted that the presence of such a place upstairs disrupted the business of the House and encouraged drunkenness among the Members who were constantly going up and down the stairs for refreshment. Legislation, he argued, could never be properly undertaken by candlelight and to the clinking of brandy bottles.

4. The 'Leghorn' hats and bonnets most women then wore in summer were so called because the straw for their manufacture was imported from Italy, home-grown straw being considered too coarse for that purpose. Cobbett was sent a straw hat which had been made in America, not from straw, but from grasses which had been dried, bleached and plaited. He soon worked out that the same grasses grew in England and that an industry that would support thousands of cottage women could be built up around the harvesting, drying and bleaching of such grasses and plaiting them into material milliners could use instead of Italian straw. He wrote a great deal about this in the *Register* and in such of his works as *Cottage Economy* and *Rural Rides*. He was delighted when the Royal Society of Arts awarded him a silver medal for his work on this matter, and even more delighted when two Orkney crofters visited him in London to tell him that there were hundreds of Orkney women earning a considerable amount of money out of his 'straw-plait' discovery.

5. This section was published as a separate article in the *Register* under the heading of 'Governing of Scotland'.

6. The reference is to the 'Ely mutiny' affair, for writing about which Cobbett was convicted of seditious libel and imprisoned in Newgate for two years.

7. Cobbett was an early example of a politician treating politics as a branch of economics, and economics as an exercise in statistics. Whether the figures were concerned with great causes, such as the growth of the National Debt or the price, over the centuries, of the gallon loaf, or whether they dealt with such a minor political argument as the treatment of the Trinity-house pensioners, he generally went for the statistics first and built his arguments and fought his political battles on a solid foundation of figures.

8. One of the most interesting and charming of all Cobbett's lesser works was *The Emigrant's Guide*, which he published in 1829. This dealt with the experiences of several of the labourers who had emigrated from Kent and Sussex to the United States. The work has never, unfortunately, been re-published and can now generally be found only in the statute libraries.

9. It is easy enough to read humbug into this passage since, for most of his life, Cobbett's England had stopped this side of the Tyne and the Mersey, and his Britain this side of the Tweed. But the reasoning behind the passage is clear, in spite of the humbug. Cobbett was concerned for Scotland, not for Scotland's sake, but England's. He feared that the example of Scotland would be copied in England and so, to prevent the contagion spreading, he had to concern himself with the wrongs done to the Scots.

PAISLEY   pp. 65 to 77

1. Cobbett's ignorance of Scotland was showing. No Scot would agree that his country was divided in this way along this line.

2. 'Van's' pamphlet, published in 1796, was called *An Enquiry into the State of the Finances of Great Britain*. When Cobbett returned to England in 1800, he would have approved of its arguments, for he was then, as Vansittart was, a Pittite and an anti-Jacobin. As such, his writings in America had assured him of a place in that small group of talented writers in the Tory cause which included such men as Canning and Vansittart. They had all, at that time, stood on an equal footing, although Cobbett, if anything, had already created a reputation for himself as the better pamphleteer and polemicist. But Canning had gone on to become Prime Minister, Vansittart had become a Chancellor of the Exchequer and Cobbett was still endeavouring to get into Parliament after thirty years in which, to a very large extent, both political and worldly success had eluded him. It would have been a part of human nature for an element of personal rancour to be added to his hatred of these men who had once been his colleagues and had since become his political opponents and enjoyed the fruits of office that might have been his.

3. Cobbett became a Radical for economic rather than egalitarian or doctrinal reasons. He believed, oddly enough, that Radicalism must inevitably lead to less government, cheaper government and sound money. One of his principal reasons for desert-

ing the Tories had been his belief that Pitt's inflationary economic and fiscal policies were bringing greater ruin to the country than ever the French could. Those policies had, by 1811, led to such a fall in the value of bank notes that a Bullion Committee had recommended to Parliament that they should all be withdrawn within a period of three years, and that the country should return to the gold standard. It was this recommendation that Vansittart, then Secretary of the Treasury, had spoken against and eventually defeated.

In 1819 Peel's Bill once again provided for a return to cash payments over a period of three years. But, when that period had elapsed, such a reduction in the amount of money in circulation had clearly become impossible and Vansittart, then Chancellor of the Exchequer, passed an amending Act which allowed bank notes of smaller denominations to remain legal tender.

4. The editor of the *Scotsman* at that time was Charles Maclaren (q.v.).

5. Before the introduction of the penny post in 1840, Members of both Houses of Parliament could send ten letters and receive fifteen every day free of charge. It was a valuable privilege which was frequently made use of by their friends. All the Member needed to do was to sign his name on the cover and it was then 'franked'. That is, it could go anywhere in the kingdom, irrespective of who sent it, without any payment.

6. Mr Spiers (Speirs) had, in Reform and Radical terms, married into the purple, as was entirely fitting for 'the oldest reformer'. Laurence, second Baron Dundas had been one of the pioneers of Reform and, although William Wentworth, second Earl Fitzwilliam, had once been a Pittite Whig, he had grown more Radical with age and had finally won Cobbett's approval when he was dismissed from the Lord Lieutenancy of the West Riding for presiding at a meeting at which the Manchester magistrates had been censured for their conduct in the Peterloo affair. Wentworth was, thereafter, enrolled in the Radical's Book of Martyrs.

HAMILTON   pp. 78 to 80

1. 'My corn' was Maize, or Indian Corn, which Cobbett attempted to popularize as a grain crop in England, he having obtained the seed of a French strain which he found would ripen in his Kensington nursery. He wrote a great deal about the virtues of this

crop and distributed seed of his own growing widely throughout the country. The enthusiasm he engendered in the farming community waned when it was discovered that the grain could not be relied upon to ripen in the British climate. None the less successive generations of English farmers continued to refer to Maize as 'Cobbett's Corn', although they might as well, considering all he had claimed for it, have called it 'Cobbett's Folly'.

2. i.e. Francis Jeffrey (q.v.).
3. It has been impossible to discover what this particular jibe refers to.
4. 'The Regiment' and 'The room' were two terms of radical slang. The first referred to the great collective of placemen and sinecurists, the second to the House of Commons.
5. i.e. Dr. Johnson.
6. Cobbett was eager to show that he had given a fairer account of Scotland, and was less prejudiced against the Scots than the celebrated author of *Journey to the Western Isles*.

NEW LANARK   pp. 81 to 96

1. The 'paper' mentioned was Cobbett's *Important Considerations for the People of this Kingdom*, which was published anonymously in 1803 at a time when the Peace of Amiens had broken down and Napoleon was threatening to invade. What Cobbett had written was, in essence, a stirring call to arms. As such it was given to the government which caused copies to be sent into every parish in England and Wales, there to be read and displayed in every parish church. It was, however, slightly perverse for Cobbett to refer to it thirty years later. It belonged to his unregenerate, Tory, 'warmongering' and anti-Gallican past, when he thought it to be every Briton's duty to defeat the atheistical and 'democratical' French.

2. It is difficult to separate the personal from the political in Cobbett's long and increasingly savage vendetta against Burdett. The two had once been close political allies. But Burdett was an exceedingly rich landowner (he had married the daughter of Coutts the banker), and, as the agitation for Reform grew rougher, Burdett retreated into moderation as rapidly as Cobbett advanced into populism. That, in brief, was the political reason for their split.

But there was also a question of money between them. When Cobbett faced financial ruin because of his imprisonment in Newgate, Burdett had advanced him two sums of £2000 and

£700. Cobbett never repaid him and never admitted the debt. Burdett behaved rather well in the circumstances. When Cobbett finally went bankrupt in 1820, he never filed his claim as a creditor. Human nature being what it is, Cobbett held even this against him.

3. The lady-and-child' jibe referred to the scandal over Burdett's affair with Lady Oxford, whose son, Lord Harley, was commonly believed to be Burdett's bastard. When Burdett sued Lady Oxford's brother, William Scott, in 1811, for repayment of a loan of £5000, the defence advanced was that this had been money paid for the support of Lord Harley.

4. From the first time he put himself forward as a Parliamentary candidate — at Honiton in 1805 — Cobbett had made much of the fact that he would never, under any circumstances, accept public money if elected. From 1824 onwards, however, he never fought an election without asking the public to subscribe to his election fund. That fund, he declared, was needed for three reasons. It would cover his election expenses. It would compensate him, if elected, for what he would lose through not being able to devote all his time to earning his living as a writer, farmer and publisher. It would help him to qualify as a candidate. In those days no one could be elected unless he was in possession of property worth £600 a year if it was a county seat, and £300 if it was a borough one, and after his bankruptcy Cobbett was not always in that position.

The amount he invited the public to subscribe amounted, in his latter years, to £10,000. There were those amongst his enemies who argued that his undertaking never to take public money if elected went oddly with his readiness to take public money in order to get elected.

5. Cobbett, in his Radical years, made much of the fact that he had started life as a ploughboy. But he was never, in any true sense, a farm labourer apart from having worked, as a boy, for his father, who was a middling prosperous farmer and publican. Cobbett had, in fact, been born into what was then the largest and most important class in England, one that stretched, through almot imperceptible gradations, from peasant proprietors to great landowners. He was, as a consequence, so close to being classless that he was as much at his ease with the aristocrats whom he eventually attacked so bitterly as with the chopsticks whose champion he became.

6. Cobbett had long fought for the abolition of Stamp Duties on paper, newspapers and newspaper advertisements, and all the

more bitterly after these had been manipulated to kill off his *Twopenny Register*, the first mass-circulation political weekly in England. His efforts were partly responsible for some easing of these Duties after 1825, although newspapers had to be stamped until 1855. It is probable, however, that such men as Carlile of *The Republican* and Wooler of *The Black Dwarf* achieved more than he did in this respect. They defied the law, issued their papers unstamped, and kept going to prison as a consequence until, in the end, juries refused to convict them.

No one of his day did more than Cobbett in providing 'workmen opportunities of acquiring useful knowledge'. Almost every book he wrote was directed to that purpose. It is worth adding that one of the most effective speeches Cobbett made in Parliament was in favour of a motion to reduce the number of hours children could work in factories. All in all, then, he did as much as any man to further the causes the Radical 'operatives of Glasgow' held so dear.

7. 'All jaw and no Judgement' was 'that nasty palaverer', Brougham.

8. This was unusually coy of Cobbett. His *Political Register* had been, and possibly still was, the most influential and widely-read political weekly in England – perhaps even in Europe.

9. Cobbett was, for those days, an abstemious man, and one who always ate sparingly. On the other hand, he took a great interest in food, and considered himself an excellent judge of the quality of almost anything that could be eaten. He had what could be described as advanced ideas on diet, but retained eighteenth-century tastes for such things as enormous joints and excessively fat meat.

10. At this point the book departs slightly from the account published in the *Register* of 10 November 1832. In the latter, the *Glasgow Chronicle's* account of the dinner given in Cobbett's honour at Glasgow (*see* Appendix A) is given in full. The book, having promised to revert to that account, fails to do so.

NEW MILNE pp. 96 to 114

1. This short passage, written out of chronological order, was for no apparent reason, published in the book but not in the *Register*.

2. The fertile, and then still unspoilt Valley of the Wey.

3. This is a reference to the Tsar Nicholas 1 of Russia, and to his suppression of the Polish uprising of 1830. He had visited Britain

in 1816 in the course of a European tour. 'The present Lord Chancellor' was, of course, Brougham.

4. Owen had taken William Allen and certain other Quakers as his partners at New Lanark, but when he began to embark on schemes for converting the world to co-operation and socialism, these partners took over the running of New Lanark. Owen's connections with that place were finally severed completely in 1828.

5. The 'large building' was Owen's 'New Lanark Institution for the Formation of Character'. He had opened this in 1816 in the hope of proving his theory that men are the products of their environments, and that their characters are 'made for them and not by them.' Cobbett, as can be seen, thought little of Owen for a number of reasons. His common sense made him reject Owen's determinism. Owen's rejection of established religion shocked him. He found his theories of education and moral training laughable. But, above all, he argued that the Utopia Owen sought to construct through co-operation, and on the ruins of capitalism, led men away from their true salvation, which could speedily be achieved, and would only be achieved, through a reform of Parliament,

Both men, many might say, were misled. But Owen's is a more hallowed name than Cobbett's these days.

6. Cobbett, who believed in self-education, did not approve of any school. But ever since he had moved to Bolt-Court he had particularly disapproved of the school situated next door to him. This was of the Lancasterian variety, where a system of 'mutual instruction' was practised and a great deal of noise was created as a consequence, since knowledge was supposed to be acquired by a communal chanting of texts.

7. Robert Owen's theories led him to deny, at least implicitly, the existence of free will. He argued, as Locke had before him and many have since, that men are the products of their social environment, and this, as Cobbett saw it, 'made minds a fiction'.

8. This must be one of the earliest criticisms of education as a form of 'social engineering'.

9. In his earlier days at New Lanark, Robert Owen had succeeded in combining enlightened policies as an employer with running the mills at a profit. As he began to devote more and more of his time and thought to co-operation and socialism he may have laid the foundation of his modern reputation as a prophet and founder of socialism, but he persuaded many of his contemporaries, his partners and Cobbett included, that he was little more than another Millenarian crack-pot.

10. For the great majority of the population home-grown fruit was almost the only fruit they could enjoy in their diet. Cobbett, it should be remembered, carried on a large trade in fruit-tree stocks and grafts, and he had written two gardening books in which fruit growing had been treated as a matter of the greatest importance if the garden was to be any aid towards self-sufficiency and a wholesome diet.

11. The reference is probably to the damage caused by the woolly aphis (*a. lanigera*).

12. There never was, and possibly never will be, a more intensely political animal than Cobbett. He never made the mistake, how-ever, of believing politics to be everything, and he claimed to be prouder of what he had done for agriculture and arboriculture in England and America than he was of anything else he had achieved. 'My efforts have, all my life long . . . been to cause additions to be made to the food, the drink, the raiment of the industrious classes.'

13. They must have been trees of considerable girth, for Cobbett was, in his later years, exceedingly stout. He admitted to riding at eighteen stone, and he was described, after his election to Par-liament, as one of the stoutest men in the House. Cobbett's first act on entering the House had been to measure the bench space available to the six hundred odd Members. When he discovered this amounted to no more than fifteen inches a man he decided that this was quite inadequate as far as he was concerned and accordingly he established himself, contrary to all precedent, on the Front Bench, in the place normally occupied by the Leader of the House.

14. Cobbett, who hated all taxes, hated those on Malt and Hops the most, since they stopped cottagers brewing their own beer from materials they could, for the most part, grow or gather them-selves. He once commented angrily on a snooping Excise man who, seeing wild hops growing in a cottager's hedge, immedi-ately charged him to tax.

15. Descendants of these "wild cattle" have survived on the Hamilton estates, though whether they are of the same wild breed as the more famous herd at Chillingham is not certain.

16. Although Cobbett was insistently and almost prudishly mono-gamous, he had retained, from his soldiering days, a quick eye for a pretty face. In his rides around England he developed a habit of cataloguing the different forms of female beauty according to their different districts, occupations and diets. This somewhat ludicrous exercise eventually led him to conclude that

Welsh girls had harder faces than Sussex ones solely because the
Welsh reared store cattle, whereas in Sussex they fatted them
and then ate them.

17. This should have read Charles II. One might have assumed a
typographical slip were it not that the original version in the
Register is even more adrift historically, for there the passage
runs: 'We went over the bridge called Bothwell-Bridge where the
famous battle was fought between CROMWELL and the Covenanters; or, as Hudibras would have called it, between the land-
saints and the water-saints.'

18. Cobbett was not, for once, blowing his own trumpet unreason-
ably. All contemporary reports describe him, in his private life,
as a pleasant, amiable and soft-spoken man, quite unlike the
hectoring, scurrilous, loud-mouthed one who spoke through the
columns of the *Register*.

19. Several cartoonists, in America as well as in Britain, had por-
trayed Cobbett in various guises as the agent of the Devil.

20. When Peel's Bill for a return to cash payments was passed in
1819, Cobbett declared that it would prove impossible to
withdraw all paper money without bringing ruin to the country.
He added that, if he were proved wrong, he 'would give Castlereagh leave to put me on a gridiron and broil me alive, while
Sidmouth stirs the fire, and Canning stands by making a jest of
my groans'. When the Small Notes Act had to be passed in 1822
in order to keep a sufficient amount of currency in circulation,
Cobbett claimed to have been justified, and thereafter adopted
the Gridiron as his symbol.

21. Brougham had been one of the founders of that Society for the
Diffusion of Useful Knowledge which Peacock had satirised as
The Steam Intellect Society. Cobbett derided it as part of the
'hedukashional' system designed to reconcile the poor to their
lot. The *Penny Magazine* which was the Society's chief instrument, was greatly resented by publishers and booksellers as an
attempt to undersell them in a developing market.

22. Establishments which had been purpose-built as barracks were
rare in Britain before 1792. Until then troops had either been
kept in royal castles and forts, or in tented or hutted camps, or
billeted on the civilian population. The threat of invasion led
Pitt to embark on a programme of barrack-building to house the
greatly enlarged army needed to defend the country. Cobbett
came to look on such barracks as symbols of the hated 'Pitt
system'.

23. Mr Archibald Hamilton's father, General Hamilton of Dalzell,

was, at that time, still alive. He died in 1834 at the age of ninety-one. His son, despite Cobbett's 'fervent prayers', died in the same year at the age of forty-one.

24. In those days, land close to a large town would generally be in good order irrespective of its intrinsic fertility. The carts and waggons taking produce in to the townspeople would, as often as not, return loaded with the night soil and stable wastes of the town which would be used to enrich the surrounding farmland. In an age when manure of any sort was always a limiting factor in crop growing, this was a much valued benefit.

25. Cobbett was remembering an old grudge. After the savagely fought Coventry election of 1820, Cobbett, who had lost, withdrew to the Bull's Head Inn at Meriden, some five miles from Coventry, in order to recover from a severe cold which had troubled him throughout the election campaign. The Earl of Aylesford, who was the local great landowner, threatened the innkeeper with the loss of his custom and his innkeeper's licence if Cobbett was allowed to remain at the Bull's Head. This was followed by a letter to a Coventry newspaper, signed by Aylesford and most of his tenants, expressing astonishment and disgust at the conduct of the Proprietors of the Bull's Head Inn in having entertained Cobbett for so long a time, 'contrary to our general feeling and loyal spirit'.

   Cobbett replied in the *Register* with a *Letter to the Earl of Aylesford*. After giving his version of what had happened at Meriden, he added, '*You* may come and reside at the Inn at *Botley*, and not a soul in the country will either know or care when you come or when you go away; or will ever hear who or what, you are. What a poor thing, in the creation, *you are*, when compared to me! What an insignificant thing!' Cobbett, one would think, had the better of it overall.

CARLISLE   pp 115 to 122

1. Cobbett, in fact disliked music. He was once very cross when, on arriving at Gloucester, he discovered 'what should there be here, but one of those scandalous and beastly fruits of the system, called a MUSIC-MEETING'.

2. The coat that covered the great Radical agitator also covered a markedly conservative countryman, and the two seldom quarrelled with each other, or even thought they were keeping strange company. Joseph Hume (q.v.) had long argued in Parliament for national and standardised weights and measures to replace the

varying regional ones that were still in use. He was successful
when, in 1824, the Weights and Measures Act was passed, and
the Imperial yard, pound and gallon were declared the only
legal standards. Any contract or bargain in which other meas-
urements were used could be declared null and void. Thus, to
the annoyance of more people than Cobbett, local and traditional methods of weighing and measuring disappeared. Our recent
adoption of the metric system has probably brought as much
annoyance to as many people.

3. The Mechanics' Institutes which began to appear in many of the
cities and industrial towns after 1820, had been founded, in the
first instance, by working class men for working class men. The
Society for the Diffusion of Useful Knowledge, which had been
started by such eminently middle class men as Brougham, Birkbeck and Hume, sought to take over the Institutes in order to instil
sound Benthamite and 'feelosofical' principles into the lower
orders. It was, needless to say, a 'reform' which Cobbett resisted.

4. 'The Old Lady' — i.e. The Bank of England.

5. Richard Potter (q.v.) was the Radical candidate at Wigan.
Cobbett's crude 'bull-baiting' of him referred to current problems over which they had disagreed and quarrelled. Thus — 'The
Whig War' was the one that threatened to break out with France
over the British government's support for the newly acquired
independence of Belgium. Cobbett disapproved of the British
nominee, Leopold of Saxe-Coburg, who had been placed on the
throne as King of the Belgians, and thought it best for the peace
of Europe if Belgium were once again made part of France, as it
had been from 1793 to 1815.

'The Church Reform' referred to the changes brought about
by the Ecclesiastical Commission Act of 1831, which Cobbett objected to because of the powers of control over Church revenues
given to the Commissioners.

'The expansion of the currency' is probably an ironical reference to Cobbett's bugbear, Peel's Bill of 1819.

6. Although Joseph Hume had his home at Sommerton Hall in
Norfolk, had made his fortune in India, and spent most of his
time at Westminster, he had still been born in Montrose. This,
in Cobbett's opinion, made him another 'renegado Scot'. Moreover, he was a Benthamite and one who failed to hate the Whigs
as heartily as Cobbett expected Radicals to do.

7. When it came to the commoner weaknesses of the flesh, such as
lechery, gluttony and insobriety, Cobbett was very proud to be
what, in other circumstances, he despised — a Puritan.

8. The 'pensioner' was the new King of the Belgians, Leopold of Saxe-Coburg. On his marriage to the Princess Charlotte in 1816 he had, as husband of the heiress to the British Throne, been voted a pension of £50,000 a year by Parliament. He surrendered part of this pension when he departed, in 1830, to become King of the Belgians. But, to Cobbett's disgust, he kept part of his British pension in order, as he said, to maintain his English establishment.

9. The Duke of Newcastle's nominee at Leeds was Michael Sadler, who failed to get elected.

10. Brougham's nominee was Thomas Babington Macaulay, later Lord Macaulay. He was a 'placeman' because he had previously sat for the rotten borough of Calne and had recently become a commissioner in bankruptcy. His father, Zachary Macaulay, had been 'in our pay' only to the extent that he had once been Governor of Sierra Leone.

11. Cobbett never returned to Scotland. He did, in 1834, at last manage to visit Ireland, but no book resulted from that trip, although his *Ten Letters to Charles Marshall*, written from Ireland, were published in the *Register*. The Scottish tour, therefore, was the last excursion of the man G. K. Chesterton referred to as 'the horseman of the shires' to be recorded in a book. It must therefore rank, so far as posterity is concerned, as the last of Cobbett's Rides.

OLDHAM and DAVENTRY   pp. 122 to 125

1. At that time the truth of a statement was no defence in a prosecution for criminal libel. though it was in a civil action for libel. The anomaly was eventually removed under 6 & 7 Victoria (1843).

2. The *Register* article went: 'I will, however, do it in a more complete manner than I have been able to do in the *Register*. The volume shall be compact and cheap, well printed and on good paper; and it will live long after the whole of the "feelosofers" and all their stupid and tyrannical supporters shall be rotten and forgotten.

The summary of this speechifying tour is as follows:

Speeches out of doors to great assemblages of people 25
Lectures to persons in-doors 50
Speeches at dinners 3
                                                                                                  ___
                                                                                                  78

I left London on the 27. of August, so that I shall have been eighty-seven days from home. I have written, during the same time, thirteen *Registers*, each containing more matter written by myself than is usually contained in a two-shilling pamphlet. During the same time, I have travelled one thousand four hundred and sixty-four miles, and have slept in five different cities and twenty-four different towns; and, if that is not a pretty good eighty-seven days' work, let the gin-drinking *"feelosofers"* look out for better. To the *"Temperance Societies"* who would cut my throat because I call them despicable drivelling quacks, this one fact is worth more than all their volumes of trash and all their botheration meetings; namely, that all this prodigious labour has been rendered light, only, because I have eaten very sparingly, during all the time, and have never drunk a drop of wine, of spirits, of the beer kind, or of the cider kind; and that my drink has been, very little in quantity in the first place, and in kind, tea, milk, or water.

WM. COBBETT

HIGHLANDS of SCOTLAND   pp 125 to 129

1. This account of the Highlands, amounting to a postscript, was never published in the *Register*.
2. No one could have disliked factory processes and machinery more than Cobbett. But when it came to mechanical gadgets, there was something of the White Knight about him. The American stoves which he had seen in the course of his travels, struck him as something he ought to introduce into Britain, where they would, by replacing the open hearth, permit of a useful saving in fuel. He had a London blacksmith construct prototypes of such a stove, and he used the *Register* to advertise its merits.
3. Cobbett made much, in later life, of a game he had played with his brothers as a boy. It had entailed his being bundled up inside his smock and then being rolled down a sand-hill 'as steep as a house roof'. It had been, he insisted, a better form of character training than anything provided at Winchester College or Westminster School. It was also eminently suitable training for a future Member of Parliament, something he had been trying to become for the past twenty-five years. It would also produce better Prime Ministers, for Cobbett was not so modest as to believe that any Prime Minister that century had been as good a

man as himself. Indeed, when Goderich ('Prosperity' Robinson), resigned in 1827 after a remarkably short tenure of that office, Cobbett wrote to the King suggesting that he should be his replacement, and there was some element of seriousness in the jest.

APPENDIX A   pp 130 to 133

1. Cobbett always maintained, and probably with some justification, that on at least four occasions the government of the day would have given him wealth, or its equivalent in position or power, in exchange for some sacrifice of his independence or his principles. The first occasion was in Philadelphia in 1798, when Liston, the British Minister to the United States, offered to reward him, on behalf of the British government, for the part he had played as Peter Porcupine in advancing the British cause. When he returned to England in 1800 the Tories offered him the title and presses of *The True Briton*, one of the two government newspapers. In 1806, when the Ministry of All Talents was formed, William Windham, then Cobbett's patron, is reputed to have offered him an Under-Secretaryship. Finally, in 1817, an emissary from Lord Sidmouth is believed to have offered Cobbett £10,000 if he would give up the *Political Register* and retire into private life. Cobbett chose exile in the United States instead.

2. William Huskisson (1770–1830) was a man whom Cobbett disliked for a variety of reasons, not least because he had been one of Canning's followers. This had, in due course, ensured him the posts of President of the Board of Trade followed by that of Colonial Secretary. Cobbett could never forget that, at the turn of the century, Canning and he had been fellow writers in the Tory cause, and that he, at that time, had been thought at least Canning's equal. Huskisson, incidently, was the first man ever to be run over and killed by a train.

APPENDIX C   pp 144 to 156

1. When Cobbett fled to the United States in 1817, he took up his residence at Hyde Park Farm on Long Island. He was visited there by a number of American, French and British travellers, all eager to interview the great man in his exile. One of the last was a certain Thomas Fearon, who later published a candid, if not unflattering account of his visit in his book *Sketches of*

America. What he put into that account so infuriated Cobbett that he attached a postscript to his own book, *A Year's Residence in the United States of America,* in which he attacked Fearon with even more than his customary brutality. One of the passages in Fearon's book Cobbett had particularly objected to ran, 'He feels no hesitation in praising himself, and evidently believes that he is eventually destined to be the Atlas of the British nation.' It was probably this that the *Fife Herald* journalist had in mind when he referred to him as 'quite Sir Oracle'.

BIOGRAPHICAL INDEX

Cobbett, as the reader will have noticed, used names somewhat erratically. He would refer to a man by his surname as often as by his title, and by a nickname or an opprobrious description as often as either. In this way the Earl of Ripon would become 'Prosperity Robinson' and Baron Brougham and Vaux 'that nasty palaverer'. In what follows I have, wherever I thought it might help the reader, followed Cobbett rather than Debrett and included nicknames as well as proper ones. The very brief biographical details have been extracted from the *DNB, Chambers Biographical Dictionary,* the far more detailed Biographical Index G D H Cole provided for his three-volume edition of *Rural Rides* and my own *Great Cobbett: The Noblest Agitator.*

ABERCROMBY, James 1776–1858   79
Later Lord Dunfermline. Whig politician, Speaker 1835.

ADDINGTON,
See Sidmouth

ALDERSON, Sir Edmund 1787–1857   10
Judge of the Common Pleas. Sent to the Eastern and Southern Counties in 1830 as a member of the Special Commission trying those arrested during the riots of the 'Captain Swing' rebellion.

ALTHORP, John Charles 1782–1845   46
Viscount Althorp, later third Earl Spencer. Whig politician. Chancellor of the Exchequer and Leader of the House in Grey's administration.

ANGLESEY, Henry William Paget 1768–1854   46
Son of the first Earl of Uxbridge. Created Marquis of Anglesey for his services at Waterloo, where he commanded the cavalry. Later second Earl of Uxbridge.

ATTWOOD, Thomas 1783–1856   103
A well-known Birmingham banker, economist and Radical Member
of Parliament whose views on the currency Cobbett strongly opposed.
The two had a public debate in August 1832 which went on for two
days.

AYLESFORD, Heneage Finch 1786–1859   114,117n
Fifth Earl. A great landowner with estates in Kent, Surrey and
Warwickshire.

BAINE, Messrs   65,66,67,68
Merchants in Greenock.

BARING, Sir Thomas 1772–1848   23,121
Second Baronet. Grandson of the German, John Baring, who had set
up as a cloth manufacturer in Honiton, and son of Sir Francis Baring
(1740–1810) who established the great banking house of Baring
Brothers. Cobbett had a number of reasons for disliking the Barings,
and made full use of every one of them.

BAXTER, Edward c. 1770–1856   48,49,50,58,79,90,119
A Manchester merchant, and a prominent, albeit 'moderate'
Reformer. As such he was one of the 'low, filthy wretches at
Manchester' associated with the Potters.

BELHAVEN AND STENTON, Lord, Robert Montgomery Hamilton   105
1793–1868
Eighth baron.

BELL, David ?–1863   52,54,55,56,65,79,94,99,104,109,112
A well-known Glasgow manufacturer and Radical. One of the
founders of the Glasgow Royal Exchange. Cobbett's host during his
stay in Glasgow.

BISSETT, Messrs   78
The Bissett's were silk-manufacturers and merchants established in
Paisley and other locations around Glasgow.

BLACK, John ('Doctor') 1783–1855   12,19,20,22,29,91,123
A self-educated, self-made Scot who eventually became editor of the
Morning Chronicle, at that time a leading Radical newspaper.
Cobbett, who disliked him because he was a Benthamite, tended to
sneer at his intellectual pretensions, which was why he generally gave
him the quite gratuitous title of 'Doctor'.

BLANTYRE, Robert Walter Stewart 1775–1830   66
Eleventh Lord Blantyre. Soldier and landowner.

BONTINE, Robert Cunninghame Cunninghame Graham   77
1799–1863
The eldest son of the Grahams of Gartmore took the name of Bontine in respect of the estate of Ardock until inheriting from his father. This Bontine was Radical candidate for Renfrew at the time of Cobbett's Tour.

BOSWELL, James 1740–95   80
Lawyer, man-of-letters and celebrated biographer and companion of Doctor Johnson.

BOYES, John of Owselbury   23,49
'Farmer' Boyes. A small farmer whose trial for the part he played during the 1830 agricultural riots became something of a cause célèbre. The jury refused to find him guilty, whereupon Sergeant Wilde (q.v.) who was prosecuting secured a re-trial in a different court and Boyes was sentenced to transportation for seven years.

BRODIE, Mrs Anna   65,77
Wife of Rev Alexander Brodie and daughter of John Walter the First, the coal merchant and jobbing printer who founded The Times in 1785. Ownership of that paper was, by his will, vested in members of his family, principally Anna Brodie, Fanny Wraight (q.v.) and John Walter the Second (q.v.). Cobbett, who hated The Times, liked to think that the two sisters were responsible for what the paper published, which was very far from the case, it being managed and edited by their brother 'Jack' Walter until he retired into politics and handed the management over to Thomas Barnes.

BROUGHAM, Henry 1778–1868   xxii,xxviii,11,15,19,22,48,50,57,
                               85,91,104,111,123,173n,176n,178n
First Baron Brougham and Vaux: Politician, author, educationalist and polymath. A Radical Whig, he was Lord Chancellor under Grey. He and Cobbett had both acted as advisers to Queen Caroline at the time of the Bill of Pains and Penalties, and they had fallen out over how her defence should be conducted. Thereafter there was no politician Cobbett disliked more. Brougham was only half a Scot: nevertheless he seemed to Cobbett the archetypal 'renegado Scotch feelosofer' so often mentioned and abused in this work.

BROWN, Timothy   84
A wealthy paper merchant and a prominent Reformer. He stood surety for Cobbett when the latter had served his sentence in Newgate. In 1820, when Cobbett went bankrupt, Brown remitted the £2000 owed him.

BRUCE, James 1730–94   47
The famous explorer, known as 'the Abyssinian' because of his travels
in that country. Author of *Travels to Discover the Sources of the
Nile.*

BUCCLEUCH, Walter Francis Scott, Fifth Duke. 1806–84   122

BURDETT, Sir Francis 1770–1844   15,16,22,46,79,84,90,171n
'Old Daddy Burdett', 'Sir Glory'. Leader of the Radicals in Parliament, and one of the men who converted Cobbett to Radicalism. He
eventually withdrew into moderation, Whiggery and, in the end,
Conservatism. Cobbett quarrelled bitterly with him, both on account
of this backsliding, and over the money Burdett had either lent or
given him.

BURNET, Bishop Gilbert 1643–1715   108
The Whig churchman, author and politician. Wrote *History of the
Reformation* and *History of My Own Time.* Cobbett was always rude
about him because he was a Scot, a Whig, and was thought to be in
some way responsible for the 'funding system' — i.e. the National
Debt.

BURNS, Robert 1759–96   120
The poet. Cobbett heartily approved of his political views, loved and
quoted his poetry, but deplored his fondness for women and whisky.

CANNING, George 1770–1827   9,158n,169n
Tory politician, versifier and, for a few months, Prime Minister.
Cobbett had collaborated with him in his Anti-Jacobin days, and had
attacked him ever afterwards.

CASTLEREAGH, Robert Stewart 1769–1822   69
Viscount Castlereagh, later second Marquis of Londonderry. First a
Whig, later a Tory politician. Foreign Secretary from 1812. Cut his
throat with a penknife, to the great joy of Cobbett and all other
Radicals.

CHADWICK, John   38
An Edinburgh merchant who helped arrange Cobbett's stay in
Edinburgh.

CLEMENT, William   84
Newspaper proprietor. Part-owner of *The Observer.* Owned
Morning Chronicle 1821–34. Was for a time publisher of Cobbett's
Political Register until the two fell out over money.

COBB, Captain Nathan   69
Commanded the packet boat *Hercules* on which Cobbett returned to
England from the USA in 1819.

COCHRANE, Sir Alexander Inglis 1758–1832   105
Admiral and uncle of Lord Cochrane (q.v.)

COCHRANE, Thomas, Lord 1775–1860   45,48,166n
Later tenth Earl of Dundonald. Next to Nelson the most famous
seaman of the period. Radical Member of Parliament and close
friend of Cobbett's. Imprisoned in 1814 for his alleged complicity in
the De Berenger swindle. Dismissed from the British Navy, he
commanded the Chilean, Brazilian and Greek Navies in their Wars
of Independence, was re-instated in the British Navy in 1832 and
made Rear-Admiral of the United Kingdom in 1854.

COOK, Henry, of Micheldever 1811–31   23,49
'Poor Cook'. An agricultural labourer who was hanged for striking
Bingham Baring during the agricultural riots of 1830. Since he did
no more than stove Baring's hat in, the sentence seemed excessive.
The legend is that snow never lies on Cook's grave in Micheldever.

COULSON, Walter 1794–1860   15,22
'The Reporther'. Started his career as secretary to Jeremy Bentham,
which was one reason why Cobbett disliked him. After a time as
parliamentary reporter to the *Morning Chronicle* he was made editor
of the *Globe*, 'that rumble-tumble of filth and beastly ignorance', so
providing Cobbett with another reason for abusing him. Two more
reasons were provided by the fact that he was a Poor Law
Commissioner and supported Brougham in founding The Society for
the Diffusion of Useful Knowledge.

CRAIG, Hugh   116
A merchant and Baillie of Kilmarnock and a prominent leader of
local Radicals. Cobbett breakfasted with him.

CRANSTOUN, George 1771–1850   99
Later Lord Corehouse. A prominent Scottish lawyer who was
appointed a Lord of Session in 1826.

CREEVEY, Thomas 1768–1838   12,159n,162n
A minor and somewhat seedy Whig politician now remembered only
as the author of the *Creevey Papers*. He was at one time friendly with
Cobbett whom he visited in Newgate. Later, however, he referred to
him as 'a foul-mouthed malignant fellow' and proposed to stand
against him at Oldham.

DALE, David 1739-1806   100
The celebrated Glaswegian industrialist, banker and philanthropist.
He founded the New Lanark Mills in conjunction with Richard
Arkwright, these being taken over by Robert Owen when he married
Dale's daughter.

DENMAN, Thomas 1779-1854   10,49,57,121
First Baron. Lawyer and Whig politician. Grey appointed him
Attorney-General in 1830 and Lord Chief Justice in 1832. Denman
was once the darling of the Radicals because of his brilliant defences
of such as Queen Caroline, Burdett, Cochrane and Carlile. He
became an ogre to the Left, however, when he had, as Attorney-
General, to prosecute the farm labourers involved in the Captain
Swing riots, and Cobbett for his articles concerning those riots.

DONKIN, Armorer 1779-1851   9
A Newcastle solicitor whose gardens and plantations Cobbett greatly
admired, not least, perhaps, because Mr Donkin had followed the
methods Cobbett had laid down in his works *The Woodlands* and
The English Gardener.

DOUGLAS, Archibald, of Mauldslie Castle   102,105,109
He was Cobbett's host.

DOUGLAS, John, of Barlock.   56,65
Lawyer and Radical politician. Stood unsuccessfully for Glasgow in
the 1832 Election. Acted as one of Cobbett's guides in Glasgow.

DRAYTON, Edmund   58
'The Auctioneer'. An auctioneer who was involved in the unsavoury
case of Griffith ('Taffy') Jenkins, (q.v.)

DUN, B Finlay 1775-1853   33,36
A music teacher in Edinburgh who was secretary to the North-
Western Political Union and organised the Edinburgh Address to
Cobbett.

DUNDAS, Henry 1742-1811   49
First Viscount Melville. Pitt's closest friend and the 'uncrowned king
of Scotland' prior to his impeachment in 1805. It was his case that
first set Cobbett off on his lifelong task of smelling out corruption in
high places.

DUDLEY, Rev Sir Henry Bate 1745-1824   68
A fairly notorious parson, politician, journalist and sportsman who
was made a baronet by the Prince Regent in 1813. Playwright,
pamphleteer, and one-time editor of the *Morning Post* and the

Morning Herald. He shared Cobbett's love of coursing, and once gave him a brace of greyhounds.

ELDON, John Scott 1751–1838   39,65
First Earl. Lawyer and Tory politician. Lord Chancellor 1801–27. Thought responsible for much of the repressive legislation of the period and a great sinecurist. But he did advise against prosecuting Cobbett over the failed court martial case of 1792, and he gave him an early discharge from bankruptcy in 1820, neither of which acts did anything to endear him to Cobbett.

ELGIN, Thomas Bruce 1766–1841   40
Seventh Earl. Diplomat, art lover and landowner in the county of Fife. Remembered principally for his acquisition of the 'Elgin' Marbles, subsequently sold to the nation and a present cause of some chagrin to Greek Socialists.

ELLIS, George 1753–1815   9
Scholar, poet and satirist. Co-founder with Canning of the *Anti-Jacobin*. Cobbett, on his return from the United States in 1800, had once toiled with him in the same Tory vineyards.

ERSKINE, Thomas 1750–1823   46
First Baron Clackmannan. Brother of the Eleventh Earl of Buchan. A lawyer noted for his forensic skills and for his failings as Lord Chancellor. A one-time Jacobin sympathiser, he defended Horne Tooke, Hadfield, Tom Paine and other Radicals. Cobbett, who greatly enjoyed making fun of him, found his title of Baron Clackmannan has such a ridiculous ring to it that he dragged it in whenever he could. As Hazlitt put it in his *Essay on Mr Cobbett,* 'What could be better than his pestering Erskine year after year with his second title of Baron Clackmannan?'

FIELDEN, John 1784–1849   xx,xxi
A member of the firm of Fielden Brothers of Todmorden, one of the largest textile firms of the period. He was MP for Oldham from 1832–47 and had Cobbett, for a time, as his fellow Member, both of them standing as Radicals. John Morgan Cobbett, William's son, was his son-in-law and sat for a time in his father's place as the other Member for Oldham. Fielden was one of William's greatest admirers and someone with whom not even William could contrive to quarrel.

FOLKESTONE, Viscount
See Radnor.

FORDYCE, John 1738–1800   12
When he ws Receiver-General of the Land Tax in Scotland he had

the misfortune to be out in his accounts by the sum of £100,000. Creevey had at one time thought of moving a vote of censure on him for this, but withdrew it when it become apparent that the deficiency was not Fordyce's fault. Fordyce was married to the Duke of Gordon's sister-in-law.

FOX, Mrs Elizabeth Bridget 1750–1842   80
As 'Mrs Armistead' she was Charles James Fox's mistress until he married her in secret in 1795. The secret was revealed in 1802 and when Fox died in 1806 she was awarded a pension of £1,200 a year. Since she did not die until she was 92 she proved a considerable expense to the nation.

FRERE, John Hookham 1769–1841   9
Diplomat, poet, wit, friend of Canning's and contributor to the *Anti-Jacobin*. A friend of Cobbett's in the latter's Tory days.

FULTON & SON   78
The Fultons were Paisley worthies engaged in muslin manufacture, banking and other activities in Paisley and Glasgow.

GAWLER, Henry 1764–1852   22
Brother of 'Duke' Gawler, barrister and a Poor Law Commissioner, he acted as Burdett's agent, for which reason alone Cobbett disliked him.

GAWLER, John 1765–1842   xxviii,15,16,160n
'Duke Gawler'. Second cousin to William Ker fourth Duke of Roxburghe, who wanted to make him his heir. George III gave him the right to assume the name Bellenden Ker in 1804, but when the fourth Duke died in 1805 his will was put aside after a deal of litigation and the estate and title went to Sir James Innes. Gawler was Burdett's second when he fought his duel with Paull during the Westminster election of 1807, and anyone connected with Burdett was unlikely to get fair treatment from Cobbett.

GERRALD, Joseph 1763–96   98
Was, with Margarot (q.v.) sent by the London Corresponding Society to the second Scottish Convention held in Edinburgh in 1793. He was one of those tried and sentenced by the Lord Justice Clerk (Robert M'Queen q.v.) to transportation and he died of consumption in Botany Bay shortly after landing there. Together with Muir and Skirving these men were thought of as the earlier martyrs of the Reform movement.

GILLON, William Downe 1801–46
Was at that time the Radical Member for Selkirk and Falkirk Burghs.

GRAY, John Boyle   56,65
A prominent Glasgow lawyer and Radical who accompanied Cobbett on part of his Tour.

GREY, Charles 1764–1845   xxii,xxviii,xxx,38,48,49,50,57,
                                                                  81,110,111
Second Earl. Whig politician. As Lord Howick he was Foreign Secretary and Leader of the House in 1806 and was Prime Minister from 1830 to 1834, during which time he got the Reform Bill through Parliament. He was almost the only Whig Cobbett had any respect for, although he could never forgive him for ordering his prosecution in 1831.

GREY, General Henry George 1766–1845   9
Brother of the above. He thought Cobbett a 'humbug'.

GURNEY, Richard Hanbury 1783–1854   16,85
A member of the Norfolk Quaker family who founded that Gurney's Bank whose failure in 1866 caused a market panic. Cobbett disliked bankers, Quakers, and any friend of Burdett's and 'Dick' Gurney qualified on all three counts.

GUTSELL, James   xxv
A one-time tailor who became Cobbett's secretary and general factotum in the last years of the latter's life. He was probably the 'amanuensis' mentioned in the text.

HADDINGTON, Thomas Hamilton 1780–1858   16
Ninth Earl. A Tory peer who was at one time First Lord of the Admiralty and Lord Privy Seal. He was, according to Greville, a politician of very little merit or importance.

HALSEY, Mrs Sarah   107
Was married to Joseph Whately the MP for St Albans, who assumed her name.

HAMILTON, Archibald James of Dalzell 1793–1834   102,103,104,
                                                          105,108,109,112,176n
A soldier and landowner who held strong Radical views and was, in addition, an Owenite. The son of the General Hamilton referred to in the text.

HAMILTON, Alexander Hamilton Douglas 1767–1852   80,83,106
Tenth Duke. A patron of the arts and, like his father-in-law, William

Beckford, fond of extravagant architectural conceits. These included Hamilton Palace and the vast mausoleum built to contain his sarcophagus.

HAMILTON, David 1768–1843   94
The celebrated Glasgow architect who, amongst other buildings, designed the Palace of the Duke of Hamilton and the Glasgow Exchange.

HASTINGS, Francis Augustus George Rawdon-Hastings 1808–44 144
Second Marquis. His mother had been Countess of Loudon in her own right and it was from her that he inherited Loudon Castle.

HOBHOUSE, John Cam 1786–1859   16,46,48,49,57,60,77,90,165n
Later first Baron Broughton. 'Little Sancho', 'the brewer privy-councillor'. Laywer, Radical politician, and friend of Byron. Wrote *Journey Through Albania with Lord Byron*. His close association with Burdett made him one of Cobbett's favourite targets.

HOLLAND, Henry Richard Vassall Fox 1773–1840   13,53,99
Third Baron. Whig peer, nephew of Charles James Fox and husband of the celebrated Holland House hostess. He was one of the few Whigs Cobbett respected and he had asked for his protection before he fled to the USA in 1817.

HOWICK, Henry George Grey   17,22
Viscount Howick and later third Earl Grey. Whig politician, Colonial Secretary under Canning. Member of the Poor Law Commission.

HUME, Joseph 1777–1855   116,117,119,178n
A one-time surgeon and Radical politician and Member of Parliament. He was a Benthamite and a 'moderate' Reformer, which was why Cobbett fell out with him, and all the more because he supported the Potters (q.v.)

INNES, Sir James
See Roxburghe.

IRELAND, Richard   38,165n
An Edinburgh bookseller who was Cobbett's agent in that city and one of the men responsible for his lectures there.

JAMIESON, John, DD 1759–1838   25
A Scottish minister and lexicographer, author of an *Etymological Dictionary of the Scottish Language*.

JEFFREY, Francis, Lord Jeffrey 1773–1850   3,79,163n
Scottish judge, politician and man-of-letters. Founder and editor of
the *Edinburgh Review* ('Old Mother Mange'). Member for Perth
1830 and for Edinburgh 1932. Lord Advocate under Grey. Greatly
disliked by Cobbett.

JENKINS, Griffith   49
('Poor Taffy'). A somewhat feeble-minded farmer who had figured
in a scandalous law-case in which Wilde and Drayton (q.v.) were
accused of having got him drunk in order to cheat him out of an
estate worth £40,000. It was the sort of scandal Cobbett revelled in
and he never let either Wilde or Drayton forget it.

JOHNSON, Samuel 1709–1783   80,108,122,128,165n,171n
The great lexicographer. Cobbett often quoted him and must have
had that respect for him which one outstanding hack will always owe
another. On the other hand Johnson was a Tory and had been in
receipt of a pension from the Crown in his latter years, both reasons
for Cobbett to despise him. He also thought that the Doctor had
given a quite false picture of Scotland in his *A Journey to the Western
Isles of Scotland.*

JOHNSTON (properly Johnson), Colonel (properly General)   85
William Augustus
A Radical and Member first for Boston and, when Cobbett died, for
Oldham. Keenly supported Sir Thomas Beevor in his plans for
establishing a fund in order to send Cobbett to Parliament.

KEITH, George Elphinstone 1746–1823   47
Viscount Keith. The celebrated Admiral, son of the tenth Lord
Elphinstone.

LAUDERDALE, James Maitland 1759–1839
Eighth Earl. He started in politics as a Jacobin and was a Tory before
he withdrew from politics. He and Cobbett came together, perhaps,
over their passionate interest in agriculture.

LIVERPOOL, Robert Banks Jenkinson   71
Lord Hawkesbury and second Earl of Liverpool. Prime Minister
1812–26.

LONG, Charles 1761–1838   74
First Baron Farnborough ('Charley'). Paymaster General from
1810–26 and a man who was commonly believed to have made half a
million out of his politics.

MACAULAY, Thomas Babington, Lord Macaulay 1800–59
xxvii,179n
Poet, historian, politician and lawyer. Cobbett disliked him because he was a Whig and because of his connections with the *Edinburgh Review*. He recorded his belief that Cobbett, in his last years, was out of his mind.

MACAULAY, Zachary 1768–1838   121,179n
Father of the above. Became an abolitionist as a consequence of his experiences managing plantations in the West Indies. Later Governor of Sierra Leone. An Evangelical and member of the Clapham Sect.

MACLAREN, Charles 1782–1866   75
'Mortified, spiteful and ridiculous reptile'. One of the founders of the *Scotsman* and its editor from 1820–45.

MacQUEEN, Robert 1722–99   98
Later Lord Braxfield. The Lord Justice Clerk who presided over the trials of the Scottish Reformers in 1793–4 and became infamous for the short and savage justice he dealt out. Thought to have been the model for R L Stevenson's *Weir of Hermiston.*

MALTHUS, Rev Thomas Robert 1766–1834   22,91,92,123,162n
The celebrated author of the *Essay on the Principle of Population.* Of all the 'feelosofers', he was the one Cobbett most preferred to hate and always chose to misunderstand.

MARGAROT, Maurice 1745–1815   98
A Frenchman by birth, he was one of the founders of the London Corresponding Society, and was sent with Gerrald (q.v.) as one of its delegates to the Edinburgh Convention. For this he was arrested, tried and sentenced to transportation for fourteen years.

MARTIN, William   125
Cobbett's agent in the Birmingham district.

McCULLOCH, John Ramsay 1789–1864   150
The economist and one-time editor of the *Scotsman.* He was a disciple of Ricardo and, so far as Cobbett was concerned, the very model of a 'scoundrelly Scottish feelosofer'.

MELBOURNE, William Lamb 1779–1848   79,85
Second Viscount. He was, for a short time, Home Secretary in Grey's Administration and was held responsible for the severity with which the rioters of 1830 were treated. He was Prime Minister 1835–41.

MONTEITH & Co   55,56,99
The Monteiths were leading cotton manufacturers in the Glasgow area.

MUIR, Thomas 1765–98   74,76
A Glasgow lawyer and early Reformer. Was tried for sedition in 1793 and sentenced to transportation. He escaped and eventually died in France of wounds received in a fight against British ships. He was then planning an invasion of Scotland.

MURRAY, Lady Augusta   83
The daughter of the fourth Earl of Dunmore whose marriage to the Duke of Sussex was declared void under the Royal Marriage Act. She and the two children of that union were in receipt of several handsome pensions.

MURRAY, Charles Augustus 1806–95   83,84
Son of the fifth Earl of Dunmore and so nephew of the above. He was the Whig candidate for Selkirk.

MURRAY, Colonel Sir George 1772–1846   45,165n
Colonial Secretary 1829–30, Master of the Ordnance 1835–46. He was Lady Louisa Paget's (q.v.) second husband.

MYLNE, Rev James 1756–1839   55
A leading Glaswegian Radical and Professor of Moral Philosophy at Glasgow University.

NEWCASTLE, Henry Pelham Fiennes Pelham Clinton 1785–1851
                                                      121,179n
Fourth Duke. A notorious borough-monger.

O'CONNELL, Daniel 1775–1847   xx,19,22,161n
'The Liberator', according to his countrymen and 'Big O' according to Cobbett. The two were alternatively allies and opponents over a good many years.

OWEN, Robert 1771–1858   100,101,102,174n
The industrialist, Socialist and millenarian. What Cobbett understood of Owen's ideas he disliked, and what he could not understand he laughed at. He did, however, join Owen's National Regeneration Society in 1834 in order to canvass for an eight hour working day.

PAGET, Lady Louisa   45,80,165n
The daughter of the first Earl of Uxbridge and the sister of the first Marquis of Anglesey. She married firstly Sir James Erskine and then Sir George Murray (q.v.)

PALMER, Thomas Fyshe 1747–1802   98
A Scottish Unitarian preacher and one of the early Reformers
transported for sedition in 1793. He survived his time at Botany Bay
but died of dysentry on the voyage home.

PEARSON, Charles 1794–1862   50,79,121
'Our Charley'. One of the Westminster Radicals and Under-Sheriff
for London and Middlesex 1832–4. As such he was one of the
'guttlers and guzzlers' attacked by Cobbett in this work. Pearson was
deeply interested in penal reform and became MP for Lambeth in
1847 in order to promote his views on this subject.

PEEL, Sir Robert 1788–1850   72
The Tory politician and Prime Minister 1841–46. As Chairman of
the Bank Committee he had been responsible for the Act of 1819
providing for a return to cash payments, for which reason Cobbett
continued to attack him till the day he died.

PERCEVAL, Spencer 1762–1812   71
Tory politician and lawyer. As Attorney-General he had been
responsible for prosecuting Cobbett in 1805 and as Prime Minister
(1809–12) he did something to ensure Cobbett's imprisonment in
Newgate. It was not strange, therefore, that such a vindictive man as
Cobbett should gloat when Perceval was assassinated by Bellingham
in 1812.

PERCY
See Smithson.

PIOZZI, Mrs Hester, née Salusbury 1739–1821   80
Perhaps, as Mrs Thrale, the most famous widow in English literary
history. When she married again, however, Doctor Johnson, who had
been part of her household for the past sixteen years, split from her
and the two only met again in their correspondence. The lady had
literary pretensions of her own, but it is only through her connections
with Doctor Johnson and her *Anecdotes of Doctor Johnson* and
Letters to and from Doctor Johnson that she is now remembered.

PITT, William 1759–1806   9,49,70,71,74
It would probably be true to say that Cobbett stopped being a Tory
when he stopped being a Pittite. This happened as a consequence of
the Peace of Amiens. Thereafter he would attribute every ill in
Britain to the Pitt System, and cheerfully maligned 'The Great Pilot'
until the day he died.

PLATT, Jesse   103
One of the Long Island farmers who had been Cobbett's neighbours
during his Long Island exile. The two had remained friends and
corresponded frequently.

POTTERS, The   xx,xxviii,50,54,58,86,90,118,119
('The Tadcaster fellows' etc.) The Potters were a wealthy Manchester
family whose fortunes were based on their position as drapers and
bankers. They were leaders of the Reform movement in that area
and incurred Cobbett's wrath by being no more than 'moderate' and
middle-class Reformers and opposing his candidature in the 1832
Election.

SIR THOMAS POTTER 1773-1845
The first Mayor of Manchester one of the founders of the *Manchester
Guardian* and a leader of the Anti-Corn Law movement.

RICHARD POTTER 1778-1842   xx,xxviii,50,54,58,86,90,118,119
Eventually became MP for Wigan and was active in Poor Law
reform. It is a pity that Cobbett devoted as much time as he did to
abusing this worthy but otherwise dull pair who should, perhaps, be
best remembered today as ancestors of Mrs Sidney Webb, which
seems predictable, and of Beatrix Potter, which is rather more
surprising.

PRENTICE, David 1783-1837   55,65,102
Owner and editor of the *Glasgow Chronicle* and a prominent
Glaswegian Reformer, Abolitionist and Radical.

RADNOR, William Pleydell-Bouverie 1779-1869   47,75
Viscount Folkestone and third Earl of Radnor. Was educated in
France where he acquired Jacobinical ideas. Sat in the Commons as
an extremely Radical Whig from 1801-26. He was a close friend of
Cobbett's and one of the few he was never able to quarrel with,
although they differed over Poor Law reform and Cobbett addressed
several Open Letters to him on this subject.

RENNIE, George 1749-1828   16
A large-scale farmer and brewer and one of the leading Improvers of
his day. His bankruptcy made a considerable stir in Scotland.

ROBINSON, Frederick John 1782-1859   13,71,85,160n
Viscount Goderich and first Earl of Ripon, 'Prosperity Robinson'.
Tory politician, Chancellor of the Exchequer 1823 and Prime
Minister for a short while in 1827.

ROSE, George 1744–1818   70,71,74
'Old George Rose'. A Tory politician who acted as unofficial patronage secretary to Pitt and was arguably the most active and successful
political jobber and sinecurist of his day. The Radicals accused him
of having made over a million out of the post of Treasurer to the
Navy. Cobbett was befriended by him in his Tory days but attacked
him savagely in 1817, when he had turned Radical, in a *Register*
article called *A New Year's Gift to Old George Rose.*

ROSEBERY, Archibald John Primrose 1783–1868   39
Fourth Earl. Sat in the Commons as a Whig and in the Lords as a
Scottish representative peer.

ROSS, Lady Mary, née Fitzgerald   99
Had married General Sir Charles Ross of Bonnington Castle. She was
a niece of Major Lord Edward Fitzgerald who had been Cobbett's
commanding officer when the latter was Regimental Sergeant Major
of the 54th of Foot, and who had been the only officer Cobbett ever
expressed any admiration for.

ROXBURGHE, Duchess of   xxviii,15
The Sir James Innes who became fifth Duke of Roxburghe in 1812
had, in 1807, taken as his second wife Miss Harriet Charlewood, who
duly became his Duchess and bore him a son when he was seventy-
eight and she was twenty. It was that son who frustrated 'Duke'
Gawler's hopes of inheriting.

RUTHVEN, Lady Mary 1789–1885   107
Wife of James, seventh Baron Ruthven.

SCOTT, Sir Walter 1771–1832   68,119
The poet, novelist and lawyer. Cobbett despised him as the author of
'trashy romances', as a Tory, and as the author of the *Letters of
Malachi Malagrowther,* in which Scott had defended the use of
paper money.

SENIOR, Nassau William 1790–1864   15,22
The economist and first Drummond Professor of Political Economy
at Oxford. He was a member of the Royal Commission on the Poor
Laws, and was largely responsible for its report on which Poor Law
reform was based.

SHUTTLEWORTH, John 1786–1864   49,50,58,79,90,119
A Manchester cotton merchant, Reformer, Radical and member of
the Potter 'gang', which last was why Cobbett fell out with him.

SIDMOUTH, Henry Addington 1757–1844   132
First Viscount, 'the Doctor' Tory politician. Speaker 1789–1801,
Prime Minister 1801–04, Home Secretary 1812–21. In the latter
capacity was largely responsible for many of the repressive measures
passed from 1816 onwards and for the notorious Six Acts of 1819.
Sidmouth was, perhaps, too undistinguished a man to have deserved
the amount of hatred devoted to him by the Radicals.

SINCLAIR, Sir John 1754–1835   17,103
A Pittite and the first President of the Board of Agriculture. He was
an Improver and a great compiler of statistics, a word he is said to
have invented. He wrote a pamphlet to prove the authenticity of
Macpherson's *Ossian* and held eccentric views on the currency.

SMITHSON, Sir Hugh 1715–86   9
Married the Percy heiress, assumed the name of Percy and was made
Duke of Northumberland in 1766. The Duke of Cobbett's day
—Hugh Percy (1785–1847)—was a Tory politician and a staunch
opponent of Reform, which was why Cobbett may have taken evey
opportunity of reminding him that his name was rightly Smithson.

STAFFORD, George Granville Leveson Gower 1758–1833   60,128
Second Marquis, later Duke of Sutherland. A great landowner and
the richest man in England who acquired the great estates of the
Earls of Sutherland when he married the Countess of Sutherland.
Their names will always be associated with the controversy
surrounding the 'Clearances'.

SPEIRS, (Not Spiers) Archibald of Elderslie House 1758–1832
                                                 66,76,77,107n
Was the largest landowner in Renfrewshire and had been the
Member for that county for many years. He was a Reformer.

STEUART, Sir Henry Seton 1759–1836   104
Carried out many experiments in arboriculture on his estate of
Allanton in Lanarkshire. He was the author of *The Planter's Guide;
or a practical essay on the best method of giving immediate effect to
wood by the removal of large trees and undergrowth.*

STEUART, Sir James, of Coltness 1744–1839   105
A one-time General and MP for Lanark 1784–1807.

STURGES BOURNE, William 1769–1848   19,28,29,91
A member of Parliament, Privy Councillor, a member of the Special
Commission which tried the rioters of 1830 and of the Poor Law
Commission of 1832. He brought in the Bill distributing votes in

parish vestries according to the amount of property held, which duly became law in 1818, and was still advancing what Cobbett saw as noxious proposals for Poor Law reform fourteen years later.

SWANN, James   84
Owned the Wolvercote paper mills and supplied Cobbett with paper for the *Political Register*. He was one of Cobbett's principal creditors when the latter was imprisoned in 1810 and when he went bankrupt in 1820. On both occasions he refrained from pressing his claim.

THOMSON, Charles Edward Poulett 1799–1841   48,49,57,60,79,
                                                            86,90,166n
First Baron Sydenham, 'the tallow-man'. Son of Poulett Thomson who was head of the firm of Thomson, Bonar & Co, Russia merchants. He was an economist and a Benthamite and was put up by the Potters to stand against Cobbett at Manchester. He became Vice-President of the Board of Trade under Grey and was made Governor-General of Canada in 1839.

TROTTER, Sir Coutts 1767–1837   68
A senior partner in Coutts Bank and was made a baronet in 1821 by George IV.

TURNER, James   112
A merchant of Glasgow and a prominent Radical he accompanied Cobbett on part of his Tour.

VANSITTART, Nicholas 1766–1851   70,71,72,73,169n
First Baron Bexley, 'Little Van'. Lawyer, Tory politician and pamphleteer. Chancellor of the Exchequer 1812–1823. One of Cobbett's favourite butts.

VAUGHAN, Sir John 1769–1839   10
Lawyer and politician. Attorney-General 1816. Member of the Special Commission of 1830 sent to try the rioters.

WALTER, John, 'Jack' 1776–1847   65,77
Son of the founder of *The Times,* he was the paper's sole manager and editor until 1810, after which it was formed into a Company. Despite Cobbett's repeated attacks on him he was elected for Berkshire in the 1832 election.

WAKEFIELD, Edward Gibbon 1796–1862   124
The economist and expert on colonial affairs. He was imprisoned for persuading a rich schoolgirl, Ellen Turner, to run away with him to Gretna Green. Whilst in prison he wrote *A Letter from Sydney* which was later expanded into *A View of the Art of Colonisation*. He had

much to do with the founding of South Australia and with the annexation of New Zealand. He also published a pamphlet in 1830 called *Swing Unmasked* which was what had evoked Cobbett's wrath.

WILDE, Thomas 1782–1855   10,49,50,57,79,121
Later Lord Truro. A Whig lawyer who became Sergeant Wilde in 1827 and Lord Chancellor in 1850. He was Crown prosecutor in the Captain Swing trials of 1830, was responsible for the re-trial and transportation of Farmer Boyes (q.v.) and was cleared of the charge of having cheated Griffith Jenkins (q.v.) all of which provided reasons for Cobbett to dislike him.

WILKINS, Charles   48,50,79,86
'The Mountebank'. A strolling player who turned, successively, school teacher and lawyer. He became a successful barrister but was unable to keep out of debt and he had to flee to France to escape his creditors. He was connected with the Potters and with the candidacy of Poulett Thomson, which was why Cobbett was so vehement about him.

WRAIGHT, Fanny   65,77
A daughter of John Walter the First and, together with her brother John and her sister Anna Brodie a principal proprietor of *The Times*.

YOUNG, Arthur 1741–1820   125
The first Secretary to the Board of Agriculture and one of the greatest writers on agriculture in the language. His various *Tours* in England, Ireland and France, published between 1768 and 1771 were precursors of Cobbett's own *Rural Rides* and may well have served as models for them. Young was a frequent contributor to Cobbett's *Political Register*, although the two of them differed over politics and over various agrarian problems.